# THE THEATRE OF TENNESSEE WILLIAMS

GW00642983

# THE THEATRE OF TENNESSEE WILLIAMS

*Brenda Murphy*

*Series Editors: Patrick Lonergan and Erin Hurley*

B L O O M S B U R Y

LONDON • NEW DELHI • NEW YORK • SYDNEY

**Bloomsbury Methuen Drama**

An imprint of Bloomsbury Publishing Plc

50 Bedford Square            1385 Broadway
London                      New York
WC1B 3DP                    NY 10018
UK                          USA

**www.bloomsbury.com**

**Bloomsbury is a registered trademark of Bloomsbury Publishing Plc**

First published 2014

**British Library Cataloguing-in-Publication Data**
A catalogue record for this book is available from the British Library.

ISBN: HB: 978-1-7809-3025-1
PB: 978-1-4081-4543-2
ePub: 978-1-4081-4533-3
ePDF: 978-1-4081-4532-6

**Library of Congress Cataloging-in-Publication Data**
A catalog record for this book is available from the Library of Congress.

Typeset by Deanta Global Publishing Services, Chennai, India
Printed and bound in India

*To George*

# CONTENTS

# ACKNOWLEDGMENTS

My heartfelt thanks are due to the libraries and their staffs that made the research for this volume not only possible but also pleasurable: my home library, the Homer Babbidge Library of the University of Connecticut, which provided me with research space as well as help and resources; the Harry Ransom Humanities Research Center at the University of Texas at Austin, which has the richest source for Williams manuscript materials and one of the kindest and most helpful library staffs I have ever encountered; and the Harvard Theatre Collection, Houghton Library, Harvard University, the Rare Book and Manuscript Library of Columbia University, and the Billy Rose Theatre Collection of the New York Public Library for the Performing Arts, all of which provided important material for this study.

I am grateful to Mark Dudgeon at Bloomsbury Methuen Drama and series editor Patrick Lonergan for their invaluable advice and support, and for giving me the opportunity to write this book, which is the result of 30 years of thinking about, writing about, and teaching the works of Tennessee Williams. I would also like to thank my students in two courses on Tennessee Williams at the University of Connecticut in 2011–12. They inspired me with the sense that Williams's works are exceedingly relevant to life in the twenty-first century and were not only tolerant but enthusiastic as I tried out many of the ideas in this book on them. As always, my husband, George Monteiro, contributed his unique critical acumen at crucial stages and moral support throughout the writing of this book.

# LIST OF ABBREVIATIONS

C        Devlin, Albert J. (ed.), *Conversations with Tennessee Williams* (Jackson: University Press of Mississippi, 1986).

CP       *The Collected Poems of Tennessee Williams*, eds. David Ernest Roessel and Nicholas Rand Moschovakis (New York: New Directions, 2002).

CS       *Tennessee Williams Collected Stories* (New York: New Directions, 1985).

L1       *The Selected Letters of Tennessee Williams: Volume I 1920–1945*, eds. Albert J. Devlin and Nancy M. Tischler (New York: New Directions, 2000).

L2       *The Selected Letters of Tennessee Williams: Volume II 1945–1957*, eds. Albert J. Devlin and Nancy M. Tischler (New York: New Directions, 2004).

M        *Memoirs* (Garden City, NY: Doubleday, 1975).

N        *Tennessee Williams: Notebooks*, ed. Margaret Bradham Thornton (New Haven: Yale University Press, 2006).

NSE      *New Selected Essays: Where I Live*, ed. John S. Bak (New York: New Directions, 2009).

P1       *Tennessee Williams Plays: 1937–1955* (New York: Library of America, 2000).

P2       *Tennessee Williams: Plays 1957–1980* (New York: Library of America, 2000).

T1-T8    *The Theatre of Tennessee Williams*, 8 Vols (New York: New Directions, 1971–1992).

# INTRODUCTION

As she tries to explain her son Sebastian's life to Dr Cukrowicz in *Suddenly Last Summer* (1958), Violet Venable says, "his life was his work because the work of a poet is the life of a poet. . . . I mean you can't separate them" (P2: 102). This was famously true of Tennessee Williams. From the time when he made the decision to be a playwright and entered the University of Iowa's playwriting program in 1937, his life was arranged around writing. His intimate relationships were either short-term liaisons that did not interfere with his work or, as with Frank Merlo and Amado Rodriguez y Gonzales, arrangements in which his partner also served as his "secretary," or what would now be known as his personal assistant. This is the way he generally referred to Merlo, with whom he shared an intimate 14-year relationship, outside his close circle of friends, and it was not simply a cover for a gay relationship in the homophobic 1950s. He paid him a salary, and it was well known in Williams's circle that Merlo not only helped with his work, but also ran the household, made the travel arrangements, and generally removed the burdens of everyday life from Williams so he would be free to write without annoyance.

The home in Key West, Florida that Williams shared with Merlo, with its little studio built to his specifications for writing, was his favorite and most productive place to work, but his house in New Orleans and the many apartments and hotel suites he occupied after he could afford something more comfortable than a room at the YMCA were also arranged around his writing. Williams traveled often, sometimes by himself, but most often with Merlo or, after Merlo's death in 1963, with a paid "travel companion" who took care of the details. Besides escape from whatever demands were pressing at the moment, what he was seeking in his travels was a place where he could write, which meant access to a swimming pool where he could get the self-prescribed therapy for his nerves that he found so necessary, as well as both new scenes, sensations and experiences, which stimulated his creative juices, and a quiet place where he could be alone with his typewriter in the mornings.

As described by many observers, Williams's daily writing was obsessive. His longtime friend, director Elia Kazan, remarked that, every morning, no matter where he found himself, what condition he was in from the night before, or whom he was with, he would get out of bed, roll a sheet of paper into his portable typewriter, and become Tennessee Williams. This was his life. During the few periods when he experienced writer's block, he suffered from terrible bouts of anxiety which did not subside until he was able to write again. When Dr Lawrence Kubie, with whom he was in analysis in 1957 and 1958, prescribed a hiatus from writing as a way to "lie fallow" and recharge his creative power, he wrote to Kazan that without his work, he was "unbearably lonely" and his life "unbearably empty" (N: 711). He was soon writing again.

The extent to which Williams's life was his writing and vice versa has emerged even more clearly since 2000, with the publication of primary texts such as the two volumes of selected letters edited by Albert J. Devlin and Nancy Tischler and the prodigious edition of his "notebooks," or journals, by Margaret Bradham Thornton. The publication of these primary texts and a number of previously unpublished plays by Williams's longtime publisher, New Directions, volumes that normally would have appeared immediately after the writer's death, was delayed for nearly 20 years because of the circumstances of Williams's will, which appointed his friend Maria Britneva, the Lady St Just, as his executor. Since her death in 1994, when the University of the South took over as executor, permission to publish manuscript materials, and for scholars to quote from them, has been more forthcoming, and a good deal of basic scholarship has been done.

With this new wealth of information, the standard narrative of Williams's life, essentially beginning with the failure of *Battle of Angels* (1940) and the triumph of *The Glass Menagerie* (1945), and ending with the 20-year decline after *The Night of the Iguana* (1961), is gradually being revised. Once New Directions published the plays from the 1930s, we were able to see Williams in the context of his roots in a theatre of social engagement. And thanks to the work of critics like Annette Saddik, Linda Dorff, Felicia Londré, Philip C. Kolin, and William Prosser, as well as the publication by New Directions of many of the previously unpublished plays that were written after 1961, the later part of Williams's career is undergoing a major reassessment. One of the aims of this book is to place the familiar narrative of Williams's career in this new context, and to consider his better-known plays in the context of his earlier and later work. In addition to the individual chapters on the 1930s and the later plays, these works occupy a good deal of attention in the critical perspectives section from John Bak, Annette Saddik, and Felicia Londré.

The new depth of knowledge about Williams and his *oeuvre* opened up at a time when scholarly and critical analysis of his work, and of literature in general, was benefitting from the perspectives of Gay and Queer Studies. Beginning with studies by John Clum and David Savran, the last two decades have seen an explosion of interest in Williams's treatment of sexuality, gender, and sexual identity, subjects that are central to much of his writing, especially beginning in the mid-1950s, when he was actively considering his identity as a gay man in the homophobic culture of mid-twentieth-century America.

While his sexual identity, and his sex life generally, were very important to Williams, it is also important to see these elements in the larger perspective of his self-declared identity as an artist and bohemian. From a Queer Studies perspective, the queer identity—marginalized, transgressive, destabilizing—that he recognized as his own was very much tied up in the particular nexus of things implied by the phrase "gay bohemian artist." He considered all three facets fundamental to his identity and his marginalized place in the world, and also the source for his rebellion against the standard American middle-class culture in which he had grown up, whose limits and strictures he was constantly testing. Yet at the same time, it was vital to him that his plays be successful. At first that meant success in the Broadway theatre, with both critical accolades and monetary rewards, but as the accolades and the money diminished in the 1960s and 1970s, he began to redefine success largely in terms of rebuilding an audience for his work. His desire to *épater le bourgeois* existed simultaneously with his desire to win his love.

Williams's other creative obsession has long been recognized. If his life after 1937 might be seen as a staging ground for his writing, his life before that was the source of much of its material. In his imaginative and creative life, Williams returned again and again to the early life with his family. The presence of his sister Rose pervades his work, and he sought to dramatize some aspect of her in the very different characters Laura Wingfield, Alma Winemiller, Blanche DuBois, Catherine Holly, and Clare in *The Two-Character Play/Out Cry* (1967, 1971). In his *Memoirs*, he wrote that "some perceptive critic of the theatre made the observation that the true theme of my work is 'incest,'" and that, while "my sister and I had a close relationship, quite unsullied by any carnal knowledge . . . our love was, and is, the deepest in our lives and was, perhaps, very pertinent to our withdrawal from extrafamilial attachments" (M: 119–20). Williams's parents and maternal grandparents and his brother Dakin also provided significant material for his characters. The publication of Williams's *Notebooks* has helped to deepen our understanding of his imaginative use of his family and early life, and I think the broad look at his work that this volume affords helps to show its evolution.

An important subtext in Williams's work that has received less attention from critics is what Violet Venable calls "looking for God, I mean for a clear image of Him" (P2: 107). The grandson of a beloved Episcopal minister, Williams described himself throughout his life as a Christian and a believer, although the images of God and religion that he presents are mostly dark ones: the hysterical practice of atonement by the evangelical congregation in the story "Desire and the Black Masseur" (1948); the Darwinian cruelty of Sebastian Venable's image of God in *Suddenly Last Summer*; the angry, petulant "senile delinquent" of a God that the Rev T. Lawrence Shannon describes in *The Night of the Iguana* (1961). But he also created the comforting images of the "Angel in the Alcove" (1943) and the vision of the Blessed Virgin who watches over the misfits and the marginalized in *The Mutilated* (1966). Williams saw a deity that encompassed all of these elements, and his sometimes desperate search for religious truth and faith underlies a good deal of his work.

Literary engagement also emerges often in this book as an important subtext in Williams's plays. The imaginative sources of his work were in his voluminous reading as well as in his lived experience. This is of course most evident in the "literary" characters who appear in his plays—D. H. Lawrence, Hart Crane, Lord Byron, Camille, the Baron de Charlus, Scott and Zelda Fitzgerald, Ernest Hemingway—but it is much more significant in the literary images, symbolism, and language that pervade his work. It is impossible in the scope of a broad study like this one to do justice to the literary subtexts of the plays, but I have tried to point it out where it is most important.

This book is arranged roughly chronologically, and although the subtexts of Williams's perennial concerns run through it from beginning to end, the greatest attention is given to the plays that have proven most significant to the theatre and to critics. I have tried to present the plays as creations of the theatre as well as the imagination and the typewriter of Tennessee Williams, and to present them in the context of the theatre and the culture of his time.

In his essay in the Critical Perspectives section, John Bak makes use of primary materials like Williams's unpublished essays and his letters to critics responding to their criticism of his plays in his detailed analysis of the theatrical culture of Williams's time and his evolving role within it. Each of the other essays in the Critical Perspectives section offers a different point of departure from which to consider Williams and his work. Bruce McConachie's analysis of *A Streetcar Named Desire* illustrates the value of approaching Williams with a fresh critical eye and new theoretical tools, in this case applying the theory of cognitive science to the reception by audiences of the play in 1947 and the film in 1951. The remaining essays, by two critics who have already contributed a great deal to our understanding of the later plays, shed more light on these neglected works. Felcia Londré uses the poem "Cyclops Eye," which first appeared in Williams's novel *Moise and the World of Reason* (1975), to illuminate three of his later plays, *In the Bar of a Tokyo Hotel* (1969), *The Two-Character Play/Outcry,* and *Vieux Carré* (1977), and Annette Saddik provides a rich context for *Kingdom of Earth* (1968), *A Cavalier for Milady* (c. 1976), and *A House Not Meant to Stand* (1982) in the theory of the grotesque.

Despite the eclipse of his reputation during his lifetime, in the 30 years since his death, Williams has continued to occupy his place as one of the three or four great playwrights the United States has produced. If my students at the University of Connecticut are a good measure, he holds a fascination for a new generation who approach his work within a new cultural context in which theatrical experimentation is expected and it is homophobia rather than homosexuality that is seen as unacceptable. Scholarly interest in Williams is at a high point as well. In 2011, the centennial of his birth sparked a good deal of activity. Centennial conferences and celebrations were held at the University of Perugia in Italy, the Université Nancy in France, Georgetown University and Arena Stage in Washington, D.C., the Tennessee Williams Literary Festival in New Orleans, and a centennial festival in his hometown of Clarksdale, Mississippi.

Many revivals assure Williams's constant presence on the stage. *The Glass Menagerie* and *A Streetcar Named Desire* receive multiple revivals in theatres throughout the world every year. The ongoing activity in a variety of venues testifies to the vitality of Williams's work, early and late, well known and unknown in the theatre. In 2010, for example, besides the acclaimed Cate Blanchett production of *Streetcar*, which was done in Australia, Britain, and the United States, there were several revivals of both this play and *Menagerie*, as well as productions of *A Lovely Sunday for Creve Coeur* (1979), *The Night of the Iguana*, *Eccentricities of a Nightingale* (1964), *Clothes for a Summer Hotel* (1980), and *Cat on a Hot Tin Roof* (1955). In addition, the early play, *Spring Storm*, which had never been produced in New York or London, was produced at London's Cottesloe Theatre; New York's Wooster Group did an experimental adaptation of *Vieux Carré* at the Edinburgh Fringe Festival; and *Now the Cats with Jewelled Claws* (1981) was done at the venerable Off-Off Broadway Club at La MaMa. Popular revivals with bankable stars, such as Emily Mann's multiracial production of *Streetcar* with Blair Underwood in 2012 and the 2013 *Cat on a Hot Tin Roof* with Scarlett Johansson, testify to Williams's continued presence in the Broadway theatre 30 years after his death.

## A Note on Texts

Tennessee Williams revised his plays many times before, during, and after their productions, often making changes in the scripts for revivals, or for new editions of the published plays. In cases like *Summer and Smoke* and *Battle of Angels*, he reworked the scripts so drastically that he considered them new plays, and had them produced and published under new titles. In other words, in the case of Tennessee Williams, the text of a play is a protean thing, and deciding which of the published versions to use can be as vexing for scholars as for directors. In most cases there are at least three published versions of a Williams play: the "acting version," published by Dramatists Play Service, which is the script based on the original production, with stage directions, property lists, etc., for those who want to produce the play; the "reading version," usually published in a single volume by New Directions, Williams's longtime publisher; and later New Directions versions, including the eight-volume edition of his collected plays, *The Theatre of Tennessee Williams*, published between 1971 and 1992.

In most cases, the eight-volume edition is the standard edition that scholars use in discussing the text. This does not include all of Williams's plays, but it usually contains the last version of the text approved by Williams during his lifetime. In addition, the readily available Library of America volumes, *Tennessee Williams Plays*, edited by Mel Gussow and Kenneth Holditch in 2000, contain by design the first editions of the plays in book form. I have mostly used the Library of America volumes in my overview of Williams's career because my discussion of the plays is in the context of the original productions, and these are the closest reading versions to the original scripts. The essays in the Critical Perspective sections mostly use the *Theatre of*

*Tennessee Williams* volumes in discussing the text. Single-volume New Directions versions are used throughout the book for plays that do not appear in either of these collections. These are rules of thumb, however, and it is important to remember that, when dealing with Williams texts, no rule is hard and fast.

# CHAPTER 1
## THE 1930S' PLAYS (1936–1940)

## Williams in the Thirties

Much of Williams's early playwriting was shaped by the social, economic, and artistic environment of the 1930s. His most important theatrical relationship at the time was with director Willard Holland and The Mummers of St Louis, a group dedicated to the drama of social action that was vital to American theatrical culture in the 1930s. *Candles to the Sun* (1937), based on a coal mining strike, and *Fugitive Kind* (1937), about the denizens of a seedy urban hotel, were both produced by The Mummers, and *Not About Nightingales* (1938), about brutal abuses in the American prison system, was intended for them, although they disbanded before the play was produced.

The other major influence on Williams's early development as a playwright was the playwriting program at the University of Iowa, which he attended in 1937–38. Its director, E. C. Mabie, had worked for the Federal Theatre Project (FTP), the only federally subsidized theatre in American history, which existed briefly from 1935 until 1939, when its funding was cut by a Congress that objected to its leftist leanings. In the FTP, Mabie had worked with agit prop and other social action techniques in the Living Newspaper, a theatrical form that he brought to Iowa. As part of a Living Newspaper, Williams wrote a one-act dramatization of a prison hunger strike, called *Quit Eating!*, which became the basis for *Not About Nightingales*. Williams's other instructor in playwriting at Iowa was E. P. Conkle, who had had a successful Broadway production of his play about Abraham Lincoln, *Prologue to Glory*, just the year before Williams came to Iowa.

With this background, it is not surprising that Williams worked hard during the 1930s to produce drama of political and social significance. At the same time, the perennial themes and tropes that make a Tennessee Williams play recognizable were beginning to be established during these early years. The misfit, the marginalized, and the "fugitive kind" who need to escape from the trap of confinement by middle-class mores are evident from the beginning, as well as the artist, who often is also the misfit, and the bohemian lifestyle that he seeks as escape. Williams's interest in the representation of sexuality, particularly the divergence from, or the transgression of, the heteronormative, is there as well. And permeating all his work is his lifelong obsession with his mother, his father, his grandparents, and especially his sister Rose, which would fuel much of his art. These themes are particularly evident in *Spring Storm*, written in 1937–38, and *Stairs to the Roof*, written in 1940, neither of which was produced during his lifetime. Both dramatize concerns that were immediate to Williams at the time: sexual conflict and confusion, the situation of the artist, and the necessity of escaping the trap of a mechanical, dehumanizing job and a joyless, drearily conventional middle-class life.

## A Literary Bohemia: *The Magic Tower*

*The Magic Tower* was Williams's first produced play, staged on 13 October 1936 by an amateur theatre company in Webster Groves, Missouri, a wealthy suburb of St Louis. In a playwriting contest sponsored by the Webster Groves Theatre Guild, the play won first prize, which included production of the play. Perhaps because it was not a play written for The Mummers or for the seminars at Iowa, there is no striving for social significance in this one-act play about a bohemian artist, Jim, and his wife, Linda, a former vaudevillian.

Williams's depiction of the bohemian lifestyle is straight out of the traditional literature of bohemia deriving from Henri Murger's *La vie bohème* (1849) and Giacomo Puccini's opera *La bohème* (1896), a bohemia that was popularized in the United States by the writers and artists of the Greenwich Village Little Renaissance that flourished before World War I. Williams's play could easily be one of the one-act plays of the Provincetown Players, which often indulged in the self-depiction of the bohemian community of Greenwich Village. Williams was to alter his view of the bohemian lifestyle as he gained in experience and broadened his views, embracing particularly the gay element in the bohemian subcultures of New Orleans, New York, Key West, Southern California, and Puerto Vallarta. But at this stage in his life, Williams clearly took his view of bohemia from literature.

*The Magic Tower* has many of the tropes of traditional bohemian literature. The penniless artist and his wife are living a life of poverty devoted to art and love in an attic apartment they call their "enchanted tower" while they dodge the landlady and wonder where their next meal will come from. But like many of the Provincetown plays, it engages in an ironic self-criticism by dashing the cold water of reality on the bohemian fantasy. Jim, a very young artist, pins his future hopes on a meeting with an art dealer who is looking for fresh new talent to invest in, while his wife Linda is tempted back to her show business career by two former colleagues who try to convince her that she is just a drag on her husband's artistic ambitions. They nearly succeed until Jim returns, revealing he has failed to impress the art dealer, and Linda feels the need to stay and take care of him.

In a final twist, though, Jim reveals that he is not as dedicated to the "enchanted tower fantasy" as Linda is, exploding with "magic tower, boloney! It's Mrs. O'Fallon's attic that we're up in, Linda! Mrs. O'Fallon's lousy, leaking attic! And we're five weeks behind on the rent! Do you know what's going to happen to us, Linda? We're going to get kicked out on our ears, that's what!" (Williams 2011: 36). When he responds to her statement that in "this state of enchantment–in which we lived–nothing ever happened–nothing ever mattered except our having each other" (36–7) with the flat "those were pretty words" (37), Linda decides to leave him after all, assuring him that it will be "much healthier to live in a dry, bright attic–than a magic tower with a leaking roof!" (38). For Williams, who was living in his parents' attic in 1936, this notion of combining the artist's garret with the regular meals, clean laundry and other comforts of middle-class life was an attractive compromise. It would be 2 years until he finally broke out of the parental nest and made his first foray into the authentic bohemian lifestyle of the New Orleans French Quarter.

## "Group consciousness": *Candles to the Sun*

*Candles to the Sun* was the first full-length play by Williams to see production. It was actually his development of a one-act play, *The Lamp*, by Joseph Phelan Hollifield, a writer who was a friend of his grandparents in Memphis. The two had worked together on the play in 1935 when Williams was in Memphis, and Hollifield eventually turned it over to Williams to do what he could with it (N: 52, n. 81). As Dan Isaac notes in his Introduction to the play, Williams wrote a note on a draft of the play that he submitted to Holland, explaining that Hollifield had written the original one-act play, and he was "doing the writing on the present manuscript" while Hollifield was contributing material about the Red Hills section of Alabama where the play is set (Williams 2004: xxv).

The play, which dramatizes the brutal living conditions in a mining camp and the efforts to improve them with a labor strike, culminates in the miner's widow Fern's choice to spend her savings to sustain the strikers rather than to save it for the college tuition that will free her son from the mine. The play was tailor-made for the Mummers, and Williams worked with Willard Holland in a close collaboration that was the first of several such partnerships between playwright and director during his career. William Jay Smith, one of Williams's close friends in St Louis, says in the play's Foreword that Holland "had almost single-handedly helped to shape the final version of the play from the more than 400 unnumbered typewritten pages of various drafts that now repose at the Harry Ransom Humanities Research Center in Austin, Texas" (ix).

As shaped by Williams and Holland for The Mummers' 1937 production, *Candles to the Sun* certainly fulfills the group's mission of social engagement. Set pieces establish the economic conditions and labor abuses the play is meant to combat. For example, when John, the oldest son of the family, dies in a coal mine, his wife Fern writes to his parents, Hester and Bram, about the conditions they had been up against in trying to save money to get him out of the mines and into a better job:

> The company stopped paying cash. Instead they paid us paper money called scrip that you couldn't use anywhere but the company store so we had to buy everything there and prices went up so high it was all we could do to keep living, and then sometimes we couldn't even get any scrip. We got behind on the rent and the company took all John's pay 'cause the house we lived in was theirs. Everything was theirs, it all belonged to the company. And for weeks at a time the mines would be shut down and there wouldn't be food in the house and the rent way behind till it got so we owed so much that we couldn't ever catch up. (19)

Familiar stages of the drama of social action are marked with equally clear monologues. The moment of rebellion against these impossible conditions comes with Hester's declaration that "I'm gonna give 'em back as good as I git frum now on. I don't care what happens. I'm gonna start fightin'. It's time somebody started fightin'. Bram won't, he's too dumb. He's a natcheral bo'n slave. But me, I'm gittin' tired of it all. . . . It's time somebody did something round here besides dig in the dirt and eat it. *I'm fed up!*' (31–2).

The conversion of the family to leftist ideas by the aptly named Birmingham Red comes gradually, as Fern's son Luke realizes, "he ain't in it for what he can get out of it like everybody else seems to be. He talks about–society. You know–you and me and everybody else that makes up the whole world. It's too big to understand all at once. It's one of those things that you have to lay in the dark and think about a long time" (41). His aunt Star, a pariah in the mining camp because of her loose morals, becomes intrigued with Red and his "screwy ideas" like "Justice. Equality. Freedom" (42), and both falls in love with him and is converted to his politics, expressing her disgust with the men who resist the strike because they are afraid of the company: "the damn fools! Red tries to make them see things but they won't! They'd rather go on as they are, the life being poisoned out of them with coal dust, over-worked and underpaid, cheated, bought and sold" (66). And her conversion to the leftist agenda has transformed her as well: "It seems I've changed into somebody else and everything that I done before I look back at and wonder how it could have really been me that done those things" (66).

The major transformation takes place in Fern, who has devoted her life to earning the money to free her son Luke from the coal mines so that he will not die as his father did. Red's argument with her anticipates Arthur Miller's *All My Sons*, which would be a Broadway success in 1947. When Red tells her that her money could sustain the 1500 people in the camp, she says, "only one of them's my son!" His response is, "why not the others?" (93). Red's major monologue makes the argument that using the money for all the strikers would be a more fitting monument to her husband than using it to free Luke from the mine:

> Do you think he'd be proud of the choices you've made? He wasn't the first to die in the mines. There was lots of others. Death after death. And some of them not so quick. They could write starvation on pretty near every death ticket they filled out around here and it wouldn't be very far off. And now these people are fighting for a chance to live. Isn't that a big enough monument for John—to give 1500 of his own people their last fightin' chance on earth? (95)

After Fern gives up the money and Red is shot by the company men, the strike is successful, and as Star says, "He didn't get killed for nothing! *More quietly.* And you didn't give your money for nothing, neither. The work'll be safe now an' I guess they'll have to pay fair wages" (107).

The argument is certainly simple and straightforward, but in an interview for the *St Louis Star-Times*, Williams claimed that the play transcends propaganda, calling it "an earnest and searching examination of a particular social reality set out in human and dramatic terms" (xv). He also provided a gloss on its theme, noting that "the candles [in the title of the] play represent the individual lives of the people. The sun represents group consciousness. The play ends as a tragedy for the individuals, for in the end they realize they cannot achieve success and happiness apart from the group but must sacrifice for the common good" (xvi).

The play also has a literary element apart from its social agenda. The influence of the Irish playwright J. M. Synge is evident in Williams's framing of the family's tragedy. Like the mother in *Riders to the Sea*, whose sons are drowned one after the other, leaving her alone with her two daughters and her grief in the end, the Pilcher women see their men lost one after another to the mines. The audience only hears about the death of John, Hester's son and Fern's husband, but it sees the corpse of the second son Joel being brought back from the mines on a plank and the shooting of Red by the company men. It also hears about Hester's death from pellagra and witnesses the father Bram's growing blindness after his long years in the mines and Star's departure to work as a prostitute in Birmingham, the only means of survival open to her after Red's death. In the end, only Luke and Fern are left, with Luke confined to the mines now that Fern's money is gone. The shadow of D. H. Lawrence, a major influence on Williams during the 1930s, is also evident in the strong primal bond between mother and son and the depiction of the domestic lives of the miners.

## "The Sensitive non-conformist individual": *Fugitive Kind*

Williams's second play for The Mummers, *Fugitive Kind*, was meant to take a step beyond realism with its suggestion of an expressionistic mood in the setting. The single set, the lobby of a flophouse, or cheap transient hotel, in a large Middle Western city, is dominated by a large glass window, which "*admits a skyline of the city whose towers are outlined at night by a faint electric glow, so that we are always conscious of the city as a great implacable force, pressing in upon the shabby room and crowding its fugitive inhabitants back against their last wall*" (Williams 2001: 3). The stage directions note that, when the set is brightly lit, it is realistic, but during the play's final scenes, *"where the mood is predominantly lyrical, the stage is darkened, the realistic details are lost–the great window, the red light on the landing and the shadow walls make an almost expressionistic background"* (3). This effect is an early instance of the subjective realism Williams would employ in *The Glass Menagerie* and *A Streetcar Named Desire*, in which expressionistic effects signal the audience when the play leaves the dimension of a putative reality shared by audience and actors, the so-called "fourth-wall illusion" that the audience is merely overhearing real events that take place on stage, and enters the subjective reality of Tom's memory or Blanche's disturbed mind. In *Fugitive Kind*, the final scene, in which *"the stage is very quiet, very dark, only the arc light shining through the door and the faint electric glow of the city outlining its towers through the big window upstage"* (135), becomes a subjective space in which the fugitive state of Terry, the gangster who is on the run, and Glory, the daughter of the flophouse's owner who has fallen in love with him, exist until Terry is killed by the FBI men who are pursuing him. This is a message play, although its message is vaguer than that of *Candles to the Sun*. The final monologue of Glory's brother Leo enunciates the manifesto of the fugitive kind as the sky can be seen faintly brightening through the big window:

They'll never catch his kind till they learn that justice doesn't come out of gun barrels.–They'll never catch *us* either– Not till they tear down all the rotten old walls that they wanted to lock us up in! *More quietly.* Look, Glory. The snow's still falling. I guess that God's still asleep. *Rising inflection.* But in the morning maybe he'll wake up and see disaster! He'll hear the small boys' voices shouting the morning's news– "The Criminal's Capture, the Fugitive Returned!"– And maybe he'll be terribly angry at what they've done in his absence, these righteous fools that played at being God tonight and all the other nights while he's been sleeping!– *Softly but with strong feeling.* Or if he never wakes up– then we can play God, too, and face them out with courage and our own knowledge of right, and see whose masquerade turns out best in the end, theirs or ours– (147)

The echo of Clifford Odets is clearly evident in this speech, particularly the famous tag line from his *Awake and Sing!* (1935), which had made him the theatrical voice of the Left: "Go out and fight so life shouldn't be printed on dollar bills" (1968: 33). In this play, Williams was grafting a perennial and very personal concept, that of the fugitive kind, onto an accepted paradigm for leftist drama, the journey to enlightenment and freedom by characters who are imprisoned in an oppressive and dehumanizing economic and social system. In 1939, he wrote to Audrey Wood, "I have only one major theme for all my work which is the destructive impact of society on the sensitive, non-conformist individual" (L1: 220).

*Fugitive Kind* was written before Williams's peripatetic bohemian lifestyle commenced with his first escape from the family home to New Orleans in 1938, but it is his first extended exploration of the concept of the fugitive kind that is central to his self-conception and to many of the characters in his work, notably Val Xavier, Cassandra Whiteside, and Carol Cutrere in *Battle of Angels* (1940) and *Orpheus Descending* (1957) and Jonathan Coffin, Hannah Jelkes, and T. Lawrence Shannon in *The Night of the Iguana* (1961). In these works, the fugitive kind is a bohemian, often an artist or writer, as is Leo in *Fugitive Kind*, who feels confined and trapped in conventional middle-class life and is constantly searching for an escape through travel.

In his own life, Williams felt trapped first in St Louis, and later in places where he could not live the bohemian lifestyle he was most comfortable with, particularly in the 1940s and 1950s when he was constrained by the need to live both as a closeted gay man and as the public figure Tennessee Williams. He was known for disappearing, leaving New York when the social stress of the literary theatrical life became too much for him, leaving rehearsals, leaving film sets. He wrote to friends that his whole life was "a series of escapes, physical or psychological, more miraculous than any of Houdini's" (L1: 214), and that he was "sure, now, that I will never find one particular place where I feel altogether at home, will just have to keep moving about and absorbing as I go" (L1: 284). In his journal, he wrote: "I can never stand still–I'm always the fugitive–will be till I make my last escape–out of life altogether" (N: 205).

In *Fugitive Kind*, Glory's brother Leo expresses Williams's state of mind in the late 1930s, as he contemplated his escape from St Louis, his parents' house, and the shoe business where his father had confined him. Leo is unsuccessful when he tries to leave school and look for a job, explaining that "it scared me to watch them doing those things they were doing, operating machines, writing figures, selling goods, bustling around with piles and piles of letters and orders and–business! That's the whole thing to them and to me it's nothing at all. It doesn't exist, it's a world that I don't belong to, full of strangers. The only thing that I'm any good for, Chuck, is putting words down on paper" (132). In a characteristic image of confinement, Leo describes the city as a big trap that people built themselves, like a man who builds a house around him but forgets to make any doors or windows: "They're all caught in it except just a few like us, you an' me, the poor bums that flop here–Us, we didn't build walls around us, we don't belong–No, we're outcasts, lunatics, criminals–the Fugitive Kind, that's what we are–the ones that don't wanta stay put" (133).

The gangster Terry is another version of the fugitive kind, the social misfit. In a gesture toward social realism that suggests Sidney Kingsley's enormously successful gangster play *Dead End* (1935), which was adapted to film in 1937, Williams gives him a background that causes him to go wrong. The child of a tubercular prostitute, Terry got his education "out of alleys and poolhalls and whorehouses and backstreet gambling joints" (101). He wanted to be a doctor, but instead quit school and escaped to Chicago, where he at first tried to "go straight," working in a packing house, then, disgusted by the job, went to sea where he loved seeing foreign places, but realized he needed money to enjoy them, and tried to earn it, but "all I ever done was to work my tail off to make some rich guy richer. I got tired of that. See? And so I started my own little private revolution. It's been going on ever since" (102).

Tired of hiding out in the flophouse, Terry plans to go East and "cash in. And then I'm through" (102). When Glory falls in love with him, she realizes that she too has become a fugitive. When she confesses that the word scares her, Terry counters "Fugitives from justice? Naw, we're fugitives from *in*-justice, honey! We're runnin' away from stinkin' traps that people tried to catch us in!" (138). When Terry is shot by the FBI men, Glory becomes a convert to his way of seeing things: "What are they killing him for? What for, oh, what for? He wanted to get away, only to get away, only to get away, that was all, a thousand miles off from this place!" (143–4). The play ends with Terry's death and Leo and Glory, the brother and sister, left to represent the fugitive kind in envisioning some freer kind of existence. As a social drama, the play is vague, but it is an eloquent statement of Thomas Lanier Williams's view of the world and what was wrong with it in 1937.

Unfortunately, the play did not receive the kind of production Williams had hoped for. The Mummers' rehearsals took place in St Louis while he was at school in Iowa, and when he first saw the set, he told his friend Margo Jones 5 years later, "I found my window was a little transom at the top of the back wall! I fled from the theatre and walked along the street, literally tearing the script to little pieces and scattering it on the sidewalk" (L1: 492). In an apparently unfinished letter to Holland at the time, he confessed to what he saw as a weakness in the hastily finished script, revised while he was pressured with other work in the playwriting program at Iowa, but he complained that, in the production, "there was hardly an effort at atmospheric build-up in the setting for [the latter] half. The lighting was all wrong – there was no large window to bring the city and snow onto the stage – what became of the cathedral-like effect which we had agreed upon? The neon sign?" (L1: 119). Holland had ignored Williams's gestures toward the symbolic and expressionist, and produced the play in the mode of social realism. The reviews were mixed, and Williams felt that the production was a failure, although *Fugitive Kind* seems to have been the only one of his plays that really pleased his father, who called it his G-Man play, and may easily have identified with Terry's hard knocks and his love for the road.

## The Lure of Escape: *Not About Nightingales*

Williams's most fully realized social drama, *Not About Nightingales*, was intended for The Mummers, but Holland was fired as Director and the group disbanded before it could be produced. It was not produced until 1998, when British actor Vanessa Redgrave became aware of the script and turned it over to her brother Corin and their theatre group Moving Theatre. Their critically acclaimed production in conjunction with the National Theatre was directed by Trevor Nunn. It premiered on 5 March 1998 in London and moved to New York on 13 January 1999, where it was equally successful, hailed as a major play by America's greatest playwright. Nunn's production was expressionistic, with a set dominated on one side by prison bars and on the other by rows of filing cabinets representing the Warden's office. The culminating scene in the "Klondike" took place in the middle of the stage, in the "no man's land" between the two. The production also evoked the agit-prop techniques of the Living Newspaper where the play had originated with its episodes introduced by captions like news headlines projected across the bars.

The one-act play *Quit Eating!*, which Williams wrote for his class at Iowa, was based on a hunger strike in the Stateville, Illinois prison. He wrote to Holland that it was staged "in protest against new Parole policies which have reduced [the] number of paroles from over 1300 last year to about 240 for the nine months of this year" (L1: 108). In the fall of 1938, at his parents' house in Missouri, Williams began *Not About Nightingales* after reading a story about the prison atrocity that had occurred in a Holmesburg, Pennsylvania prison in August. In retaliation for a hunger strike staged by the prisoners to protest their poor diet, the men had been locked in a small cell, the "Klondike," with the steam from the heating system directed at them, raising the temperature to levels as high as 150 degrees F., and literally roasting the men. Over a period of 4 days, 4 men died and several others suffered delirium and other physical effects.

Williams clearly based the dramatization of the hunger strike on his earlier play. In *Not About Nightingales*, there is a good deal of talk about the poor diet, and the men weigh the possible consequences of being thrown in the Klondike against the desire to strike. It is actually the death of the popular inmate Ollie, who kills himself when he is sentenced to 5 more days in the "Hole," another torture cell, that finally energizes the men. In a group chant *"gradually rising in volume and pitch"*

(Williams 1998: 92) that is straight out of the Living Newspaper, the men first say "they killed Ollie–Ollie's dead.–They killed Ollie–Ollie's dead–They KILLED OLLIE– THEY KILLED OLLIE– OLLIE'S DEAD!" (92). At the incitement of the prison leader Butch O'Fallon, this chant shifts to "Butch says HUNGER STRIKE!–Hunger Strike– quit eating–Quit eating–HUNGER STRIKE!" (93), followed by the voices of a newsboy shouting a headline about the hunger strike, a woman's voice reporting it, the click of a telegraph, and bulletins by the Associated Press, United Press [International] and the Columbia Broadcasting System. This provides a climactic curtain for the end of Act I. The strike's becoming news also sets the stage for the Warden's brutal retaliation against the strikers.

In addition to the hunger strike, Williams includes several elements that are intended to arouse the audience's emotional engagement, ultimately to take action against such abuses. The opening scene introduces Mrs B., the mother of Sailor Jack, a young prisoner who has been driven insane by a stint in the Klondike. Not knowing this, she has been kept waiting for days to see her son. The audience sees Sailor Jack hallucinating and singing French songs to himself. When she finally gets in to see the Warden, his mother finds out that after spending 3 days in Klondike, he has been "transferred to the psychopathic ward. Violent. Delusions. Prognosis–'Dementia Praecox'" (32). His mother finally speaks out, accusing the Warden of torturing him until he had driven him crazy.

In a long monologue that did not make it into the 1998 version of the script published by New Directions, Butch gives a rousing speech reminiscent of the James Cagney characters of the 1930s' prison films and calculated to arouse the audience's admiration for the tough endurance of Butch and the other prisoners:

You're scared of Klondike? I say let 'em throw us in Klondike!–
Maybe some of you weak sisters will be melted down to grease-chunks. But not all twenty-five of us! Some of us are gonna beat Klondike! And Klondike's dere las' trump card, when you got that licked, you've licked everything they've got to offer in here! You got 'em over the barrel for good! So then what

**21**

happens? They come up to us and they say, "You win! What is it you want?" We say, "Boss Whalen is out! Git us a new Warden! Git us decent livin' conditions! No more overcrowdin', no more bunkin' up wit' contajus diseasus; fresh air in the cell-blocks, fumigation, an' most of all—WE WANT SOME FOOD THAT'S FIT TO PUT IN OUR BELLIES!" (122)

As Williams wrote it, this speech suggests an improbable naivete about the system on Butch's part, but it gets across the sense of solidarity among the men and the abuses they are opposing. Even more improbably, Butch goes on to articulate a progressive agenda for prison reform, claiming that the men can make the prison "like the Industrial Reformatory they got at Chillicothe! A place where guys are learnt how to make a livin' after they git outa stir! Where they teach 'em trades an' improve their ejication!" (123). This part of the speech was obviously meant to rouse the audience to action rather than the inmates.

Like Williams's other leftist plays, this one has a trajectory from arousal of the characters' social conscience toward enlightenment and action. The romantic relationship between Jim Allison, the Warden's assistant who the prisoners assume is the informer, or "canary," and Eva, the new secretary, parallels the characters' growing sense of social responsibility. At first, Eva, who had been down to her last dime before she was hired, values keeping her job above revealing the abuses at the prison, and Jim is anxious to accumulate enough goodwill with the Warden to earn his parole. As they begin to fall in love, Eva plans to leave in a month or so and tell the story of the prison to the newspapers. Jim, who has been educating himself, hopes to write an article exposing the abuses once he gets out. Meanwhile, he believes in "intellectual emancipation," as he tells Ollie: "They can tell us what to read, what to say, what to do— But they can't tell us what to *think*! And as long as man can think as he pleases he's never exactly locked up anywhere. He can think himself outside of all their walls and boundaries and make the world his place to live in" (38). Sounding the collective note, he insists, "you're not alone, though, cause you know that you're part of everything living and everything living is part of you" (39).

When Jim tells Butch about his plan to write an article about the prison after he gets out, Butch is scornful. Jim earns Butch's respect when he engineers the breakout from the Klondike, and he gives up his chance for parole when he lets Butch take his revenge on the Warden, beating him with the same rubber hose he has used on Butch and Jim in the past and throwing him out the window into the water that surrounds the island where the prison is located. Jim's final escape is left ambiguous, as he jumps out the window, hoping to swim to the *Lorelei*, the tour boat that is aptly named for the Rhine maidens that lure men to their doom. Although it lends a troubling ambiguity to the drama of social action, this ending had deep personal significance for Williams. In an image that would become familiar in the Williams canon, Jim speaks of being "pent up here, in these walls, locked in 'em so tight it's like I was buried under the earth in a coffin with a glass lid that I could see the world through! While I felt the worms crawling inside me" (126). This was a feeling that the playwright expressed often when he was living in his parents' attic. The lure of escape was powerful.

Another of Williams's major subjects, transgressive sexuality, makes an interesting appearance in both *Not About Nightingales* and *Candles to the Sun*. In the earlier play, Star speaks of her love for Red in terms that foreshadow Williams's treatment of sado-masochistic sexual attraction in *Camino Real* (1953), the story "Desire and the Black Masseur" (1948), *27 Wagons Full of Cotton* (1945), and *Suddenly Last Summer* (1958). She tells Red, "When you were talking at the meetins [*sic*] I used to look at your hands and feel them touchin' me! Sometimes I could even feel them striking me and I liked even that! I wanted to get in front of your hands an feel them poundin' me down, down! I knew from the very beginning that it would be like that! Your hands beating me down! And still I wanted it, Red" (98). In *Nightingales*, Eva is disgusted by the Warden's sexual advances, but when she tells Jim that he has pinched her hard enough to bruise her arm, she says she felt "terribly scared–and at the same time–something else" (83). She admits to feeling attracted to him as well: "I knew that if he touched me I wouldn't be able to move" (83). Jim tells her that the pulps call this "fascinated horror," and she replies, "Yes. Or a horrible fascination" (83).

Although Williams's treatment of homosexuality is often assumed to begin in the mid-1950s with *Cat on a Hot Tin Roof* (1955) and *Suddenly Last Summer*, allusions to it are straightforward in these early plays when he was still dealing with the religious taboos around his homoerotic feelings and figuring out his own sexual identity. *Not About Nightingales* has a clearly gay character, called Queen by the other prisoners. He is treated sympathetically, but the imagery of contamination and self-destruction that would be associated with gay characters in Williams's later works is evident here as well. Queen has tested positive for syphilis, information the other prisoners try to shield him from. In the Klondike scene, when the men are being tortured with the steam from the radiators, Queen is the foil for the manly and stoic Butch, becoming hysterical, screaming *"in frantic horror,"* and *"sobbing wildly and falling on the floor"* as he says, "Oh, my God, why don't they stop now! Why don't they let us out! Oh, Jesus, Jesus, please, please, please!" (139). When Queen finally staggers blindly into the radiators, scalding himself and screaming, Butch cracks his head on the floor. Told that he has killed him, Butch says, "somebody shoulda done him that favor a long time ago" (143).

## Sexual Confusion: *Spring Storm*

There is also a homoerotic element in the two early unproduced plays that were most personal to Williams, *Spring Storm* (1938) and *Stairs to the Roof* (1941). The latter includes a stereotypical gay character, "A Designer," who works in the garment industry where the protagonist, Benjamin Murphy, is also employed. He is described as *"an effeminate young man"* who rolls his eyes heavenward and dramatically puts his hand on his forehead when he has to deal with a shirt that wasn't made according to specifications: "The stripes on the dickey should have been pale, *pale* blue but they're *al*-most *pur*-ple!" (Williams 2000: 4).

The more complex Arthur Shannon in *Spring Storm* is very much like Williams himself at this time, avidly pursuing heterosexual relationships despite, or perhaps in flight from, his homoerotic feelings.

Williams essentially came out in New Orleans in 1938, when he first began to have sex with male partners on a regular basis. When he began to speak publically about his sexuality 30 years later, he would always identify himself as homosexual, and not bisexual. He wrote in his *Memoirs* that his affair with Bette Reitz, a fellow student at Iowa, was the only consummated heterosexual relationship in his life. As late as 1940, however, when he was rather aggressively pursuing a promiscuous gay lifestyle in New York, Williams was also interested in relationships with women. He recorded in his journal a "love episode" with the young sculptor Anne Bretzfelder, whom he liked very much, and she told Williams's biographer Lyle Leverich that "he kept making advances that displeased me mightily. I felt pressured to the extreme by him—so much so that finally I would flee from him and hide from him." In her view, "it was just unfortunate for me that I happened to be in his life at that time. And I didn't realize then, not until I was older and knew more about such things, that he was probably profoundly being pulled in two directions" (1995: 351).

*Spring Storm* was written at the time of Williams's greatest conflict over his sexuality, and it clearly informed Arthur Shannon's characterization. In the play, Arthur is aggressively pursuing Heavenly, an attractive girl with natural and highly developed Southern charm, who is "*frankly sensuous without being coarse, fiery-tempered and yet disarmingly sweet. Her nature is confusing to herself and to all who know her*" (Williams 1999: 5), particularly Arthur Shannon. Tellingly, Arthur's reason for pursuing Heavenly is not romantic love or sexual attraction, but a grudge he has held against her since elementary school. As the hyper-masculine Dick Miles remembers, when Arthur was in elementary school, he was "a sissy" whose chauffeur brought him to school and who sat in a corner at recess reading *The Wizard of Oz*. The other children, including Heavenly, used to taunt him with "Artie, Smartie, went to a party!/ What did he go for? To play with his dolly" (18). After he had a nervous breakdown and went to London to study, Arthur had an affair with a girl. He tells the sympathetic Hertha, "It was her first experience and mine, too. It did us both good. We were both slightly crazy before it happened, and afterwards, we were perfectly sane" (30).

Arthur writes poetry, although he realizes that he doesn't have it in him to become anything other than a talented amateur because his poetry "isn't a terrific volcanic eruption . . . it's just a little bonfire of dry leaves and dead branches" (25). Having returned to Port Tyler, Mississippi, Arthur has been asked to join the Junior Chamber of Commerce, much to his father's delight, and is ready to pursue the conventional life of a businessman, which would of course include marriage to someone like Heavenly. But he confesses to her that he is "in a state of constant confusion . . . a pretty queer sort of person. . . . I want what I'm afraid of and I'm afraid of what I want so that I'm like a storm inside that can't break loose!" (69). He confronts her with the memory of an incident in school when some bullies cornered him in the school yard and yelled "sissy" at him until he cried, and she stood there laughing at him: "That laugh, that was why I couldn't go back to school anymore–so they had to send me to Europe and say that I'd had a nervous breakdown" (70). He tells her that he cannot get over the hatred that he has felt for her since, but still feels compelled to pursue her with what he thinks is love, or what Strindberg called "love-hatred and it hails from the pit!" (72).

When Heavenly chooses Dick over him and sends him away, Arthur gets drunk for the first time and makes sexual advances to Hertha, who backs away in dismay. Flattered that she is afraid of him, Arthur says that he had never gotten over being a sissy until that night, "when I got drunk. God! I never knew it could be so good to get drunk and feel like a man inside" (120). He dismisses literature and the arts, and "being a highbrow," and says he is going to be more like Dick Miles in the future. He kisses Hertha, and when she responds, "I love you! I love you. So much that I've nearly gone mad!" (123), he becomes disgusted, saying "I didn't know you were like that. I thought you were different" (123). He later says that he lost his desire because "she was like I was, lonely and hungry" (145).

The next evening, when Heavenly asks him to drive her to meet Dick Miles so they can run away, Arthur "*kisses her repeatedly: on the lips, throat, shoulders. Heavenly gasps for breath, stops resisting. She leans passively against him*" (139). Having discovered that she responded to Arthur sexually as much as she did to Dick, Heavenly decides not to go off to meet Dick and commit herself to a life of relative poverty, but to marry Arthur and live in the best house in town, but when Arthur finds out that Hertha has killed herself, he decides to leave town because of the guilt he would feel being with Heavenly. She calls him a coward for running away, and he responds, "Yes. That's a habit of mine" (147). In the end Heavenly becomes what is most dreaded by the young women in a small Southern town, an old maid or "front porch girl," having sacrificed her marriageability because of her well-known sexual intimacy with Dick, and she goes to sit on the porch and wait for Arthur or Dick to return and marry her.

Like Williams at this time, Arthur Shannon is clearly a young man who is struggling to understand his sexual desires, to figure out his relationship to art, and to find a way to escape from the pressures of conventional life that he finds so oppressive. He also feels guilt for the mental condition of Hertha, who bears a strong resemblance to Williams's sister Rose Williams. "*Without money or social position, she has to depend upon a feverish animation and cleverness to make her place among people. She has an original mind with a distinct gift for creative work. She is probably the most sensitive and intelligent person in Port Tyler, Mississippi*" (21), all characteristics he would ascribe to Rose. Like Rose, who was 28 when she was diagnosed with "dementia praecox" in 1937, Hertha fears becoming an old maid, and fears losing her mind because she feels so nervous, saying "lots of girls do at my age. Twenty-eight. Lots of them get *dementia praecox* at about that age, especially when they're not married. . . . They get morbid and everything excites them and they think they're being persecuted by people. I'm getting like that" (114). This is a good description of Rose Williams's symptoms at that time. Arthur's rejection of Hertha and his feeling of responsibility for her self-destruction are no doubt informed by Williams's guilt over his lack of sympathy during the early stages of Rose's illness and his remoteness from her during the early years of her confinement.

Along with its intensely personal content, the play shows the influence of Anton Chekhov. The play's anticlimactic ending and the inherent futility of its narrative trajectory, in which each of the characters pursues an unreachable object of desire, are typically

Chekhovian. In this case, Hertha loves Arthur, who pursues Heavenly, who is trying to hold onto Dick, who desires freedom. In the end, with Hertha's death and Heavenly's abandonment, each of the men becomes a different version of the fugitive kind, with Dick leaving the town and going off to do the kind of physical labor he likes and Arthur escaping the town and both of its women, presumably to discover a way of life that is more natural to him.

The intensely personal content of *Spring Storm* was not welcomed by the playwriting program at Iowa, with its strong emphasis on social drama. Williams confessed in his journal that he was "badly deflated by Conkle & class this week when they criticized my new play. Hardly a favorable comment. . . . I was horribly shocked, felt like going off the deep-end. Feared I might lose my mind" (N: 117). Two days later he was in a more healthy state of mind, writing, "I don't believe the play is really that bad—its virtues are not apparent in a first reading but I think it would blossom out on the stage—but I see plainly now that I'm a distinctly second or third rate writer—and I wonder how I ever got into it so deep—now what?" (N: 117). This was in April. After working all summer on the play, he wrote on 2 August that he had read aloud the final version of the play and "was finally, quite, quite finally rejected by the class because of Heavenly's weakness as a character." He wrote that it was "very frightening & discouraging to work so hard on a thing and then have it fall flat," but he had the confidence to think "there is still a chance they may be wrong—all of them—I have to cling to that chance. Or do I? Why can't I be brave and admit this defeat?—Because it means the defeat of everything? Perhaps." (N: 121–3). The class was right about Heavenly's weakness as a character, but Williams was interested enough in her to resurrect her in *Sweet Bird of Youth* (1959), the early drafts of the play clearly drawing on the story of Heavenly and Dick for the story of Heavenly Finley and Chance Wayne.

## An Escape for the Wild of Heart: *Stairs to the Roof*

Williams said that he wrote *Stairs to the Roof* "as catharsis for the years he spent as a clerk in the International Shoe Company" (Leverich

1995: 436). It has its aesthetic origins in the *Stationendramen* or "station plays" developed by the German Expressionists in the early twentieth century, and most recognizable in Georg Kaiser's *From Morn To Midnight* (1922). Structured as a series of episodes, this kind of play typically focuses on the "little man," the dehumanized worker, an anonymous clerk or factory worker lost in the vast machinery of a corporation or factory. An event at the beginning of the play shocks the little man out of the automaton-like state to which he has been reduced by routine and boredom, and each of the episodes that follows shows him trying to find some way to make sense of his life and what has happened to him, through his marriage, or religion, or politics, and finally through sex, or crime, or in other socially rebellious ways, and failing. The typical play ends with a primal *Schrei* or scream, which expresses the little man's final desperation, and then his incarceration or death in retaliation for his rebellion. Williams probably became familiar with the form through Eugene O'Neill's Americanized versions in *The Emperor Jones* (1920) and *The Hairy Ape* (1922), which he read for a paper he wrote on O'Neill's work as an undergraduate, and the lighter, more satirical versions in Elmer Rice's *The Adding Machine* (1923) and, more directly, *Two on an Island* (1940), an expressionistic play with a lot of similarities to *Stairs to the Roof*, which ran in New York between January and April of 1940, when Williams was conceiving and drafting the play there.

*Stairs to the Roof* begins typically for a *Stationendrama* in a dehumanizing workplace depicted expressionistically. The set of Consolidated Shirtmakers is minimal, including the boss's desk and an enormous clock:

> *The rest is suggested by the movements of the workers. They sit on stools, their arms and hands making rigid, machine-like motions above their imaginary desks to indicate typing, filing, operating a comptometer, and so forth. Two middle-aged women are reciting numbers to each other, antiphonally, in high and sing-song voices. The girl at the (invisible) filing cabinet has the far-away stare of a schizophrenic as her arms work mechanically above the indexed cases.* (Williams 2000: 3)

It was a scene that Williams knew well from his stint at International Shoe Company, perhaps filtered through *The Adding Machine*. Foreshadowing the "celotex interior" of *The Glass Menagerie*, "*there is a glassy brilliance to the atmosphere: one feels that it must contain a highly selected death ray that penetrates living tissue straight to the heart and bestows a withering kiss on whatever diverges from an accepted pattern*" (3). The play's protagonist, Ben Murphy, is a Williams self-representation, "*a small young man with the nervous, defensive agility of a squirrel. Ten years of regimentation have made him frantic but have not subdued his spirit. He is one of those feverish, bright little people who might give God some very intelligent answers if they were asked*" (5).

Having discovered that the building contains a hidden staircase to the roof, Ben has taken to going up there to take his breaks instead of smoking in the Men's room with the other clerks, and he is chastised by the boss for disappearing too often and for too long at a time, and for not having enough ambition to succeed in the company. During their encounter, Ben shares his idea that "people wouldn't be killing and trying to conquer each other unless there was something terribly, terribly wrong at the bottom of things." He suggests that "maybe the wrong is this: this regimentation, this gradual grinding out of the lives of the little people under the thumbs of things that are bigger than they are! People get panicky locked up in a dark cellar: they trample over each other fighting for air! Air, air, give them air! Isn't it maybe–just as simple as that?" (13). Predictably unimpressed with this analysis, his boss tells him that he is going to review his record, and if he doesn't find "any ray of hope for your future with Continental Branch of the Consolidated Shirtmakers" (13), he will be fired the next day. This provides the "violent shock" that sends Ben off onto his journey toward discovery. He tells his friend Jim: "Mentally I'm a submarine brought to the surface for the first time in eight years by the explosion of a terrible depth bomb. Something is going to happen to me tonight" (24).

The rest of the play is Williams's version of the journey of discovery. It begins in a bar, where Ben chides his old friend Jim, based on Williams's St Louis friend Jim O'Connor, for his deterioration.

At 30, Jim, who was an athlete in college, has become overweight and soft. "Now in your present condition I bet you would drown in the municipal birdbath," he says, "even your eyes have changed color. They used to be blue, energetic. Now they're kind of shifty-looking gray" (22). In December, 1939, Williams wrote in his journal about going to visit O'Connor and drinking "too much beautiful whiskey." He wrote that "Jim has a lovely wife and a very attractive apartment, a beautiful car. But he has gotten fat and I think is a little ashamed of his bourgeois position. Not unhappy—in fact I suppose much happier than in his wild, free days—but I felt sorry for him somehow although he certainly has an abundant supply of good whiskey and the little wife looked like good stuff, too. Alas, poor Yorick or something—I knew him well. They'll do it every time, won't they? Thank god I've gotten bitch-proof" (N: 173–5). In the play, Ben poses an existential question to his friend, noting that between birth and death "is one little instant of light—a pin-point of brilliance—right here in the very center of infinite—endless-dark! What are you going to do with it? What wonderful use are you going to make of this one instant?" (23). After establishing the dreary and joyless lives of these two conventional middle-class young men, Williams turns the traditional expressionistic play's desperate descent into self-destruction into an existential search for wonder.

Ben goes home to his pregnant wife Alma, a stout woman whose *"face is glittering with cold cream, and her hair is done up in wire curlers. She is a woman corresponding to the spider of a certain species that devours her mate when he has served his procreative function"* (26). After she berates him for being late, she guesses that he's been fired and says she is going to leave him and go home to her mother. Ben goes out for a walk and finds himself on the campus of his former university, where the scene flashes back to his romance with Helen, a poet, and Jim's warning that her lyric verse was "the perfume in the poison cup" (33) that would keep him from the life of adventure that they planned in the merchant marine. This is followed by the commencement speech at their graduation by the president of Consolidated Shirtmakers, who offers Ben a job, and Jim's determination to take a job for 3 or 4 months in order to raise the money for their trip. In the play's present,

Ben says bitterly, "Three or four *years*–five years–six years–seven–eight! You cheat! You phony! You coward! You dirty liar!" (35).

Ben goes to Jim's house to talk over his thoughts, and says he wants to "refurnish" his life with "new things! *Beliefs*–that are like steel weapons! *Ideals*–that catch the sunlight!" (41). He will look for them "in the political party of my heart! In my instinct that tells me I don't have to be caged!" (42). The subtitle for early versions of the play was "A Prayer for the Wild of Heart That Are Kept in Cages" (Leverich 1995: 436), a phrase Williams also used to describe *Battle of Angels* and *Camino Real*.

Ben's journey toward his new beliefs begins when he wanders down to his office building and encounters the Girl, a character who has come to retrieve the love letter she has written to her boss before he reads it and fires her. Ben proposes that they go "night-prowling" together: "We'll make observations in the dark of the moon; we'll penetrate to the very heart of darkness. And when the sun comes up, we'll know all the forbidden secrets" (53). They go to the zoo, where Ben begins his "career of emancipator" (58) by freeing the foxes, a probable allusion to D. H. Lawrence's novella, *The Fox*. Chased by the guards, they wind up in an amusement park they call "Wonderland," and the Girl tells Ben her story, saying that "love is one cage that there isn't any way out of" (66). Seeing a swan on the lake, Ben remarks that it is moving away from them because "it isn't domestic–it's wild. It's heard of the cages that tame creatures have built to capture the wild of heart" (68). With the Girl pretending Ben is the boss she is in love with and Ben identifying her with the wild swan, they make love to the music of the distant carousel.

From this point, the play becomes increasingly expressionistic and fantastic. The next scene, at a carnival, "*is like the set for a rather fantastic ballet as the play progresses further from realism: this may be justified, if necessary, by Ben's increasing intoxication and the exaltation of love in the Girl*" (70). As a commentary on sex, some Mummers perform "Beauty and the Beast," describing the sexual encounter between beast and virgin which ends: "He was astonished–she was not besmirched./ Her face was holy as a nun's at church" and Beauty's speech, "Do not grieve–/ I owned no beauty till it felt thy need,/

Which, being answered, makes thee no more Beast,/ But One with Beauty!" (73). This is followed by their parting on the street corner in front of the office building after facing the fact of reality, which, Ben tells the Girl, is composed of "some very harsh ingredients," the facts that he is married and probably jobless.

A scene between the Girl and her boss shows that the experience has changed her, however. She tells him that she has seen her reflection in the water, and she is not an ugly duckling, but "a snow-white swan.–And from now on I'm going to preen my feathers, I'm going to rustle and glide–and be admired by people" (85). She tosses a bunch of files into the air and takes the stairs to the roof that Ben has told her about.

The play ends with two expressionistic scenes, in the first of which the heads of the corporation, Messrs. P, D, Q, and T, discover that Ben knows about the roof, and they decide to offer him a job "on the road" to keep him from spreading the word to the other workers. In the final scene, Ben and the Girl meet on the roof and Mr E, whom Williams referred to as the play's *deus ex machina*, proposes to them that they become the settlers of a new star. He has been observing "this funny little clown of a man named Murphy," and has decided that Ben has "suddenly turned into the tragic protagonist of a play called 'Human Courage'" (97). To rectify his mistake in creating the human race, Mr E has decided, instead of exterminating it, to send Ben and the Girl "off to colonize a brand-new star in heaven" (97). As Mr E disappears in a cloud of smoke, the workers burst out of the door onto the roof. Unable to stop them, Ben's boss tells P, D, Q, and T, "Smile, you sons of bitches! Act delighted. Play like this is what you always wanted!" (98). Ben says goodbye from a long way off, and a raucous celebration hails the new Millennium.

*Stairs to the Roof* is perhaps the most joyful and life-affirming play that Tennessee Williams wrote. Departing from its expressionistic precursors, it dramatizes an existential journey toward freedom and self-acceptance rather than a journey into desperation and destruction. It is telling that Ben escapes not only his marriage and his job in the end, but also the earth itself, embarking on a cosmic journey to literally begin a new way of life. This fantasy is a fitting summary of the eventful

3 years in Williams's life after leaving his parents' attic in St Louis, coming out in New Orleans, embracing the bohemian life of the French Quarter, the road, and Southern California with his friend Jim Parrott, and living a bohemian gay lifestyle in Provincetown, Puerta Vallarta, and New York. The play is a farewell to middle-class convention, a fanciful manifesto for the life of "emancipation," and a celebration of the keynote of Williams's lifestyle in the future, "escape."

*Stairs to the Roof* was not to see a New York Production. Having been sent the play by Williams's agent Audrey Wood, producer David Merrick wrote that he found it "interesting and beautifully written," but thought it "unlikely you can get a Broadway production. I don't think a producer would be likely to risk a more than average amount of production money on a fantasy or semi-fantasy at this time. Not unless it had a chorus of pretty girls, and [referring to *Lady in the Dark*] a part for Gertrude Lawrence" (Leverich 1995: 456). The play was to be produced by the Pasadena Playhouse in 1947 to mixed reviews and did not receive another production until it was done at the University of Illinois in 2000.

The year 1940 found Williams on the brink of his entrance into the professional theatre. He had written his "apprentice work." He had found a way to write effectively for the theatre of social and political engagement, even though its theatrical and literary idioms did not come naturally to him. He had begun to develop an authentic voice in which to express things that were meaningful to him and to adapt theatrical styles like expressionism to his own vision for the theatre. Perhaps more importantly, in writing about the bohemian, the fugitive kind, the "wild of heart kept in cages," the misfit, the sexually confused, and the frustrated artist, he had explored much of the territory he was to mine for the rest of his writing life.

# CHAPTER 2
## BATTLE OF ANGELS AND ORPHEUS DESCENDING (1939–1941 AND 1957)

### "The sensitive, non-conformist individual":
### Battle of Angels

*Battle of Angels*, written in the summer and fall of 1939, during Williams's stays in Taos, in his parents' attic in St Louis, and in New York, was a combination of the ideas and tropes he had been developing in the previous four plays, and an expression of what he announced to his newly acquired agent Audrey Wood in December 1939 as the "one major theme for all my work which is the destructive impact of society on the sensitive, non-conformist individual." In *Battle of Angels*, he said, the individual was "a boy who hungered for something beyond reality and got death by torture at the hands of a mob" (L1: 220). In an essay written for the play's first publication, in the short-lived New Directions magazine *Pharos* in 1945, he explained that *Battle of Angels* was the first of his plays to "release and purify the emotional storms of my earlier youth." Referring to its setting in a small Mississippi town, he wrote that "the stage or setting of this drama was the country of my childhood. Onto it I projected the violent symbols of my adolescence. It was a synthesis of the two parts of my life already passed through" (P1: 277). This was true, but it also took on the themes and characters that would preoccupy him for the rest of his life: the plight of the social outcast, particularly the bohemian artist struggling to create art in a hostile environment; the "fugitive kind," who seek a necessary escape from the oppressive norms and institutions of society; and the individual's struggle with sexuality and sexual identity.

Having returned to his parents' house after his wandering year spent in New Orleans, Southern California, Taos, and briefly New

York, Williams wrote to Molly Day Thacher at the Group Theatre that he was "back in St. Louis, writing furiously with seven wild-cats under my skin, as I realize that completing this new play is my only apparent avenue of escape. . . . My whole life has been a series of escapes, physical or psychological, more miraculous than any of Houdini's but I do at the present moment seem to be hanging by that one thread: obtaining a fellowship and/or producing a successful play" (L1: 213–14). To Audrey Wood he wrote that his life in St Louis was "hopelessly circumscribed by the wholesale shoe business on one side and the D.A.R. [Daughters of the American Revolution] on the other although I must admit there is considerably less anxiety about the next meal than there was on the Coast. But I am one of those noble animals who would rather starve in a jungle than grow fat in a cage" (L1: 215).

Fortunately, the escape arrived in December with the news that Williams had been awarded a Rockefeller fellowship, and he quickly departed for New York. At this point, his chief anxiety about *Battle of Angels* was the "violent, melodramatic nature of the material." He was concerned that Wood would not like the "pathological characters or violent theme" (L1: 215). He was also concerned about its fire motif, particularly the conflagration that ended the Third Act, which he thought melodramatic, but as he revised the play, he thought he had integrated the fire theme enough that the ending would not seem just "a melodramatic trick to add horror to the atmosphere" (L1: 217). After Audrey Wood reassured him that a violent theme would not be detrimental to the play's chances for production, he was much relieved, sending her a draft at the end of November.

The circumstances of the play's production were a young playwright's fantasy come true. Wood first submitted it to the Group Theatre, which had shown interest in Williams's work, and awarded him a $100 prize, and to Guthrie McClintic, who she hoped would see it as vehicle for his wife, the distinguished actor Katharine Cornell. McClintic passed, however, and The Group was on the verge of disbanding. Besides, as Williams knew, *Battle of Angels* was not the sort of play that would appeal to their leftist agenda. In March he wrote to Wood that he thought a copy of the play should go to the Theatre Guild, the producer of Eugene O'Neill and George Bernard Shaw, and the first choice for any American playwright who had aspirations to literary distinction as well as commercial success. Williams had a foot in the door of the Theatre Guild because he was attending a playwriting workshop at New York's New School that was run by John Gassner, a distinguished drama scholar who was serving as play reader for the Guild, and Theresa Helburn, one of its directors. The plan worked. Gassner read the play and was so impressed that he and Helburn held a meeting of the New School workshop, at which "the play was thoroughly dissected and many changes were suggested" (L1: 241), and Williams, without consulting Wood, agreed to give the Theatre Guild the play in exchange for a $100 option. He was quite pleased with this exploitative deal, and it took some tough talk from Wood and the Dramatists Guild to extricate him from it and make an arrangement more favorable to the playwright, which abided by the Dramatists Guild's rules.

With the promise of the $100 check, Williams had immediately made his escape, stopping to visit his parents and grandparents on an intended trip to Mexico. Writing to Theresa Helburn in response to a wire she sent to his parents' house, he said that he had bolted from New York because "my residence there had become a sort of endurance contest in which I felt myself to be rapidly losing out." In true fugitive-kind style, he wrote, "I seem to be constitutionally unable to stay [in] one place more than three months and I had been in Manhattan nearly four and had an excruciating nostalgia for the beach again" (L1: 250). He agreed to return to New York to finish the revisions, however, and was back in the city a week later. While this behavior, suddenly disappearing without a word, was to become typical of Williams during productions and film shoots, in this case, he may have had a better sense of what was necessary for him to finish the script than the producers did. On 11 April, 2 days after the New School reading, he had sent John Gassner a letter that included his notes for a major revision of the script, which involved changing the setting and action of one of the Acts, and eliminating some characters and developing others.

Williams may have known that he would have a hard time concentrating on his writing amid the distractions of New York and a big-time commercial production for which he was completely unprepared. He perhaps instinctively sought to re-create the peace and solitude that had proven beneficial to his writing in Big Sur, California the previous year. In any case, he worked on the play in New York, sending the Guild a new Act 1 at the beginning of May, and commenting rather naively that "we can now regard the play as completed from the structural standpoint. What remains is simply pruning down and some manipulation with glue-pot, pencil and scissors, a purely mechanical business which perhaps can be done most effectively with the cooperation of actors and director when the play is actually in rehearsal" (L1: 252). At this point, Williams did not realize how unusual had been his working relationship with Willard Holland on the Mummers' productions. Holland had actually functioned as play-doctor as well as director, taking Williams's rather flabby drafts and working with him to turn them into producible scripts. He seemed to expect that his experience in the commercial theatre would be similar. As he wrote 5 years later:

> I realize that I had fooled these people. Because certain qualities in my writing had startled them, they took it for granted that I was an accomplished playwright and that some afternoon when I was not busy with interviews, casting, rehearsals, I would quietly withdraw for an hour or two and work out the dramaturgic problems as deftly as such things were done by men like [Philip] Barry and [George S.] Kaufmann [*sic*] and [S. N.] Behrmann [*sic*]. They had no idea how dazed and stymied I was by the rush of events into which my dreamy self was precipitated. (P1: 280)

Williams's inability to solve the structural problems and to revise the play during the rehearsal process was to prove a major stumbling block for the play's first production. He was up against a particularly difficult situation for an inexperienced playwright. The role of Myra Torrance was played by Miriam Hopkins, a somewhat faded movie star who was looking to revive her career by returning to the Broadway stage in a striking part. Besides being a difficult, strong-willed actor who wanted her own way in production matters, she also had invested money in the show, which gave her a substantial means of control. Williams had written a play whose central character is Val Xavier, the bohemian artist figure who comes into a small Southern town and encounters three women who are sexually attracted to him, Myra Torrance, the wife of the dying store-owner Jabe; Vee Talbot, the sheriff's wife whose repressed sexuality is expressed in her primitive religious paintings; and Cassandra Whiteside, the wild daughter of the town's wealthy plantation owners, who frankly tries to seduce Val the moment he arrives. In Williams's mind, these female characters were more or less equal, each bringing out a side of Val's character and sexuality. In a 1940 Broadway production, however, particularly one in which an actress owned a share, there had to be a recognizable female lead character, and that lead was Miriam Hopkins's Myra Torrance. As the rehearsals went on, there was pressure on Williams to build up Hopkins's part and to fix the play's somewhat chaotic ending, which culminated in the sensational fire about which Williams always had his doubts. The pressure only made it "impossible for me to do anything at all," he wrote later (P1: 282).

The production opened in Boston on 30 December for a 2-week tryout intended to give the production team time to do the final necessary revisions to the script and perfect the production before it opened in New York. Williams's version of opening night in Boston has become the standard narrative of this event, and he depicted it as a disaster owing to the play's staging, not its script. At the dress rehearsal, he wrote, the culminating fire was merely a series of inadequate stage effects, "little trickles of smoke under the wings, the flickering red lights, the bawling voices" (P1: 283), that neither signaled the conflagration he was looking for nor provided the background for the final cathartic scene. What's more, the music that Hopkins was supposed to dance to was discovered to be completely inappropriate, and recorded music had to be substituted. Expecting disaster at opening night, he found it. According to him, members of the audience got up periodically during the play and walked out, but "it was not until the point of the conflagration that the Boston audience was in a strategic position to vent its full displeasure." Having been told that the fire was inadequate, "the gentlemen operating the smoke-pots" had created an effect "like the burning of Rome. Great sulphurous billows rolled chokingly onto the stage and coiled over the foot-lights." Williams said that this excited "pandemonium," with "outraged squawks, gabbling, spluttering" in the front rows and "nothing that happened on the stage from then on was of any importance . . . the scene was nearly eclipsed by the fumes. Voices were lost in the banging up of seats as the front rows were evacuated." In his memory, at the curtain call, Miriam Hopkins stood gallantly waving at the smoke in front of her face as the audience turned their backs to her, pushing up the aisles "like heavy, heedless cattle" (P1: 285).

Williams's friend William Jay Smith, who was present at the opening, has written that he saw none of the chaos that Williams described, no banging of seats, no squawks, gabbling, or spluttering, and no spectators pushing up the aisles. He remembered instead a brief period of confusion when the curtain came down and then "a great hush that spread over the audience, a hush broken when Miriam Hopkins stepped forward waving and bowing and her gesture was followed by a strong wave of applause that swept through the house as if to extinguish the blaze" (2012: 53). None of the reviews mentioned the fire, although *Variety* called the final curtain "as amateurish a bit of melodrama as the Guild has ever attempted" (Libbey 1940). The references to the set design and direction were primarily positive, with the *Boston Herald* calling the acting and direction "nearly perfect" and Cleon Throckmorton's set for the mercantile store "just the thing" (Williams 1940), and the *Christian Science Monitor* opining that "the skill of the evening lies more in the production than in the play" (E. F. M. 1940). The *Boston Traveler's* description of the ending shows that Williams's symbolic intent for the fire was understood: "Throughout the play [Val] has confessed his eternal fear of fire. Now he is surrounded by it. The neurotic girl in white bids him arise and carry the corpse of the woman he had loved upstairs so they can all be temporarily above the flames from which there is no escape except to be killed by the mob" (Watts 1940). Miriam Hopkins was universally acclaimed, as were most of the other actors, but the play itself came in for a good deal of criticism. Williams was taken to task for the play's melodrama, sensationalism, and violence; the talkiness, vague construction, and confusing symbolism of the script, and the play's "disagreeable" ("Plays Here" 1940) characters. The *Boston Transcript* summed up a general impression: "Mr. Williams has tried to do a great many things in his play and has not wholly succeeded in any of them" (Hastings 1940).

It was clear that the play suffered from its proximity to the huge commercial success of Jack Kirkland's adaptation of Erskine Caldwell's novel *Tobacco Road* (1933), which was still running in its 7th year on Broadway. It had caricatured the rural South as a place of squalor, stupidity, and sexual license. In its review of *Battle of Angels*, the *Boston Post* reported that "the locale of the play is the Mississippi Delta and the characters are all pretty low grade, suggesting something like 'Tobacco Road' to some playgoers" ("Battle" 1940: 8). *Variety* observed that "the Theatre Guild may have heard that somebody struck gold down the old tobacco road and decided to dig up a little dirt down along the Mississippi Delta to see how it would pan out," describing Val as a "half-wit living a defensive life against predatory women" and Cassandra as "the in-bred daughter of the town's most prosperous old family" (Libbey 1940). Nothing in the play suggests that Val is a "half-wit." In fact he is a talented writer. Nor is there any suggestion of inbreeding in the Whitesides. But the critics' and audience's expectation shaped what they saw.

Perhaps in keeping with this expectation, there was a minor difficulty with the notorious Boston censors after a City Councillor who had not seen the play pronounced it "putrid," and demanded that it be shut down. As a result, two censors attended the production on 6 January and ordered some changes which the management accepted. John Haggot, the production manager, said that he had talked to the Police Commissioner after he had seen the show "and he found nothing particularly objectionable. We have to alter a few lines, but there will be no important changes" (Wheildon 1941). Williams, who had left town 2 days earlier and did not see the altered show, wrote that "the censors sat out front and demanded excision from the script of practically all that made it intelligible, let alone moving" (P1: 286). Once, again, Williams's narrative made a disaster out of a situation that was disastrous only in his mind.

In any case, the Theatre Guild decided to close the show in Boston and paid Williams a monthly fee so that he could finally go to Key West and rewrite it, with the hope that the script would prove strong enough for a New York opening, or perhaps another tryout at the Westport Country Playhouse, founded by Guild Director Lawrence Langner and his wife, Armina Marshall. When the revised script proved still unacceptable to Langner in July, 1941, Williams wrote to him, "if this is the parting of our ways, please believe it is with the very friendliest feelings on my part" (L1: 317). Williams was by no means finished revising *Battle of Angels*, however. He continued to work on the play, publishing a revised version in the New Directions magazine *Pharos* in 1945 and producing a much-altered version in *Orpheus Descending*, which finally made it to Broadway in 1957. He co-wrote the screenplay for the film adaptation *Fugitive Kind* in 1959, and in 1974, a revised *Battle of Angels* was produced in New York by Circle Repertory. With such a history, it is no wonder that the published play differs greatly from version to version. The Library of America volume, *Tennessee Williams: Plays 1937–1955* reprints the *Pharos* version, which, as the closest to the production, will be the one discussed here.

In revising the play, Williams felt the need to provide some background and explanation for its events, pointing the spectators toward its symbolism and educating them away from the assumption that the action is merely sensational melodrama. In a prologue and epilogue set a year after the major action of the play, Williams introduces the minor characters Eva and Blanch, who have set up a "Tragic Museum" in the mercantile store where the main events have transpired. They show a couple of tourists the "Jesus picture" that Vee has painted of Val; the Conjure Man, who "knows some things that he isn't telling" (P1: 192–3); and the confectionary, which is supposed to resemble the orchard across from Moon Lake, "where [Myra] kept her dreams" (193), a version of Anton Chekhov's symbolic cherry orchard. They hint at the coming events by emphasizing the blood stains on the floor and the newspaper description of the "cataclysm of nature" that happened there (192). Act 1 opens in the store a year earlier. A number of townsfolk have gathered for the return of Jabe

Torrance, the store's owner, from the hospital, where he has had an exploratory operation for cancer. The audience learns that the characters all know Jabe's illness is terminal, and he is established as a figure of death within the play.

Cassandra Whiteside appears, and there are references to her erratic driving and wild social life, focused on "jooking"—drinking and dancing and driving from one juke joint to another in the countryside. Williams lays out the mythical implications of Cassandra's character overtly, as she says she always ends up at the graveyard during one of these excursions, and compares herself to her Aunt Cassandra, "the second," noting that "the first was a little Greek girl who slept in the shrine of Apollo. Her ears were snake-bitten, like mine, so that she could understand the secret language of the birds" (201). Shooting her pistol out the door, Cassandra says that she has shot at "a bird of ill-omen that was circling over the store" (202). Then she talks Val into undertaking "a kind of exploratory operation" (205) on her car, taking him out of the store.

Cassandra's aggressive sexuality and entrapment of men, her gift of prophecy, conferred by snake-bitten ears, and her fate of not being believed are all components of the Cassandra myth that figures in the play. Her frankly sexual behavior and her belief that her aristocratic origin gives her the freedom to do what she likes also bring her into conflict with the oppressive mores of the South, when the town erupts over the story that she is having an affair with her black chauffeur. She makes her escape, telling Val, "you an' me, we belong to the fugitive kind. We live on motion" (257). Like the mythical Cassandra predicting the fall of Troy, her namesake predicts the destruction of the world that Myra has created in her "orchard" in the confectionary. In the final scene, when the lovers Val and Myra are threatened by the mob of townfolk, Cassandra comes to warn them, saying "my lips have been touched by prophetic fire" and "they've passed a law against passion . . . whoever has too much passion, we're going to be burned like witches because we know too much" (258). Myra of course ignores her, saying that her lips have been "touched by too much liquor" (258). Both go to their destruction, Myra being shot by the jealous Jabe and Cassandra committing suicide.

Watching Vee Talbott out the window in the opening scene, the town women refer to her primitive religious paintings of the 12 apostles, every one of which "looks like some man around Two River County" (198). It is Vee who brings Val in his snakeskin jacket to the Torrances' store, telling the women that "he's exploring the world and everything in it" (199). In Vee, Williams makes a rather simplistic application of Freudian psychology, her repressed sexuality coming out in the symbolism of her primitive religious paintings. Besides painting the men around her in the guise of the 12 apostles, she paints the local Episcopal church with a red steeple, saying "I always paint a thing the way that it strikes me instead of always the way that it actually is" (232). Williams's friend Clark Mills McBurney, who visited him during the rehearsals, remembered that Williams poked him with his elbow when the painting was being carried around, saying, "Get it? It's symbolism, Freudian symbolism" (Leverich 1995: 390).

Vee's painting of Val as Jesus is based on a vision she has "under the cottonwood tree where the road turns off toward the levee. Exactly where time an' time again you see couples parked in cars with all of the shades pulled down" (255). The torment of the "evil thoughts" she has been having as a result of the words the men write on the jailhouse walls is removed when in the vision, Jesus touches her breast, which one of the town women interprets as Jesus making a pass at her. Tellingly, the cottonwood tree is also known as the lynching tree, which is where Val is dragged by the mob at the end of the play. Symbolically, Vee's primitive vision combines the divinity of Jesus with a repressed sexuality and both her art and Val's, a vision that evokes ridicule and aggression in the people of the town. Interestingly, there was a similar response in Boston, for part of the censor's complaint against the play was based on the claim that "a picture of Christ was being torn up" onstage, but the situation was allayed when the production manager explained that "it represented Christ only to the unbalanced mind of the woman who painted it. Actually it was a portrait of another character in the drama" (Wheildon 1941).

Myra Torrance is based on Williams's sister Rose, who had been confined to a mental institution in 1937. Like Rose, she is a *slight, fair woman, about thirty-four years old . . . a woman who met emotional disaster in her girlhood and whose personality bears traces of the resulting trauma*" (202). Williams often attributed Rose's illness to her disappointment at the ending of a youthful romance. As her mental stability deteriorated, she had become, like Myra, "*frequently sharp and suspicious, she verges on hysteria under slight strain. Her voice is often shrill and her body tense. But when in repose, a girlish softness emerges— evidence of her capacity for great tenderness*" (202). As Rose Williams was overtaken by "dementia praecox" or schizophrenia, her repressed sexuality was unleashed in sexual allusions and fantasies. Visiting her in December, 1939, Williams was shocked by the "continual obscenities" in her speech, calling the visit in his journal "a horrible ordeal. Especially since I fear that end for myself." He went on to observe that "after all her naked subconscious is no uglier than the concealed thoughts of others–And is sex ugly? Not essentially–not from a cosmic viewpoint. But when it is divorced from reason–it looks like slime–it seems horrible you can't reason it away" (N: 177).

Williams put the shock of this emotional ordeal to good use in his art several times, most notably in *Suddenly Last Summer*. *Battle of Angels* is a kind of imaginative wish fulfillment in which Myra is symbolically brought back to life by her relationship with Val, after her powerful sexual nature has been awakened by her romance with David Anderson and shut down by his ending it to marry someone else, and her subsequent marriage to the death figure Jabe. Throughout the revision of the play, Williams was insistent on maintaining the symbolism of the locked door which Val breaks open when they begin their sexual relationship. Myra refers to Val's breaking through to her as well as to the symbolism of a fig tree which had come to life after being long barren when she tells him she is pregnant: "somebody comes along and breaks the door down. That's life! And that's what happened to me. Oh, God, I knew that I wouldn't be barren when we went together that first time. I felt it already, stirring up inside me, beginning to live! The first little fig on the tree they said wouldn't bear!" (264). When Jabe comes down the stairs, his face "*a virtual death-mask*" (267), and shoots Myra because she tells him she is pregnant, her dying thought is of the fig tree that was struck down in a storm just when it had become fruitful again. "For what reason?

Because some things are enemies of light and there is a battle between them in which some fall!" (270).

Val Xavier is also killed at the end of the play, in a horrible death at the hands of the mob when he is lynched and tortured with a blowtorch. The battle with the "enemies of light" behind his murder is somewhat more complex, for he combines the freedom and nonconformity of the bohemian artist with sexuality, and also takes political action that resists the oppressive order in this small town. His primal nature is symbolized by the snakeskin jacket, called by a newspaper reporter in the Epilogue "a shameless, flaunting symbol of the Beast Untamed" (273), which is a sensational way of expressing his straightforward connection to nature and sexuality. Val is confronted with female sexuality in five different guises in the play. Besides Myra, Vee, and Cassandra, there is a sort of Fury, the Woman from Waco, who accuses him of rape and hunts him down to destroy him after he has had sex with her once and rejected her, and there is the Naiad figure, his first love, a young nude girl he encountered on a Louisiana bayou, whom he refers to as having trapped him with love. He says the girl made him feel that he was "right on the edge of something tremendous" (227), and he left her in search of it. At the beginning of the play, Val is suppressing a powerful sexuality that gets him into trouble for touching "the women too much" (241) when he fits their shoes. He tells Myra that he's afraid of his hands, and "hold[s] them in so hard the muscles ache. . . . A herd of elephants, straining at a rope. How do I know the rope won't break sometime? With you or with somebody else?" (241). He resists Cassandra and gently holds off Vee, but his attraction to Myra proves too powerful, and, in combination with his sexual past in the form of the Woman from Waco, proves his downfall, when Jabe turns him over to the mob and they lynch him, a small-town retaliation for his sexual transgression.

The political side to the town's enmity is motivated directly when Val thwarts the sheriff's attempt to get a month's free labor for the state's chain gang by locking up the black character Loon for vagrancy. By buying Loon's guitar from him and engaging him for lessons, Val provides him with money and a job, making him no longer a vagrant. He explains to Myra that "a man has got to stick up for his own kind of people . . . we're both of us dispossessed" (239). The townspeople immediately accuse him of being a "Nawthun radical . . . come down here to organize our niggers" (237) as well as a Red who should "go back to Rooshuh!" (237). The mob torture and lynching is a classic destruction of the scapegoat and expulsion of his destabilizing power from their midst. To this town's eyes, Val is perceived as equally dangerous as a sexual transgressor, a bohemian artist, and a leftist, all elements that feed their desire to destroy him and expel him from their town. The mob action represents the oppressive norms and values of the society in which the free man and artist would attempt to live; the deaths of Val, Myra, and Cassandra suggest the tragic fates of those who would resist these norms and values.

## The Artist in Hell: *Orpheus Descending*

In his major revision of *Battle of Angels*, Williams took the Orpheus myth that is implicit in the relationship of Jabe, Myra, and Val and used it to provide the major symbolic structure of the play *Orpheus Descending* (1957). Jabe, as the figure of death, or Hades, lord of the Underworld, has imprisoned Myra (Lady in *Orpheus Descending*), or Eurydice, and she can only be freed by Val, or Orpheus, who is changed from a writer to a musician in this version. In the myth, Orpheus is given the chance to lead his wife out of the Underworld with one condition, he cannot look back at her. In some versions of the myth, he succeeds, but in others, he fails because he can't help turning and looking at her face. After this, Orpheus wanders the world like a lost soul and avoids women, including the Maenads, with whom he had often celebrated the rites of Dionysus. In retaliation for his avoiding them, the Maenads find him one day and tear him to pieces.

Many of these elements are in *Battle of Angels*, but they are made more overt in *Orpheus*, as Val explains the purifying influence of his art within his bohemian existence: "I lived in corruption but I'm not corrupted. Here is why. (*Picks up guitar.*) My life's companion! It washes me clean like water when anything unclean has touched me" (P2: 34). In this version, he is not a victim of sexual repression, but a master of physical control, being able to sleep whenever he wants for as long as he wants, to hold his breath for 3 minutes, to go a whole day without urinating, and to "burn down a woman" (37). He provides an image of his fugitive nature in a bird without legs that "has to stay all its life on its wings in the sky" (38). The power of art is also present in Vee, who in *Orpheus* is represented as painting not her Freudian sexual fantasies, but truly inspired visions. She and Val agree that making art has made existence make sense, and Val takes her visions seriously: "without no plan, no training, you started to paint as if God touched your fingers. . . . Yeah, you made some beauty!" (59).

With the Orpheus myth providing the play's structure, Williams dropped the Cassandra motif, changing Cassandra Whiteside's name to Carol Cutrere and making her into a clearer representation of the bohemian fugitive kind: "*she has an odd, fugitive beauty which is stressed, almost to the point of fantasy, by a style of makeup with which a dancer named Valli has lately made such an impression in the bohemian centers of France and Italy, the face and lips powdered white and the eyes outlined and exaggerated with black pencil and the lids tinted blue*" (15). In this version, a long monologue about her nature as an exhibitionist and her past history with Val in the clubs of New Orleans integrates Carol more fully into the play as a whole and balances her better with Lady and Vee in representing the play's feminine principle. A more overt connection is made between her and the wandering Conjure Man, who, as Williams said, "represents the dark, inscrutable face of things as they are, the essential mystery of life . . . omniscience, fate, or what have you, of which death, life and everything else are so many curious tokens sewn about his dark garments" (L1: 320). She asks him several times to give his Choctaw cry, "*a series of sharp barking sounds that rise to a sustained cry of great intensity and wildness*" (85), and she rejoices that "something is still wild in the country! This country used to be wild, the men and women were wild and there was a wild sort of sweetness in their hearts, for each other, but now it's sick with neon, it's broken out sick, with neon, like most other places" (86). At the end of the play, Carol gives the Conjure Man a gold ring in exchange for Val's snakeskin jacket, which he has salvaged from the mob, saying "wild things leave skins behind them, they leave clean skins and teeth and white bones behind them, and these are tokens passed from one to another, so that the fugitive kind can always follow their kind" (97).

Placing the symbolism of the confectionary more centrally, Williams connects Lady Torrance's desire to create her "cherry orchard" with her father, who had a wine garden and orchard outside of town where many of the town's young people, including Lady and David Cutrere, would enjoy a modern version of the rites of Dionysus. Lady's father was killed when the local Ku Klux Klan chapter burned down the orchard because he had sold wine to black people. When she finds out that Jabe was a leader of this group, she has added reason for her hatred of him and for re-creating the wine garden in the confectionary to spite him as she memorializes her father. For the ending, Williams got rid of the notorious fire, replacing it with the perhaps more ominous blue flame of the blowtorch as the men drag Val out to be lynched. The play ends with Carol putting the snakeskin jacket around her and walking out past the sheriff, who is ordering her to stop, as Val's screams are heard in the background.

Williams also cut the Prologue and Epilogue that appear in the published version of *Battle of Angels*, replacing the expository scene in the museum with a dialogue between two minor characters, Dolly and Beulah. Having perfected the technique of the "aria" in *Cat on a Hot Tin Roof* (1955), he placed Beulah at center stage, directly facing the audience, and gave her a long monologue about Lady's father and the orchard and wine garden, which, the stage directions note, should "*set the nonrealistic key for the whole production*" (12).

In an essay written for the revised play's premiere, Williams wrote that, "on its surface it was and still is the tale of a wild-spirited boy who wanders into a conventional community of the South and creates the commotion of a fox in a chicken coop. But beneath that now familiar surface it is a play about unanswered questions that haunt the hearts of people and the difference between continuing to ask them, a difference represented by the four major protagonists of the play, and the acceptance of prescribed answers that are not answers at all" (P2: 4). In writing this, he was signaling that the four major parts of Val, Lady, Vee, and Carol are of equal importance, rejecting the wrenching of the play that was done in 1940 to create a conventional

Leading Lady-Leading Man dynamic, and restoring something of the play's original balance. Although the part of Lady is still clearly the lead in contrast to that of Vee or Carol, *Orpheus Descending* conveys a clearer sense of the feminine principle that is divided among Lady, Carol, Vee, and the bayou girl, giving a more universal sense of the meaning of Eurydice and perhaps of Williams's view of the danger to male freedom and creativity that is posed by the lure of the feminine.

# CHAPTER 3
## *THE GLASS MENAGERIE* (1942–1945)

In the years following the failure of *Battle of Angels*, Williams tried very hard to do three things: to write literary plays that expressed some elemental truth from his personal experience; to achieve success in the theatre, both commercial and critical; and to make a definitive escape from St Louis and his parents' attic. The period from January 1941 to May 1943 was among the most desperate of his life, as he faced writer's block and rejection of his work, hit bottom financially, and was forced again and again to return to the house in suburban St Louis. In the early months of 1941, he was paid a small amount by the Theatre Guild to revise *Battle of Angels* for possible production. This enabled him to travel to Key West, Florida, one of the major discoveries of his life, as it was to become the closest thing to a home he had as an adult.

In the 1940s, Key West was a community of sponge and deep-sea fishermen coexisting amicably with an art colony whose freewheeling bohemian lifestyle was exactly what Williams was looking for. On the day of his first arrival there, he wrote to a friend, "this is the most fantastic place that I have been yet in America. It is even more colorful than Frisco, New Orleans, or Santa Fe. There are comparatively few tourists and the town is real stuff" (L1: 304). He was lucky to land at the Trade Winds, an elegant boarding house run by Clara Atwood Black and her daughter Marion Black Vaccaro, who would become his lifelong friends. They fixed up the old slave quarters for Williams, who would later re-create this cabin-as-writing-studio in the back of his own house in Key West when he was able to buy one. A letter to Lawrence Langner describes the "exciting double life" he led there: "writing all morning, spending my afternoon's [*sic*] in an English widow's cabana on the beach where I associate with people like John Dewey, James Farrell and Elizabeth Bishop and in the evening consorting, in dungarees, with B-girls, transients and sailors at Sloppy Joe's or the Starlight Gambling Casino" (L1: 305). In reality, this was something of an unrealized ideal. His journal reveals that he was lonely most of the time and that the work on *Battle* proceeded slowly, although he was able to write a number of other things.

In March, Williams received a $500 fellowship from the Dramatists Guild to write a new play, and he headed North by way of Georgia and St Louis, where he was able to do the needed work on *Battle of Angels*, and then to New York in early May. When the Theatre Guild turned down the revised script in June, he wrote in his journal that he was entering a new phase, "more dangerous, perhaps, than anything yet. Revised script rejected. $280.00=total funds. No new scripts. Two months to find some solution. Then destitution. Then what?" (N: 227). In the meantime, he spent the summer mostly in a communal house organized by his friend Joe Hazen in Provincetown, with a visit to the far more respectable Sea Island, Georgia retreat of the wealthy family of his friend Jordan Massee. His hand-to-mouth existence on the road was lengthened in August when the actor Hume Cronyn, the husband of Jessica Tandy, who was to play Blanche in the original company of *A Streetcar Named Desire*, optioned some of his one-act plays, and Audrey Wood began sending him the $200 in $25 installments. After returning briefly to New York, he spent the fall in New Orleans, where he wrote a good deal, working particularly on *The Long Affair*, which was to be a full-length play about D. H. and Frieda Lawrence and *I Rise in Flame, Cried the Phoenix,* a one-act play about Lawrence's death. When the option money ran out, and he found himself absolutely broke in New Orleans, he returned to St Louis, writing in his journal on 20 November: "Been here 2 weeks and crazy to leave. Waiting for checque from Audrey. Hatred of my father & <u>fear</u>—yes, fear—make it about as impossible as usual to live at home. Also poor Mother's gross lack of sensitivity. . . . Dream of Fla.–beach–sun–bicycle trips. How I shall ever manage I don't know but on I shall go. <u>En Avant</u>!" (N: 257). In December, he was back in New Orleans, where he found a short-lived job as a cashier, and worked on *Stairs to the Roof,* which he sent to Audrey Wood at the end of the year.

January of 1942 found Williams back in St Louis, whence he escaped to New York when director Erwin Piscator promised to produce *Battle of Angels*. When this did not happen, Williams went through one of his worst financial periods, working as a waiter in a bohemian club where he recited poetry for tips and living on the charity of his friend Fritz Bultman until he threw him out, and then with the older song writer Carley Mills, who supported him for several months until he left to spend the summer with his friend Paul Bigelow in an attic in Macon, Georgia. Landing in St Augustine, Florida, and finally out of resources, he accepted the bus fare to St Louis from his mother, but got only as far as Jacksonville, Florida, where he was able to avoid "descend[ing] helplessly into the psychological <u>horrors</u> of home, for an appallingly <u>indefinite</u> period" (L1: 398) by obtaining work as a teletypist with the War Department. Returning to New York in November, he tried similar work, but lasted only 2 days in the more frenetic office. As the Depression was ending and the war economy taking hold in the city, he was able to find short-lived jobs as a hotel clerk, elevator operator, and theatre usher. During this period, he started work with Donald Windham on *You Touched Me!*, based on D. H. Lawrence's story of that title and his novella *The Fox*. He also wrote a one-act play, "Spinning Song," "a play suggested by my sister's tragedy" (N: 281). Although it bears little resemblance to the finished play, this was the germ of the work that would become the film treatment and play *The Gentleman Caller*, revised as *The Glass Menagerie*.

In January of 1943, Williams received a letter that was to bring Rose's "tragedy" sharply into focus. Edwina Williams wrote to her son that Rose had come through a "head operation" from which she shows "marked improvement, and has co-operated through it all" (L1: 429). Williams immediately asked his mother to explain what she meant and learned of the prefrontal lobotomy that had been performed on his sister. Back in St Louis in April, he visited her, and wrote to Paul Bigelow that the operation "had accomplished something quite amazing. The madness is still present—that is, certain of the delusions—but they have now become entirely consistent and coherent. She is full of vitality and her perceptions and responses seemed almost more than normally acute. All of her old wit and mischief was in evidence. . . . It was curious to see these delusions persisting along with such a brightness and vivacity. . . . Unbalanced minds are so much more interesting than our dreary sanity is, there is so much honesty and poetry among them. But then you wonder if there is such a thing as sanity, actually" (L1: 438). In April, he wrote to director Mary Hunter about "The Gentleman Caller," which was now becoming a long play. Later that month, he wrote to the playwright Horton Foote that he had been working "with tigerish fury on 'The Gentleman Caller'" (N: 364).

On 30 April 1943, as Williams was in St Louis working "pretty well and continually on the Gentleman Caller" (N: 365), a telegram that changed his fortunes considerably arrived. Audrey Wood announced that he had been hired as a screenwriter by Metro-Goldwyn-Mayer (MGM) at a salary of $250 a week. Although the typical move to Los Angeles on this salary would have involved renting an upscale apartment and buying a car, Williams rented a two-room apartment in a rather seedy building with an eccentric landlady in Santa Monica for $45 a month and bought a motor scooter to take him the 8 miles to the studio in Culver City. Having no intention of living the Hollywood lifestyle, and already planning for his escape, he sent the bulk of his salary to Audrey Wood and his mother to keep in savings accounts for him to live on in the future. As Williams probably knew from the start, there was no way he could function as a screenwriter in the studio system. The three assignments he was given, an adaptation of *The Sun Is My Undoing* by Marguerite Steen, the construction of a "celluloid brassiere" (L1: 457) for Lana Turner, and a vehicle for the new child star Margaret O'Brien, were decidedly uncongenial to him, and he simply worked on other things, mainly a film treatment of "The Gentleman Caller," which he offered to the studio and had rejected, and a project with designer Lemuel Ayers and choreographer Eugene Loring to film the ballet *Billy the Kid*, which never materialized. Williams was laid off for 6 weeks by the studio, and his contract was not renewed at the end of the 6 months' option, but he had accumulated enough money to keep him going for a while and had written the short story "Portrait of a Girl in Glass," a fictional treatment of "The Gentleman Caller," as well as the film treatment, moving his conception of the play gradually closer to what would become *The Glass Menagerie*.

Williams was now, at age 32, more comfortable financially than at any time in his adult life. No longer the penniless dependent whom his father treated with unsparing contempt, he returned to St Louis for an extended stay, during which he witnessed the death of his beloved grandmother. His greatest enthusiasm at this time was for working on an adaptation of Robert Browning's poem, "My Last Duchess," which he entitled "The Balcony in Ferrara." He continued to be preoccupied with "The Gentleman Caller," however. In March of 1944, writing to Margo Jones, who had directed *You Touched Me!* at the Cleveland Playhouse in October, to send her his verse play about brother-sister incest, *The Purification,* which she was to stage at the Pasadena Playhouse, he told her about the new project and said that he also "did a complete re-write of the nauseous thing I read you in Pasadena, The Gentleman Caller. I was afraid to leave anything in that condition, so I did it over" (L1: 514). After winning a $1,000 grant in May, Williams left St Louis for the East Coast, first renting a cottage at Fire Island, and then going to Provincetown, where he joined an art crowd that included Jackson Pollock, Lee Krasner, Fritz Bultman, the poet Robert Duncan, and the critic Edward Denby. In July, he sent the "Gentleman Caller" play, now called "The Fiddle in the Wings," to Audrey Wood, "all done but the <u>first</u> scene, which is a very tricky one, as it must establish all the non-realistic conventions used in the play – I call it 'a play with music'" (L1: 526–7). In August, he told Margo Jones that finishing the play had been "an act of <u>compulsion</u>, not love. Just some weird necessity to get my sister on paper. Thank God it is done, however inauspiciously" (L1: 527).

In October, Williams was shocked to receive the news that Eddie Dowling, one of Broadway's most successful actor-directors, wanted to produce *The Gentleman Caller*, and at age 49 planned to play Tom himself. Since Dowling had already worked behind the scenes to secure the money he needed and line up the actors, the production proceeded very quickly. Laurette Taylor, a fine actor who had a bad history of alcoholism, was engaged to play Amanda, and Julie Haydon, a fragile beauty who was the future wife of Dowling's friend, the rather nasty theatre critic George Jean Nathan, to play Laura. Williams wrote to Margo Jones that "everybody has liked the script so far, the first time this has happened with any of my plays, and it surprises me completely. Of course I liked the material because it was so close to me, but for that very reason I doubted that it would come across to others. It was such <u>hell</u> writing it!" (L1: 535). Once again, Williams found himself in a rather overwhelming Broadway production, but this time he had the sense to secure a protector in the person of Jones, whom he called "The Texas Tornado." She had become a good friend as well as devoted director of his work, and he asked her to come to New York to help. Since Eddie Dowling was happy to have someone to attend to the day-to-day elements of the show, Jones was engaged to work on the production, eventually being named co-director with Dowling.

Luckily for Williams, *The Glass Menagerie*, on which he had been working for several years now, did not need the extensive revision that had been required of *Battle of Angels*, but Dowling still had ideas that Williams had to fight, with the aid of Jones. He suggested, for example, that perhaps a happy ending could be flashed across the screen at the end of the play, "Laura with the brace removed ('orthopoedics [*sic*] do such wonderful things!') and the gentleman caller standing again at the door!" (L1: 538). The main point of contention was the drunk scene that Dowling wanted to add because he and Nathan thought the play needed some comic relief. As Williams finally wrote it in order to curb improvisation by Dowling, this scene (Scene 4) actually expresses some of the most fundamental themes of the play. It is a scene in which Tom and Laura appear alone, and their close relationship is evident. More importantly, it establishes the play's major thematic dynamic of entrapment and escape, which reflected Williams's experience in the preceding years, in concrete terms. Tom goes to the movies and gets drunk to escape his mother's oppressive nagging and then tells Laura about the "coffin trick" with which he assisted the stage magician: "We nailed him into a coffin and he got out of the coffin without removing one nail. . . . There is a trick that would come in handy for me–get me out of this 2 by 4 situation!" (P1: 417). As he lies down, he says, "You know it don't take much intelligence to get yourself into a nailed-up coffin, Laura. But who in hell ever got himself out of one without removing one nail" (417), and he is answered by the illumination of the portrait of his grinning father on the wall.

Each of the characters in *The Glass Menagerie* is entrapped in some way, and each has found some means of escape, the grinning father being the most successful. A "telephone man who fell in love with long distance" and "skipped the light fantastic out of town," (401), he is at once an image of C. C. Williams, who escaped from home on long business trips as well as shorter drinking binges, but did not leave permanently, as perhaps his son Tom would have liked. Amanda, according to Williams's character notes, "having failed to establish contact with reality, continues to live vitally in her illusions" (394). She escapes the reality of having been deserted by her husband and scraping out a living in her dreary apartment by selling magazine subscriptions and working in department stores by means of her fanciful memories of days filled with jonquils and gentleman callers back in Blue Mountain. The process by which she escapes reality is dramatized in the play as she confronts Laura's failure at Rubicam's business college, a failure that "*is written in [Amanda's] face as she climbs to the landing: a look that is grim and hopeless and a little absurd*" (405). She is aware of the probable consequences, mapping out the humiliating future life that Laura faces as a "barely tolerated spinster" living upon the "grudging patronage" of her brother's future wife (409). She very quickly escapes this awareness by adapting her own fantasy and conceiving of a gentleman caller for Laura, "this image, this spectre, this hope," as Tom calls it, that "hung like a sentence passed upon the Wingfields" (411). When Tom tries gently to remind Amanda of Laura's handicaps, that not only is she disabled, but also "she's terribly shy and lives in a world of her own and those things make her seem a little peculiar to people outside the house" (430), Amanda demands that he not call her peculiar. When the plan to invite Jim O'Connor to dinner and make Laura into a "pretty trap" (434) for securing him fails, Amanda is forced to face the reality of their situation, "a mother deserted, an unmarried sister who's crippled and has no job," and a son who is a "selfish dreamer" (464).

Laura, as Williams writes in his character notes, is defined by her physical disability. Her leg, with the brace on it, is both the partial cause and a visual sign of her "separation" from reality, which has increased until "she is like a piece of her own glass collection, too exquisitely fragile to move from the shelf" (394). As Tom says, she "lives in a world of her own–a world of–little glass ornaments. . . . She plays old phonograph records and–that's about all" (431). Laura escapes to the phonograph records that were left there by her father, presumably a remembrance of happier times, much like Amanda's memories of gentleman callers, and to her glass collection, in which the single unicorn, her favorite piece, stands as an objective correlative of her own difference transformed into uniqueness, value, and magic. When Jim O'Connor knocks the unicorn's horn off, making it "just like all the other horses" (457), Laura accepts it as "no tragedy" and decides that she will just imagine that he had an operation to remove the horn "to make him feel less–freakish" and "feel more at home with the other horses" (457), certainly the expression of a fantasy of her own to have an operation that would remove her disability and consequently her shyness, making her feel at ease among "normal" people. Of course the progress that Laura makes during her encounter with Jim is dashed when she finds out that his kissing her does not mean he will call again, because he's already engaged to be married. With this knowledge, "*the holy candles in the altar of Laura's face have been snuffed out. There is a look of almost infinite desolation*" (460).

In Tom's case, the trap, as noted earlier, is most evident. He is trapped in the "2 by 4 situation" of the apartment, the result of his father's desertion, where he is the much-needed financial support of his mother and sister. He is trapped not only in the apartment among the "*vast hive-like conglomerations of cellular living-units*" that are "*burning with the slow and implacable fires of human desperation*" (399) in St Louis, but also in the hated celotex interior of Continental Shoemakers, where he is "a poet with a job in a warehouse" (394). He is forced to "give up all that I dream of doing and being *ever*" (414) in order to support his mother and sister. Williams writes in the character notes that "to escape from a trap he has to act without pity" (394). Tom recognizes that to do that, he has to do what his father did, and that means "I'm like my father. The bastard son of a bastard" (441). In the end, he walks out of the apartment and follows "from then on, in my father's footsteps, attempting to find in motion what was lost in space" (464–5), but of course his escape fails, as Amanda's and Laura's do, because he can't completely escape the memory of his sister and the guilt he feels for deserting her.

The tragic implications of the play are mitigated somewhat by the ending that Williams finally settled on after many revisions. As Tom gives his final monologue about trying to escape through motion and failing, the pantomime of Amanda's comforting speech to Laura, where, in silence, *"her silliness is gone and she has dignity and tragic beauty"* (464) and Laura finally looks up and smiles at her, lends a final ambiguity to the play that, while not quite the romantically comic ending Eddie Dowling asked for, presents a possibility of hope, or at least of grace in endurance, for Amanda and Laura.

The ending serves to remind the audience that "the play is memory" and "being a memory play, it is dimly lighted, it is sentimental, it is not realistic." And this is not just the subjective memory of past events that might be expected in any modernist work with a narrator, but the imaginative re-creation of memory by an artist, Tom, who is shaping it for presentation to an audience. Tom, after all, like Tennessee Williams, is a poet, and one has to expect that his presentation of events will be the product of his creative imagination as well as the memory where they originate. What made *The Glass Menagerie* unique as a play in 1944 was its overt presentation to the audience as a work of art, a play that made the subjective perception of memory into an aesthetic approach to truth. As Williams wrote in the production notes, "expressionism and all other unconventional techniques in drama have only one valid aim, and that is a closer approach to truth. When a play employs unconventional techniques it is not, or certainly shouldn't be, trying to escape its responsibility of dealing with reality, or interpreting experience, but is actually or should be attempting to find a closer approach, a more penetrating and vivid expression of things as they are" (395). Thus, Williams's use of the screen with "legends" or title cards like those of silent film, along with the lighting, the music, and the other scenic elements, creates an aesthetic estrangement of the audience that keeps it from identifying with the characters, the *mise en scène*, and the action as if it were reality. Williams's goal in the play was not verisimilitude, but something of a higher order: "I am the opposite of a stage magician," says Tom. "He gives you illusion that has the appearance of truth. I give you truth in the pleasant disguise of illusion" (400).

In creating this aesthetic onstage, Williams was aiming for "a new plastic theatre which must take the place of the exhausted theatre of realistic conventions if the theatre is to resume vitality as a part of our culture" (395). He was fortunate to have the artistry of scene designer Jo Mielziner. A protégé of the great American designer Robert Edmond Jones, Mielziner had at this point already made a name for himself with his innovative designs for such plays as *Street Scene* (1929) and *Ethan Frome* (1936). His association with Williams, and later with Arthur Miller and director Elia Kazan, was to lead to an influential form of total theatre that would be recognized throughout the world as "the American style." *The Glass Menagerie* was his first attempt at the aesthetic that Williams described in his production notes, which Mielziner expressed in scenic terms as "abstract realism," an aesthetic that suggested the artist's subjective intervention in the illusion of reality without moving entirely into a subjective vision, as expressionism does.

With his interest in lighting and translucent scenery and his absolute belief in the collaborative function of theatre artists, Mielziner was the ideal designer to work with Williams on *The Glass Menagerie*. Although he wrote in his memoir *Designing for the Theatre*, "if Tennessee Williams had written plays in the days before the technical development of translucent and transparent scenery, I believe he would have invented it" (1965: 124), Mielziner himself did the inventing when it came to the scenic expression of Williams's ideas. He wrote that his "use of translucent and transparent scenic interior walls was not just another trick. It was a true reflection of the contemporary playwright's interest in–and at times obsession with–the exploration of the inner man. Williams was writing not only a memory play but a play of influences that were not confined within the walls of a room" (124).

In devising the scenery for the play, Mielziner translated Williams's aesthetic into visual terms. In the first scene, Tom entered the stage and stood on a fire escape before what appeared to be the blank brick wall of the apartment house, which was actually a canvas wall with a translucent opening or scrim cut into it. In front of the scrim was the "present" from which Tom narrated the play, the convention being that this was objective reality, a reality the audience shared with Tom. Tom's initial stance outside the apartment gave him the freedom of the outsider to comment on the action and revealed for the audience the primary motive of escape that impels Tom's action throughout the play. As Tom came to the end of his monologue, a dim blue light came up behind the wall, revealing the apartment's interior through the scrim. Thus, the audience was let into Tom's "memory" visually as he entered the action with Amanda and Laura.

The set consisted mainly of a living room, which was Laura's subjective space, the world of the glass menagerie, where she slept and played her Victrola, and where the father's picture was. The living room functioned as Laura's safe haven, like her fantasies, a space where she retreats when faced with an ordeal like eating dinner with Jim O'Connor. Her ability to eventually accept Jim's presence in this space is a physical expression of the psychological progress she makes in her encounter with him. Upstage was an opening with portieres, also gauze, dividing the living room from the dining room, allowing the figures in the dining room to be seen dimly, as through layers of memory. As Thomas Scheye has noted, "the portieres curtain off an inner stage; they are another dividing line between illusion and reality or one kind of truth and another" (1977: 207). The dining room is also the seat of Amanda's power, where she presides over meals. Here she controls Tom and Laura by treating them like children, as she does at the Sunday dinner, or by browbeating them into doing what she wants, as she does at breakfast. Here she also re-creates the world to fit her illusions, as she does when she plays hostess to the gentleman caller as if the St Louis apartment were Blue Mountain at the turn of the century. In production, the dining room curtains opened automatically after Amanda's first speech, and shortly after Tom entered the scene with Amanda and Laura, the whole structure representing the outer wall of the apartment building ascended into the wings, to descend again after Tom left the house at the end of the play, again representing the screen of memory through which he presents his sister and mother.

Mielziner, who once spent an entire afternoon lighting a chair, was known as a master with light, and his complex lighting scheme for the play, in a precomputer age when every light cue had to be executed by hand, became somewhat legendary. The show required 57 lines on which to hang electrical equipment, 7 dimmer and switch boxes, each containing about 60 switches, and an additional 50 or 60 switches. Two electricians were kept busy with the lighting cues throughout the show, and they were compared to Swiss bell ringers as their hands were in seemingly constant motion. The dreamy blue light of the interior and the many special lighting effects completed the effect of the staging, an artist's representation of memory. When *The Glass Menagerie* opened in December for its tryout period in Chicago, it received positive reviews, with the performance of Laurette Taylor and the scene design receiving particular attention. Claudia Cassidy wrote in the *Chicago Tribune* that "paradoxically, it is a dream in the dusk and a tough little play that knows people and how they tick. Etched in the shadows of a man's memory, it comes alive in the theatre terms of words, motion, lighting and music" (1944: 11).

Despite a positive reception in the press, in the midst of the bitter Chicago winter and the holiday season, the play did not fare very well in its first week, and it was only through a spirited campaign by Cassidy and critic Ashton Stevens of the *Herald-American* that the play was kept going. It gathered steam by word of mouth, however, and ended up running in Chicago for 2 months before it opened in New York on 1 March 1945 for what would be a Broadway run of 563 performances. As Joseph Wood Krutch rather disdainfully put it, the New York critics "staged what is commonly called a dance in the streets" (1945: 424), heaping praise especially on Laurette Taylor, on the production, and on Tennessee Williams.

While most of the critics appreciated what Williams and Mielziner were trying to do, there were a few who found their theatrical aesthetic pretentious. Louis Kronenberger, who would never be an admirer of Williams, wrote that the narrator's role was "pretty otiose and pretty arty" (1945: 16). Krutch referred to the opening monologue as "a pretentious and inflated speech delivered in front of a blank wall," and thought the narrator largely unnecessary. He complained that the play's "hard, substantial core of shrewd observation and deft, economical characterization" was "enveloped in a fuzzy haze of pretentious sentimental, pseudo-poetic verbiage which I can compare only to the gauze screens of various degrees of filmy opacity which are annoyingly raised and lowered during the course of the physical action in order to suggest memory, the pathos of distance, and I know not what else" (1945: 425). In this rather testy observation, Krutch was identifying a bifurcation in Williams's art that would become more obvious as his work developed. That the shrewd observer who cut to the quick in sizing up a character and the aesthetically ambitious, sometimes pretentious poet existed side by side in Williams was a fact that he recognized, and it would prove both an advantage and a disadvantage to his work as his career developed.

# CHAPTER 4
## *SUMMER AND SMOKE* AND *ECCENTRICITIES OF A NIGHTINGALE* (1945–1948 AND 1964)

### Emotional Paralysis: *Summer and Smoke*

If *The Glass Menagerie* was an attempt to capture Rose Williams on paper, *Summer and Smoke* was even closer to home. Throughout his life, Williams would refer to its protagonist, Alma Winemiller, or "Miss Alma," as the character who was most like him. In a 1973 interview, he said that Alma was his favorite, "because I came out so late and so did Alma, and she had the greatest struggle. . . . Miss Alma grew up in the shadow of the rectory, and so did I. Her love was intense but too late. Her man fell in love with someone else and Miss Alma turned to a life of profligacy. I've been profligate, but, being a puritan, I naturally tend to exaggerate guilt" (C: 228). In 1961, he said that Alma's heart palpitations, a condition from which Williams also suffered, arose from "caging in something that was really quite different from her spinsterish, puritanical exterior," and that the caged figure was "an obsessive figure with me as a writer" (C: 83). Perhaps most tellingly, as he was sailing to Europe after the New York premiere of *Summer and Smoke*, he wrote in his journal that he was worried about overworking the particular vein in his writing of "loneliness, eroticism, repression, undefined spiritual longings: the intimate material of my own psyche is what I have filled my work with, and perhaps built it on" (N: 489). This is a pretty good description of the material of *Summer and Smoke*.

Miss Alma's particular affliction, her panic attacks, was something Williams knew intimately in the months before and while he was writing the play. In the fall of 1944, faced with the upcoming rehearsals of *The Glass Menagerie*, he was in a state of panic that was understandable, given his experience with *Battle of Angels* a few years earlier. His journal for those months contains many descriptions of his physical symptoms. In October, he wrote that he was "suffering a severe case of nerves–physical manifestations–I have attacks of panic–mostly on street–must rush into bars for drinks to steady myself–I get breathless–I have a weight on my chest–how much is sheer anxiety, how much real cardiac symptoms I don't know" (N: 415). These attacks subsided once the rehearsals actually began, and he found the experience of working with Eddie Dowling and Margo Jones much less trying than working with the Theatre Guild had been.

In the months following the success of *Menagerie*, Williams experienced a period of depression because, as he wrote in *Memoirs*, "I never believed that anything would continue, would hold. I never thought my advance would maintain its ground. I always thought there would be a collapse immediately after the advance. Also, I had spent so much of my energy on the climb to success, that when I had 'made it' and my play was 'the hottest ticket in town,' I felt almost no satisfaction" (M: 92). Pursuing his perennial strategy of travel to escape, he went to Mexico, where he found a good deal of peace throughout the summer. After traveling to New York in September, 1945, and witnessing the mediocre reception accorded by the critics to *You Touched Me!*, the play he had written with Donald Windham, he returned to New Orleans and the bohemian French Quarter where he felt comfortable. The next 2 years were a period of moving among New Orleans, Nantucket, Key West, Provincetown, Los Angeles, and New York, as he worked on the plays that would become *A Streetcar Named Desire* and *Summer and Smoke*, two very different realizations of the themes that were currently obsessing him.

Interestingly, it was when he worked on *Summer and Smoke*, then called "Chart of Anatomy," that his panic attacks returned. In November 1946, he wrote in his journal of the "nightmarish" state of his psyche: "The iron jaws of a trap seem to hold me here in a little corner, backing away from panic. I cling to little palliative devices–the swimming pool–the sleeping tablets–reading in bed–sometimes movies–the familiarity of Pancho [Amado Rodriguez y Gonzales]" (N: 447–9). His experience translated directly into Alma's attacks of "blind panic" (P1: 579) and "nervous heart trouble" (581), her "swallowing air" (582), and her growing dependence on her prescription for sleeping tablets, which Dr John Buchanan warns her could turn her into a "dope-fiend" (610), but which she calls "the telephone number of God" (642). Williams became anxious while he was working on the play, and he never felt that it fully expressed the experience that he wanted to convey. In April, he wrote to New Directions publisher James Laughlin that the play "was a disappointment and a pretty bad one. In fact, I was so depressed over it that I am surprised that I was able to go on working. . . . The basic conception was very pure and different from anything else I have tried. It was built around an argument over the existence of a 'human soul' but that got pretty thoroughly lost in a narrative that somehow slipped to the level of magazine fiction, or worse" (L2: 93).

Williams had worked most intensely on the play during the summer of 1946, which he spent in the company of Carson McCullers in Nantucket, while she worked on the stage adaptation of her novel *The Member of the Wedding*, a productive literary partnership that was reminiscent of the days of the "literary factory" he and his friend Clark Mills McBurney had set up in McBurney's St Louis basement. The play, originally intended to be produced by Guthrie McClintic for Katharine Cornell, was quickly deemed unsuitable by this grand dame of the theatre. Aesthetically, it was conceived along the lines of *The Glass Menagerie*, with a strong element of modernist subjectivity and a Jo Mielziner set to short-circuit any assumption of realism. Early versions had a narrator, but this idea was soon scrapped in favor of silent film sequences which were to be incorporated into the action. Williams put the silent film sequences in and took them out of the play several times as he worked on it, finally eliminating them completely. There are many fragments of these scenes among the *Summer and Smoke* manuscripts at the University of Texas, including a confrontation between John and his father; a scene in which Alma calls the police about the wild party that John is throwing; and a scene in which Alma helps John give inoculations to cotton pickers to help contain a fever epidemic (N: 446).

Throughout the play's composition, its production by Margo Jones at her Theatre '47 in Dallas, and its New York premiere, Williams continued to be dissatisfied with *Summer and Smoke* at the same time that he had high aspirations for it. At a low point in October 1946, he wrote in his journal that it seemed "grotesque, a creation of disease" (N: 445). Writing to Margo Jones from Rome in February 1948, after her Dallas production, he warned her that they should not open the play, which they were co-producing, in the same cities where *Streetcar* had had its pre-Broadway tryouts because "I am dead certain that Streetcar is a much, much better play . . . to me 'Summer' was a devastating failure in comparison to what I meant it to be, and one of the bitterest I have had. I am talking about the script, you understand" (L2: 157). In December, 1948, he noted in his journal that the whole history of the play was "fraught with the most abysmal discouragement: abandoned five or six times, I nevertheless picked it up again each time and went doggedly on with it, and the result is a play that is good enough to impress some people—not myself and not many but <u>some</u>—as the best of the four long plays I've had presented" (N: 489). He continued to rewrite the play and radically changed it in the version that would become *Eccentricities of a Nightingale*, first produced in Nyack, New York, in 1964.

While Williams took full responsibility for the weaknesses in the script, he came to blame Margo Jones's direction for failing to fully realize his vision on the stage. Jones was a close friend, and he gave her a great deal of credit for protecting him and *The Glass Menagerie* from the crasser instincts of Eddie Dowling, so he had been eager to have her produce and direct this poetic play to which she was passionately dedicated. In November, 1946, he was "pitching" her to Audrey Wood as the ideal director for the play because "Margo likes intensely romantic material and I think she knows how to handle it, and she believes in fidelity to the author's intention" (L2: 79). He did not attend the rehearsals or the premiere of her production in Dallas in July, 1947, but when he saw it, he wrote to film director George Cukor, whom he was hoping to interest in doing a Los Angeles production, that Margo had done "a remarkably good job under the limitations of her tiny theatre. The play has a living quality which Margo always gets in her productions and to my surprise it seems to have a strong popular appeal" (L2: 111). In his *Memoirs*, written 20 years after Jones's death, he was far less complimentary, writing that "the production was awful but I loved Margo and I pretended to like it" (M: 92).

The fact was that, while *Summer and Smoke* was coming into being, Margo Jones was being replaced in Williams's professional esteem by Elia Kazan, who directed *Streetcar* to great critical and commercial success in December 1947. Writing to Audrey Wood in April, he asked her to make sure there would be an out-of-town tryout for the play before it reached New York, adding, "if you want to (<u>dare</u> to) bring up the subject of Kazan directing, do so, but I doubt that you will get anywhere with it as our girl Jones unquestionably regards herself as the American Stanislavsky which it is still faintly possible that she may be however much we may doubt it" (L2: 178).

On the other hand, Williams's confidence in Jo Mielziner as a scene designer had only grown as a result of his work on *Streetcar*. He wrote to Jones just before the Dallas premiere of *Summer and Smoke* that "Jo's designs for Streetcar are almost the best I've ever seen . . . it will add immensely to the poetic quality. He must also do Summer" (L2: 109). By the end of December, he had talked with Mielziner, and had told him that "it should be designed completely away from Streetcar and Glass, using very pure colors an almost abstract design with Gothic effects and sky, sky, sky!" (L2: 140). If the design for *The Glass Menagerie* was a visual representation of memory, the design for *Summer and Smoke*, as finally realized by Mielziner for the New York production beginning 6 October 1948, was a visual representation of its theme, the eternal struggle between body and soul. Mielziner wrote that, "after reading his notes in the early script for *Summer and Smoke*, I felt that it would be truly difficult to design a setting for this play that was poor in concept" (1965: 153). In the final version of the production notes published with the play, Williams emphasizes that the entire action of the play must take place against "a great expanse of sky," which should be "a pure and intense blue." (569). In production, the sky was a cyclorama, with, as Williams suggested, the familiar constellations of the stars projected onto it at night.

Describing the set design in the script, Williams indicates that the set should consist of three major spaces, the fountain at the center, capped by the statue of the angel named "Eternity," and flanked by the two American-Gothic-style houses, the rectory at stage right where the Winemillers live and the home of the Buchanans at stage left, which also houses the father-and-son physicians' consulting room. As Williams suggests, there were no doors, windows, or walls in the set, with the buildings indicated by delicate frameworks of Gothic design. Symbolizing the contrasting outlooks of Alma Winemiller and the young Dr John Buchanan, the wall of the rectory was indicated by a gilt-framed romantic landscape and the wall of the doctors' office by a chart of anatomy. As Williams suggests, the set formed "an harmonious whole like one complete picture rather than three separate ones" (570), and Mielziner executed almost all of the scene changes fluidly through lighting. The one exception was Scene 6, the scene at Moon Lake Casino, where a small arbor was set up in front of the fountain.

The overall effect of the stage's scenic image was to suggest the unearthly, soaring spirit of the Gothic cathedral, which Alma describes to John as an ideal to place against the sensual "self-satisfaction" that he says he pursues because "it's yet to be proven that anyone on this earth is crowned with so much glory as the one that uses his senses to get all he can in the way of–satisfaction" (611). In contrast, Alma evokes the image of the cathedral in which "everything reaches up, how everything seems to be straining for something out of the reach of stone–or human–fingers . . . to something beyond attainment!" (611–12). To Alma, "that is the secret, the principle back of existence–the everlasting struggle and aspiration for more than our human limits have placed in our reach" (612). The set establishes the struggle between these two points of view visually and at the same time establishes the ontological realm of the play. Williams struggled in the writing to integrate the symbolic action of the play—in which Alma, "the soul," or spirituality, battles with sensuality in the person of John—with the realistic story of unrequited love, which, as he observed, had the tendency to degenerate to the level of a radio soap opera. The symbolic, antirealistic set reminded the audience that there was more to the play than the rather melodramatic plot, in which John's intermittent attraction to Alma is played off against his sensual affair with Rosa Gonzales, whose father shoots the elder

Dr Buchanan, shocking John into a greater appreciation for Alma's spiritual values and marriage to the innocent and healthily attractive Nellie Ewell.

Similarly, Williams makes the point in his stage directions that the characters represent something beyond their roles in the love story. John is presented as a "*Promethean figure, brilliantly and restlessly alive in a stagnant society*," with the "*fresh and shining look of an epic hero*," but subject to "*demoniac unrest*" (575). Alma, on the other hand, is "*prematurely spinsterish*," marked by "*an excessive propriety and self-consciousness . . . nervous laughter . . . quaintly and humorously affected*" (577). From the start, it is fairly evident that Williams stacks the deck in favor of the body in the duel between body and soul here, and the same is true of Alma's internal struggle, which is the psychological enactment of this duel.

To John, Alma's hysterical laughter and panic attacks are clear symptoms of an enormous sexual repression, or, as he puts it, a sensuous "*doppelganger*" (582) within her that is struggling to emerge. In a schematic way, the two characters change places as Alma realizes the sexual nature of her attraction to John and John comes to see that, despite the fact that there is no "soul" in his anatomy chart, Alma is right that love can be something beyond mere sex because "there are some people . . . who can bring their hearts to it, also—who can bring their souls to it" (614). Alma first rejects John's sexual advances because he is "*not a gentleman*" (615), maintaining her ideals against his sensual desire. But John undergoes a change as a result of his relationship with Alma, and though she ultimately finds that "the girl who said 'no' . . . died last summer—suffocated in smoke from something on fire inside her" (635), she also finds that "the tables have turned with a vengeance" (638) when he says that he couldn't have sex with her now. He tells her, "I've come around to your way of thinking, that something else is in there, an immaterial something—as thin as smoke . . . and knowing it's there—why then the whole thing—this—this unfathomable experience of ours—takes on a new value, like some—some wildly romantic work in a laboratory" (636). And he realizes that "it wasn't the physical you that I really wanted," but a "flame, mistaken for ice. I still don't understand it" (637).

The symbolic scheme and the psychological struggle come together when John rejects Rosa Gonzalez, to whom his attraction is purely sexual, and becomes engaged to Alma's former music pupil, Nellie Ewell, the daughter of a somewhat notorious woman who picks up salesmen at the train depot. At the end of the play, Nellie has escaped from her mother and has been educated at Sophie Newcomb College. She combines a straightforward, vibrant, and youthful sexuality with a reverence for Miss Alma, whom she calls "an angel of mercy" (632), and the influence Alma has had both on her and on John. John's future looks to be stable and bourgeois, a conventional if loving marriage which will clearly include a healthy sexual element.

Alma's future, on the other hand, is less conventional. The final scene, in which she picks up a young salesman in front of the fountain, is more ambivalent. Having taken one of her sleeping tablets, which makes her feel "like a water-lily on a Chinese lagoon" (642), she prepares to go off with him to the Moon Lake Casino, the scene of her earlier rejection of John's advances. Clearly she has different intentions this time, but the meaning of the play's ending is ambivalent. On the one hand, she is walking in the footsteps of Mrs Ewell, and is probably about to be ostracized by the town. If she continues this way, as Stanley Kowalski says of Blanche DuBois, her future is mapped out for her. On the other hand, she has accepted a part of her nature whose denial had reduced her to painful loneliness, hysteria and debilitating panic attacks, and seems for the first time to be at peace. As she jokes with the young salesman, she laughs *"in a different way than she has ever laughed before, a little wearily, but quite naturally"* (642). The overall sense at the end of *Summer and Smoke* is of integration and peace for its two tortured main characters, as well as loss. In the terms of Williams's symbolic scheme, the fierce flame of spiritual and sexual tension that glowed between them is quenched, leaving the smoke.

Williams had been worried about the ability of *Summer and Smoke* to reach audiences from the beginning, and his worry increased as *Streetcar* became a major hit, imprinting Williams's name on the national consciousness as the creator of Blanche DuBois and Stanley Kowalski. The response to the production was mixed, but it proved him right. Its tryout in Detroit was greeted as "a depressing letdown after 'The Glass Menagerie' and 'A Streetcar Named Desire,'" sounding, "disturbingly, as if it were written years before the other two" (Taylor 1948: C12). In New York, John Chapman called it "the third version of the FFFD (Frustrated Female from Dixie)," and "the least successful." The *Hartford Courant* was "inclined to put it down as third-rate Williams on the conviction that this author started out in fine form with 'The Glass Menagerie' and has been going down hill ever since" (Carey 1948). A few reviewers saw something unique in the play and production, however. Reviewing its tryout in Cleveland, Ward Marsh wrote that it was "no ordinary play and cannot, therefore, be judged by ordinary standards. Here is a strange, new and unnatural theatrical world, and it is not easy to accept it at once nor can it be quickly encompassed" (1948). The *Boston Globe* called it "a drama of enormous poetic power and of an indescribably hypnotic mood" (Durgin 1948). The *New York Times*'s Brooks Atkinson, who had seen the earlier production in Dallas as well as the New York premiere, called it the only play of the season "that has the imagination and quality of a work of art." He praised its "character analysis of incomparable tenderness and ruthlessness"; "the incandescence of its search into the private agonies of a human being"; "the unostentatious beauty of the dialogue"; and the "ethereal loveliness of Jo Mielziner's production" (1948: X1). The praise for the set design was almost unanimous, while the opinion on Jones's direction ranged from "brilliant" (Marsh 1948) to "fussy" (Durgin 1948).

The original Broadway production ran for 102 performances, a respectable run, but nothing like *Streetcar*'s 855. It was not until the Off-Broadway Circle in the Square Theatre produced it in 1952, directed by José Quintero, with Geraldine Page as Alma, that the play's quality was widely recognized. In their former night club, with the barest of staging, this group managed to bring out "the full delicate sensitiveness of the script which was somehow lost uptown in the large theater" (Hammerman 1952: 8). The production was to become a landmark in American theatre history, establishing the professional credibility not only of Circle in the Square, but also of Off-Broadway itself. Never feeling that it fully expressed what he hoped it would convey, however, Williams continued to revise the play. In the summer of 1951 in Rome, he had made substantial revisions that he hoped would be included in the London production that fall, but, in his own words, he "arrived with it too late" (P2: 432) This version became *Eccentricities of a Nightingale*, which received its first production in Nyack, New York, in 1964.

## "The different and odd and lonely": *Eccentricities of a Nightingale*

In his author's note with the published script, Williams makes it clear that "*Eccentricities of a Nightingale* is a substantially different play from *Summer and Smoke*, and I prefer it. It is less conventional and melodramatic . . . it is a better work than the play from which it derived" (432). There are several major differences between the two plays, primarily relating to the character of John Buchanan. In *Eccentricities*, he is not a carousing young libertine, rebelling against his father, but a rather sedate young doctor. His father does not appear in the play, but is replaced by a domineering mother, and Williams added a whole scene (Act 2, Scene 1), entitled "The Tenderness of a Mother," with Oedipal overtones, in which Mrs Buchanan, wearing a negligee, visits John in his bedroom, dries his hair and his feet, describes for him her ideal daughter-in-law, and tries to talk him out of seeing anything more of Alma. The characters of Nellie Ewell and Rosa Gonzales are eliminated, along with Rosa's father, the Moon Lake Casino, the cockfight, and the shooting of John's father by Papa Gonzales, and there is no suggestion that John is undergoing any kind of struggle between sensuality and spirituality. In fact, the focus of the play is shifted from the body-soul division to the difficulties of the eccentric, of which Alma is the prime example.

In the new play, Williams emphasizes Alma's eccentricities even more than he does in *Summer and Smoke*, particularly in a scene in which her father takes her to task for her peculiarities, such as the "fantastic highflown–phrases" she uses in conversation, her wild gestures, her breathlessness, her stammering, and her hysterical laughter, which he says are "just mannerisms, things that you could control, that you can correct" (445). He also tells her she should give up "this little band of eccentrics, this collection of misfits that you've gathered about you which you call your club" (446). The scene in which John comes to a meeting of this group (Act 2, Scene 2), which Mrs Buchanan calls "the freaks of the town . . . a certain little group that don't fit in with the others, sort of outcast people that have, or imagine they have, little talents for this thing or that thing or the other–over which they make a big fuss among themselves in order to bolster up their poor little, hurt little egos!" (459–60), was revised to make the group more sympathetic, with less of the silliness and bickering that characterizes it in *Summer and Smoke*.

Besides his identification with Alma and the disabilities he shared with her, Williams also had a good deal of experience with such groups, several of which had been part of his St Louis days. As recently as 1944, while he was staying in St Louis, he told Margo Jones that his society consisted of "one lady sixty-years-old, whose poetry I revise . . . last week I addressed a small poetry group on Hart Crane's poems, two old queens and eight middle-aged women were the audience, appreciative but mystified" (L1: 512). Here is perhaps the germ of the play's meeting and Rosemary's paper on William Blake. As he revised the play, his attitude toward such people, and perhaps his own youth, had become less judgmental, and more tolerant. Significantly, in *Eccentricities*, the meeting is broken up by Mrs Buchanan's coming to fetch John away and Mrs Winemiller's interruption, not by the participants' own bickering as it is in the earlier play.

Alma's ongoing discussion with John in *Eccentricities* is not about the battle between flesh and spirit, but about his superiority to "my little collection of–eccentrics, my club of–fellow misfits . . . my little company of the faded and frightened and different and odd and lonely" (470). In their New Year's Eve scene in front of the fountain, Alma admits that her eccentricity may be stamped on her in big letters, "This Person Is Strange" (477), but she makes a plea for acceptance that goes for all the eccentrics and misfits in the play: "I may be eccentric but not so eccentric that I don't have the ordinary human need for love. I have that need, and I must satisfy it, in whatever way my good or bad fortune will make possible for me" (477). While the Alma in *Summer and Smoke* makes a tentative offer of herself to John after it is too late for him to respond to her, the new Alma tells him straightforwardly that she would like to go with him to a hotel on New Year's Eve, although she knows he doesn't love her and that it will lead to nothing further. John expresses his admiration because she talks "as straight as a man and you look right into my eyes" (480). Williams uses an overt symbolic scheme in the subsequent hotel room scene, in which John and Alma try to warm the chilly room by lighting a fire, which goes out as they fail to connect sexually. With Alma's statement that "I'm not ashamed of tonight! I think that you and I have been honest together, even though we failed" (484), the fire miraculously revives itself, "*a phoenix*" (484). They come together, Alma asking where the fire came from and John saying, "no one has ever been able to answer that question" (484).

While *Summer and Smoke* valorizes the integration of soul and body, *Eccentricities of a Nightingale* valorizes honesty in human communication and makes a stand against the social ostracism of the eccentric, the misfit, the freak. John Clum has suggested that the play had become more about "Queerness and its synthesis of flesh and spirit, sex, and politics," as Williams "understood and experienced that term" (1996: 34–5). While the Epilogue of *Eccentricities* essentially repeats the action of *Summer and Smoke*'s, there are telling differences that emphasize the play's thematic changes. This is a much more confident Alma, who criticizes the singer at the Fourth of July celebration, using her own characteristics, which have been ridiculed by the town, as artistic criteria: "I didn't think she sang with any emotion. A singer's face and her hands and even her heart are part of her equipment and ought to be used expressively when she sings" (485). When some townspeople stop behind her and whisper and laugh at her, instead of shrinking away in embarrassment, she "*turns about abruptly, imitating the laughter with a rather frightening boldness: the figures withdraw*" (486).

It is also clear that this is not the first time Alma has hooked up with a salesman. She points out the stone angel of the fountain to the young man as "the loveliest thing in Glorious Hill" (486), but she also tells him about the part of town that is concealed by the Square, Tiger Town, which is "the part of town that a traveling salesman might be interested in," including "rooms that can be rented for one hour" (486). As the salesman goes off to get a taxi, a rocket explodes, lighting up the angel, which Alma salutes, touching the plume on her hat which is associated with her Aunt Albertine, who created a scandal by running away with the owner of the Musée Mécanique. While the Alma in the earlier play is seeking casual sex for the first time, partly as compensation for her failure with John, it is clear that the later Alma has embraced a life in which such casual relationships are a regular occurrence, and she doesn't care what the town thinks about it. As Alma no longer has music pupils and her father is dead, Williams seems to imply that she makes her living this way. While she may have been ostracized by the town that is represented by the courthouse and the churches she points out on the Square, she apparently has no problem accommodating both the beauty of the stone angel and the reality of Tiger Town in her own life.

Few audiences and critics have agreed with Williams about the superiority of *Eccentricities of a Nightingale* to *Summer and Smoke*. When it was first produced in Nyack, New York, in 1964, in a production that "ranged from indifferent to catastrophic," Norman Nadel suggested that "'Summer and Smoke' never looked better than it does in comparison with this revision," complaining that Williams had made both Alma and the play "more, rather than less melodramatic," had "almost erased the personality of John," and had exaggerated John's mother to the point of caricature (19). The 1968 self-described "American premiere" in Mineola, New York, in which Alma was "blasted . . . into ultimate non-recognition by Kim Hunter and a lunatically miscast cast" (Tallmer 1968: 58), did not do much better. Jerry Tallmer complained that Williams was "badly, blindly wrong" in his revisions, that John Buchanan had been "de-raked; he is now at best a neuter," and that Williams had taken the life out of the play (58). In 1976, a television adaptation with Blythe Danner and Anthony Langella was well received, but in the same year its only Broadway production, which led critic John Simon to the conclusion that *Summer and Smoke* "had much more texture, variety, intensity and, yes, steaminess . . . the hero and heroine had flesh-and-blood complexities rather than being stripped down to single characteristics, and those insufficiently analyzed" (26), closed after just 24 performances. There has been no major revival since.

# CHAPTER 5
## *A STREETCAR NAMED DESIRE* (1945–1947)

Williams worked on *A Streetcar Named Desire* and *Summer and Smoke* at the same time, between 1945 and 1947, exploring his sense of the split self from opposing vantage points. While Alma Winemiller's character is a case of emotional paralysis because of the repression of her sexual desire in favor of her "spiritual" side, Blanche DuBois' claims to "beauty of the mind and richness of the spirit and tenderness of the heart" (P1: 551) are undermined by her awareness that she is equally driven by sexual desire. Blanche's chosen identity is rooted in the tradition of Southern gentility which is materially represented in Belle Reve ("beautiful dream"), the plantation that has slipped from her grasp despite her hysterical claim that she has "fought for it, bled for it, almost died for it" (479).

The loss of the security represented by both the home place and the identity conferred by the tradition has sent Blanche on a desperate search for something to replace it: "I've run for protection, Stella, from under one leaky roof to another leaky roof—because it was storm—all storm, and I was-caught in the center" (515). Partly because of her complicated past, which involves her "failing" (527) her husband sexually and calling him disgusting after she has caught him with another man, as well as his subsequent suicide, her search for protection has included an element of compensation: "After the death of Allan—intimacies with strangers was all I seemed able to fill my empty heart with. . . . I think it was panic, just panic, that drove me from one to another,– hunting for some protection–here and there, in the most–unlikely places–even, at last, in a seventeen-year-old boy" (546). At the time of the play, dismissed from her teaching position and financially and emotionally destitute, she is driven to seek protection in the home of her sister Stella and her brother-in-law Stanley Kowalski, who, although from a recent immigrant and working-class background completely divorced from the Southern tradition, may be, Blanche admits, "what we need to mix with our blood now that we've lost Belle Reve and have to go on without Belle Reve to protect us" (492).

Blanche finds her own version of Stanley in Mitch, who, although of the same working-class background as Stanley, has "a sort of sensitive look" and seems to her "superior" (495) to his other friends. Mitch becomes the "cleft in the rock of the world that I could hide in" (546), and Blanche admits to Stella that she wants "to *deceive* him enough to make him–want me" (517). The deception involves her acting out the tradition, refusing any sexual activity beyond a kiss because, she tells Mitch, she has "old-fashioned ideals" (525). Williams makes sure that the audience is aware of Blanche's acting, as she rolls her eyes when she says this, and, perhaps more dangerously, compares herself to the most famous courtesan in literature, Alexandre Dumas fils's Camille, when she tells him "*Je suis la Dame aux Camellias! Vous êtes Armand!,*" and after Mitch assures her that he doesn't understand French, asks him, "*Voulez-vous couchez avec moi ce soir?*" [Would you like to sleep with me tonight?] (523), which it wouldn't take a great knowledge of French for someone who frequents the French Quarter of New Orleans to understand. There is a dangerous flirtation with self-exposure in Blanche's behavior with Mitch that is related to her guilt over her behavior with Allan and her reckless promiscuity subsequently. Nonetheless, she succeeds in deceiving Mitch until Stanley discovers her past, with its "intimacies with strangers," and she is forced to admit it to Mitch, who finds her no longer "straight" or "clean enough to bring in the house with [his] mother" (547) despite her plea, "I didn't lie in my heart" (546).

Blanche is fully aware of the disjunction between the ideals she holds and the reality of her past experience. As she tells Stella, the streetcar named Desire has "brought me here.–Where I'm not wanted and where I'm ashamed to be" (509), but she truly believes in a culture that represents human progress beyond the values of a "stone age" Stanley Kowalski, whose "*animal joy in his being,*" as Williams describes it, is based on "*pleasure with women,*" and, branching out from this, "*his heartiness with men, his appreciation of rough humor, his love of good drink and food and games, his car, his radio, everything that is his, that bears his emblem of the gaudy seed-bearer*" (481). Blanche believes that "such things as art—as poetry and music—such kinds of new light have come into the world since then! In some kinds of people some tenderer feelings have had some little beginning! That we have got to make *grow*! And *cling* to, and hold as our flag!" (511). She believes that "beauty of the mind and richness of the spirit and tenderness of the heart" (551) are things that should be valued, but she also realizes that they are not, or at least not by the Stanley Kowalskis who control the world outside the magic bubble of the Tradition, which, after World War II, has become more and more a delusion in which she takes comfort than any kind of social reality. In this regard, she is much like Amanda Wingfield, who creates a sustaining myth to which she can retreat when reality becomes overwhelming.

Williams wrote in *Memoirs* that *Streetcar* began with an image of Blanche, "sitting alone in a chair with the moonlight coming through a window on her, waiting for a beau who didn't show up" (M: 86). In an interview, he connected this image with his sister Rose, who had been in love with a young man who worked with her father: "Whenever the phone would ring, she'd nearly faint. She'd think it was he calling for a date, you know? They saw each other every other night, and then one time he just didn't call anymore. That was when Rose first began to go into a mental decline. From that vision *Streetcar* evolved" (C: 330–1). The play was originally called "Blanche's Chair in the Moon." By March of 1945, the draft was about 60 pages long, and the play had evolved enough that Williams was ready to send a synopsis to Audrey Wood, writing that he intended it for Katharine Cornell. He wrote that it was "about two sisters, the remains of a fallen southern family" (L1: 557), but also suggested as alternate titles "The Moth," "The Poker Night," and "The Primary Colors," which indicates that he had not yet decided whether it is Blanche, who is frequently imaged as a moth in the play, or Stanley who was at the center. In 1945, he wrote that after Blanche arrives at the home of Stella and her husband, then called Ralph, "a strong sex situation develops, Ralph and Blanche being completely antipathetic types, he challenged and angered by her delicacy, she repelled and fascinated by his coarse strength" (L1: 557). Ralph who has "unconsciously fallen in love with Blanche" (557), "takes her by force" (558) after a violent scene between them.

Much of Williams's subsequent work on the play focused on the relationship between Blanche and Stanley, which was complicated by the mixed feelings of attraction and repulsion between them, as well as Blanche's contempt and Stanley's anger at her superior attitude, and the danger to his dominance over his home represented by her attempt to alienate Stella from him. The attractions of Stanley are evident to Blanche, as she expresses them in her first attempt to gain his protection by flirting with him: "You're simple, straightforward, and honest, a little bit on the primitive side I should think . . . life is too full of evasions and ambiguities, I think. I like an artist who paints in strong, bold colors, primary colors . . . when you walked in here last night, I said to myself—'My sister has married a man!'" (488). Her contempt for him is far more evident throughout the play, however, from her statement that she will burn Allan's letters after he has touched them, to her descriptions to Stella and Mitch of his "commonness" and brutality, to the fatal scene which ends with his raping her, in which she says she has been "casting my pearls before swine" (551).

The development of Blanche's relationship with Stanley owes a good deal to Williams's life experience at the time, particularly his relationship with Amado Rodriguez y Gonzalez, "Pancho," who was his love interest at the time. Pancho was a young man with a fiery temper and little self-confidence, who constantly feared the loss of Williams and was extremely jealous of the casual sex partners he continued to pursue. They often had violent arguments in which Pancho, larger, younger, and stronger than Williams, had the upper hand. Elia Kazan, who directed *Streetcar* and began his lifelong friendship with Williams at this time, wrote of a violent argument, complete with smashing china, a broken chandelier, and death threats, that he witnessed in a hotel, after which "Tennessee burst through his door, looking terrified, and dashed into my room" (1988: 346). He later told Kazan that he had been teasing Pancho, and he blew up. Of Williams, Kazan wrote, "wasn't he attracted to the Stanleys of the world? Sailors? Rough trade? Danger itself? Wasn't Pancho a Stanley? Yes, and wilder. The violence in that boy, always on trigger edge, attracted Williams at the very time it frightened him" (350). This dynamic of attraction and repulsion, he thought, was what gave *Streetcar* its uniqueness and kept it from being a mere melodrama about a weak woman who is victimized by a brutal villain.

That Williams himself was aware of the contradictory complex of feelings he had for Pancho is evident in a letter to him in which he wrote: "Of all the people I have known you have the greatest and warmest heart but you also unfortunately have a devil in you that is constantly working against you, filling you with insane suspicions and jealousies and ideas that are so preposterous that one does not know how to answer them. It is a terrifying thing" (L2: 130–1). Williams's friend and sometime roommate, the artist Fritz Bultman, told his biographer Donald Spoto that "Tennessee behaved very badly toward Pancho . . . and he did so by using Pancho for real-life scenes which he created–and then transformed them into moments in *A Streetcar Named Desire*" (Spoto 1986: 136). During the pre-Broadway tour of *Streetcar*, Pancho threw Williams's typewriter from a hotel window. This direct hit at his writing was the last straw, and Williams sent him packing with a check and a train ticket to New Orleans, very like the bus ticket to Laurel that Stanley gives Blanche for her birthday. In his ending of the affair, Bultman said he saw "something opportunistic and abusive in Tennessee. I must say that I thought he mismanaged things with Pancho, and I didn't trust him after that . . . he was more callous than I'd imagined anyone could be. After Kip [Kiernan] and Pancho, something seemed to go sour in him, to harden" (Spoto 1986: 150–1). Williams was not without self-knowledge on this point. In October of 1947, shortly before the break-up, he wrote to Margo Jones of his feelings about Pancho. "I don't know what has happened but something has flown out the window, maybe never to return. Sympathy is not enough. There must be respect and understanding on both sides. . . . I am terribly troubled. I don't think I am acting kindly, and that is what I hate above all else" (L2: 129). As Blanche says, "deliberate cruelty is not forgivable. It is the one unforgivable thing in my opinion" (552).

It is evident from Williams's interactions with Pancho that he saw things from both Blanche's and Stanley's points of view. He often said that he had to be able to see every character in a play with sympathy if it was going to succeed. A letter he wrote in April 1947 to Kazan, who had a tendency to want to see things in somewhat melodramatic black-and-white terms, eloquently expresses the complex dynamic between the characters that he was aiming for in the play:

> I think its best quality is its authenticity or its fidelity to life. There are no "good" or "bad" people. Some are a little better or a little worse but all are activated more by misunderstanding than malice. A blindness to what is going on in each other's hearts. Stanley sees Blanche not as a desperate, driven creature backed into a last corner to make a last desperate stand – but as a calculating bitch with "round heels." Mitch accepts first her own false projection of herself as a refined young virgin, saving herself for the one eventual mate – then jumps way over to Stanley's conception of her. Nobody sees anybody truly, but all through the flaws of their own ego. That is the way we all see each other in life. Vanity, fear, desire, competition – all such distortions within our own egos – condition our vision of those in relation to us. Add to those distortions in our own egos, the corresponding distortions in the egos of the others – and you see how cloudy the glass must become through which we look at each other. (L2: 95)

The difference between this condition of life and its presentation in art, he thought, was that, "in creative fiction and drama, if the aim is fidelity, people are shown as we never see them in life but as they are. Quite impartially, without any ego-flaws in the eye of the beholder. We see from outside what could not be seen within, and the truth of the tragic dilemma becomes apparent" (96). In *Streetcar*, the tragedy emerges from the situation in which "it was not that one person was bad or good, one right or wrong, but that all judged falsely concerning each other, what seemed black to one and white to the other is actually grey – a perception that could occur only through the detached eye of art" (96). He warned Kazan that the play does not "present a theme or score a point, unless it be the point or theme of human misunderstanding" (96). He stated clearly that *Streetcar* is "a tragedy with the classic aim of producing a katharsis of pity and terror, and in order to do that Blanche must finally have the understanding and compassion of the audience. This without creating a black-dyed villain in Stanley. It is a thing (misunderstanding) not a person (Stanley) that destroys her in the end. In the end you should feel–'If only they had all <u>known</u> about each other!'" (96). Kazan has written that this letter was the "key to the production" (1988: 330) for him, and it is an essential document for understanding the play. As for any tragic hero, the weaknesses and flaws in Blanche's nature contain the seeds of her ultimate demise, and Williams has written a modern tragedy in which her antagonist is not a single character, but an existential condition of misunderstanding.

The details of Blanche's demise are intimately connected with Williams's inspiration for the character, his sister Rose, and, as always, his own experience. Like Rose, and Williams to a lesser degree, Blanche suffers from what Williams calls in the popular psychological language of the 1940s, hysteria. She exhibits this condition when she "*laughs shrilly*" (516) and screams when her coke spills on the night of her date with Mitch; when she screams "Fire! Fire! Fire!" (548) on the night Mitch rejects her as a wife, and in "*hysterical exhilaration*," (548) decks herself out in an evening gown and pretends to be at a party; and when she exhibits "*hysterical vivacity*" (557) in the final scene when she thinks she will be meeting Shep Huntleigh. She also suffers "*the utter exhaustion which only a neurasthenic personality can know*" (520) after her disappointing date with Mitch and takes hot baths "for [her]nerves. Hydro-therapy, they call it" (539), something Williams had done since his 20s. Although troubling, these aspects of Blanche's personality are not disabling. It is when, like Rose's, Blanche's condition goes beyond this that she is no longer able to cope. The aural hallucination of the "Varsouviana" that she hears when confronting the memory of Allan and after Stanley presents her with the bus ticket out of town is followed by "*inhuman voices like cries in a jungle*" and "*shadows and lurid reflections [that] move sinuously as flames along the wall spaces*" (553) when she confronts his menacing behavior on the night of the rape, and she finally enters a delusional state in the last scene when she believes that Shep Huntleigh is coming to take her on a vacation trip.

This is similar to Rose's condition, diagnosed as "dementia praecox," in which she was often delusional.

Besides her own emotional and psychological vulnerability, Blanche is also up against the events of her past, both her sexual promiscuity, unacceptable to Mitch or any similar future husband from whom she seeks protection, and her "failure" of and cruelty to Allan, which makes her feel inadequate and guilty. Externally, she is faced with Stanley, with his need to defeat what he sees as a threat to his home and his dominance of Stella, and also Stella's attachment to Stanley, which finally causes her to abandon Blanche despite the guilt that torments her because she "couldn't believe her story and go on living with Stanley" (556). This may be a reflection not only of Williams's perennial feeling of guilt for deserting Rose, but also of his mother's going along with her lobotomy, partly to quiet her accusations that her father had abused her.

From March of 1945, when he sent the first synopsis to Audrey Wood, Williams had difficulty in seeing how the play should end. After Stanley rapes Blanche, he wrote Wood, there were three possible ways for the play to end:

One, Blanche simply leaves – with no destination.

Two, goes mad.

Three, throws herself in front of a train in the freight-yards, the roar of which has been an ominous under-tone throughout the play. (L1: 558).

He discarded the third, Anna Karenina, option rather quickly, but he continued to play with the ending as he revised, even devising a happy ending in which Blanche leaves seemingly content with her future, much like Alma Winemiller in *Eccentricities of a Nightingale*. He decided early on that the trajectory of the play was tragic, however, and his main dilemma was how bleak to make Blanche's situation at the end of the play. By August of 1947, he was quite concerned that the ending of the play in the scripts that went out to the production team not be the one in which Blanche is a helpless victim, called catatonic by the doctor, and crouching in a grotesque, twisted position, screaming, before she is led away in a straitjacket. For Williams, who had been horrified by his visits to his sister in the state mental hospital, this was realism, but it went too far.

After working throughout the summer writing various versions of the ending, which he felt was "the crucial scene upon which the success or failure of the play may very well depend" (L2: 115), he told Audrey Wood that he was worried that the office of Irene Selznick, the play's producer, had lost it. Kazan, who was about to start his intense preparation for the production, had been sent the earlier version of the script. The new version of the scene was found, but in September, Williams wrote to Selznick that he was still tweaking the dialogue between Stella and Eunice and the "relative sympathetic treatment of the doctor. . . . We mustn't lose the effect of terror: everybody agrees about that" (L2: 123). The final version balances the sense of Blanche's extremity, as she screams and is held down by the Matron, with the doctor's "*personalized*" quality and his "*gentle and reassuring*" (563) voice as he dispenses with the straitjacket and takes Blanche's arm to lead her off, a personification of "the kindness of strangers."

The premiere production of *A Streetcar Named Desire*, which opened on 3 December 1947, was a notable event in American theatre history for several reasons. It was the beginning of Williams's partnership with Kazan, who was not only to be a lifelong friend and artistic advisor for Williams, but was also to direct *Camino Real* (1953), *Cat on a Hot Tin Roof* (1955), and *Sweet Bird of Youth* (1959), as well as the film version of *Streetcar* (1951) and the movie *Baby Doll* (1956). It was also the breakout performance of Method actor Marlon Brando, which had a tremendous effect on American acting. The production came together quickly after Audrey Wood sold the script to Irene Selznick, the daughter of movie mogul Louis B. Mayer and the former wife of producer David O. Selznick, who was trying to begin a career for herself as a producer. Having seen the recent production of Arthur Miller's *All My Sons* that Kazan directed, Williams decided that he would be the perfect director for *Streetcar*, and he felt comfortable with him because he knew him through his wife, Molly Day Thacher Kazan, who had been a friend and supporter of his since she had convinced the Group

Theatre to award him a cash prize back in 1939. Selznick agreed, partly because Kazan had also directed the film of *A Tree Grows in Brooklyn* (1945). It was Molly who talked an initially dubious Kazan into taking on the play, and the negotiations at first did not go smoothly. Williams wrote the long letter explaining the play that is quoted above as part of the campaign to interest Kazan, but he also suggested Margo Jones as a backup if the negotiations with Kazan should fail. Fortunately they eventually succeeded.

In casting the play, Selznick first thought of movie stars. John Garfield was her first choice and acceptable both to Williams and to Kazan, who had known him since their days in the Group Theatre during the 1930s. Margaret Sullavan, her first choice for Blanche, proved unacceptable to Williams, according to Kazan, because "Miss Sullavan seemed to be holding a tennis racket as she spoke his lines; Tennessee doubted that Blanche would have been a tennis enthusiast" (1988: 337). Kazan's response to Williams's suggestion of Pamela Brown was "Oh, please, not an Englishwoman" (1988: 337). He was eventually to direct Jessica Tandy in the play and Vivien Leigh in the film, both Englishwomen, to great acclaim. Tandy was cast after her husband, Hume Cronyn, who had provided Williams with much-needed money in 1941 when he had optioned several one-act plays, invited him and Selznick and Kazan to see Tandy in his Los Angeles production of Williams's *Portrait of a Madonna*, whose protagonist Lucretia Collins shares many of the elements of Blanche's character. All agreed that Tandy would make an excellent Blanche DuBois, and the main casting choice was made. When negotiations with Garfield broke down, Williams worried a good deal about Stanley, for whom Selznick was pushing the movie star Burt Lancaster. Kazan suggested Marlon Brando, a young actor from his Actors Studio class who had had several small parts in plays on Broadway, including Maxwell Anderson's *Truckline Café*, which he had directed.

The story of Brando's casting is legendary, as Kazan loaned him $20 to take the bus from New York to Provincetown where Williams and Pancho were spending the summer, and Margo Jones was visiting. According to Williams's account in *Memoirs*, Brando showed up 3 days later, having hitchhiked to save the money for food, fixed the old house's broken plumbing and electricity, and sat down to give a brilliant reading of Stanley Kowalski. "After less than ten minutes, Margo Jones jumped up and let out a 'Texas Tornado' shout. 'Get Kazan on the phone right away! This is the greatest reading I've ever heard–in or outside of Texas!'" (M: 131). Williams claimed that he kept his cool, but according to Kazan, he received "an ecstatic call from our author, in a voice near hysteria. Brando had overwhelmed him" (1988: 341–2). With the two main parts cast, the rest was much easier. Karl Malden, another Actors Studio member, was cast as Mitch, and Selznick brought in Kim Hunter, who was cast as Stella. The rest of the cast came primarily from the Actors Studio, as was to be Kazan's future practice, ensuring an ensemble performance from the beginning.

Kazan worried from the beginning that the classically trained Tandy might be unable to connect with the Method actors, particularly with Brando. The Method, an American version of the acting technique of the Moscow Art Theatre's Constantin Stanislavski, had been developed by Lee Strasberg and Harold Clurman in the Group Theatre, of which Kazan was a member, during the 1930s. Kazan, Strasberg, and Robert Lewis used The Method in training their students in the Actors Studio. The primary goal of The Method is to produce acting that is, to quote Kazan, "the spontaneous expression of an intense inner experience" (1988: 343). In order to achieve this, Method actors attempt to re-create emotions they have actually experienced by digging into their memories and reproducing the associated emotions on stage. The challenge is to do this authentically every night, and the results can be uneven and unpredictable as well as spontaneous and exciting. In The Method, little attention is paid to such things as diction and movement, and, as a result, Kazan admitted, Brando, the actor who is most famously associated with the Method, "had mannerisms that would have annoyed hell out of me if I'd been playing with him" (342). His playing of a scene constantly varied; he made his own time lapses, causing awkward pauses for the other actors; and there was his famous mumbling, an attribute he thought was endemic to Stanley's character, but which has been associated with both Brando and the Method in the popular mind ever since the production. To Kazan's relief and admiration, Tandy rose to the occasion, never complaining about the challenges of acting with Brando and adapting her own approach to Kazan's.

Jo Mielziner was engaged to do the scene design, for which he further developed the techniques he had established in *The Glass Menagerie* for introducing the subjective element into realism. Upstage, a backdrop with a distorted expressionist representation of a New Orleans street corner served as the street behind the apartment. In front of it was a series of transparent walls that represented the apartment. The rear wall had gauze appliques that represented windows, fanlights, and shutters. The front wall at first concealed the apartment, showing only the street in front. As in *Menagerie*, the walls could be lit from the front to appear opaque, or from behind to become transparent and reveal what was behind the wall. This allowed for fluid temporal transitions from scene to scene and spatial transitions from the apartment to the street, as well as expressionistic effects like the "*flores para los muertos*" scene and the expressionistic jungle effects that indicate Blanche's dissociation from reality in the rape scene. Juxtaposed with a stark realism in the costumes and props, this set produced the infusion of modernist subjectivity into the play's realism that Williams was after. As with *Menagerie*, the lighting was tremendously complex and expensive. A newspaper article described the backstage area, with its endless maze of cables, as "the cave of a black octopus family." In this pre-computer age, the design required two electricians to execute the light cues, and at one point, "one of the electricians is gradually operating four separate dimmers with his hands and another one with one knee" ("A *Streetcar* Runs").

The music, scored by modernist jazz composer Alex North, included the Novachord, a primitive version of a synthesizer, on which the "Varsouviana" was played. The rest of the music, which Williams indicates with the phrase "blue piano," was supplied by a four-piece jazz band composed of piano, clarinet, trumpet, and drums. Although the Novachord was located backstage, space being limited, the jazz band was located in a broadcasting booth on the theatre's upper floor and cued by an assistant stage manager who watched the play from the wings. Kazan and North worked together on the music so that it intensified the shifting moods of the play and emphasized its emotional climaxes.

Kazan wrote in his autobiography about his worry during the tryout period that Brando had taken over the play and Williams's assurance that Tandy would match him in the end. Kazan was convinced that "in the end, the play was the event; not the cast, not the director. The play carried us all. In years to come, this masterful work, written out of Tennessee's most personal experience, asking no favors, no pity, no special allegiance, always moved its audience. There was no way to spoil *Streetcar*" (1988: 347). *A Streetcar Named Desire*'s New York production was indeed an enormous success, running for 855 performances, and winning a collection of awards, including the Pulitzer Prize. While praising all aspects of the production, *New York Times* critic Brooks Atkinson barely noted Brando's performance, but called Tandy's "superb . . . one of the most perfect marriages of acting and playwriting . . . it is impossible to tell where Miss Tandy gives form and warmth to the mood Mr. Williams has created" (1947: 42). More typically of the critical response, the *Los Angeles Times* said that Tandy "moves with sure, almost inspired pace in the role of the unfortunate girl, but it is Marlon Brando as the tough, untutored brother-in-law who gives power and impact to the best scenes" (1947: A9). Brando went on to solidify his identity with the role in his performance in the 1951 film, directed by Kazan, with most of the Broadway cast reprising their roles. The glaring exception was Jessica Tandy, replaced by Vivien Leigh, who had played Blanche in the London production directed by her husband, Laurence Olivier. The play was not as well received in Britain as in the United States, with one critic explaining, "all we saw . . . was a squalid anecdote of a nymphomaniac's decay in a New Orleans slum" (Trewin 1949: 7).

Williams did worry about the fact that some of the audience did not shift their allegiance from Stanley to Blanche in the course of the play. In the script prepared for actors and published by Dramatists Play Service, he preceded Act II, Scene 1, (Scene 5 in the reading version) with the stage direction, *"The scene is a point of balance between the play's two sections,* BLANCHE'S *coming and the events leading up to her violent departure. The important values are the ones that characterize* BLANCHE: *its function is to give her dimension as a character and to suggest the intense inner life which makes her a person of greater magnitude than she appears on the surface*" (1947: 52). The ultimate test of a *Streetcar* production is its ability to do this, to afford to Blanche, as Williams put it, "the understanding and compassion of the audience" without "creating a black-dyed villain in Stanley" (L2: 96). As Bruce McConachie's analysis in this volume amply shows, the audience's response to the production is a complex and multifaceted dynamic that cannot easily be predicted by the artists who create it.

# CHAPTER 6
## THE ROSE TATTOO AND CAMINO REAL
## (1951 AND 1946–1953)

Symbolism was always an important element in Williams's writing, whether poetry, fiction, or drama, but in two plays from the early 1950s, he entered into a symbolic aesthetic with an exuberance beyond that of his other plays. *The Rose Tattoo* (1951) is rife with symbolism, a unique case in which the rose that is usually associated with Williams's sister in a pathetic or tragic way is instead associated with a vibrant, healthy sexuality. In his Foreword to *Camino Real* (1953), he wrote that "more than any other work that I have done, this play has seemed like the construction of another world, a separate existence" (NSE: 68). The symbolism he used to create it, he said, has "only one legitimate purpose" in a play, which is "to say a thing more directly and simply and beautifully than it could be said in words" (NSE: 70).

### Modern Fabliau: *The Rose Tattoo*

While vacationing in Provincetown, Massachusetts, in the summer of 1947, Williams had a brief affair with Frank Merlo, a young Italian-American 11 years his junior, which affected both of them more than they expected. By October, Merlo had moved in with Williams, beginning the 14-year relationship that was the longest and most stable of his life. *The Rose Tattoo*, which Williams dedicated "To Frank, in exchange for Sicily," was very much inspired by the early years of their loving and exuberantly sexual relationship, especially the summers they spent together in Italy. It is one of Williams's few comedies, based on the medieval fabliau, or bawdy tale, which also underlies Giovanni Boccaccio's *Decameron* and Geoffrey Chaucer's *Canterbury*

*Tales.* The play is full of earthy, simple humor, with a group of peasant characters Williams refers to as clowns, a goat that is chased through the yard at strategic times to emphasize the sexuality in the scene, physical humor involving a girdle and a condom, and broad sexual puns about driving truckloads of bananas.

In form, *The Rose Tattoo* (1951) is what literary theorist Northrop Frye refers to as a Normal Comedy, in which a flawed old order is disrupted by a threat that is often sexual, but a freer, more natural and more inclusive new order replaces it in the end. As the play begins, Serafina delle Rose, a seamstress, waits for her husband Rosario, the banana-truck driver, to come home. She wears a rose in her hair and her "*voluptuous figure is sheathed in pale rose silk*," but she also sits with "*plump dignity*" and is wearing a "*tight girdle*" (P1: 657). Serafina is a former peasant who is proud of having married a baron back in Sicily. She is also inordinately proud of having made love with her husband every night of her married life, believing that her husband has never been touched by anyone but her. This pride suffers a great fall, and the constraints that have channeled Serafina's sexuality within her marriage collapse. Rosario is shot because the bananas are hiding a load of drugs he is hauling for the mafia. Against the local priest's orders, Serafina has him cremated and keeps the ashes in a shrine, along with the statue of the Blessed Virgin, to whom she prays. Three years later, she has become slovenly, no longer wears a girdle, and even goes outside in a dirty slip. She also locks up her daughter Rosa, who has fallen in love with Jack, a young sailor, and takes her clothes so that she can't go out to meet him.

This state of prolonged grief and unnaturally sexless gloom is relieved when Serafina discovers that her husband was not the ideal lover she believed him to be, but that he was having an affair. In Act 3 she acknowledges her own sexuality when she sleeps with Alvaro Mangiacavallo ("eat a horse"–Williams's nickname for Frank Merlo was "the little horse"). Alvaro, who is the humorous mirror image of Rosario, her "*husband's body* with the head of a *clown*" (704), also drives a banana truck, and has a rose tattooed on his chest to match Rosario's. After Jack promises in front of the statue of the Virgin to respect Rosa's innocence, Serafina allows them to go out together.

At the end of the play, Serafina has accepted Alvaro as her lover despite his clownish face and behavior, and, because she momentarily sees a rose tattoo on her own breast, she believes that she has conceived a baby with him that will be some compensation for the miscarriage she suffered when Rosario died. She allows Rosario's ashes to blow away, and lets Rosa, who plans one afternoon with Jack in a hotel before he ships out, to "go to the boy" (737), wearing clothes from her wedding trousseau. Thus a new, far less constrained and falsely idealized order is established in which natural sexual desire is acknowledged. Serafina even sheds her girdle, which she had put on for her date with Alvaro, but takes it off because it is so uncomfortable.

Williams intended *The Rose Tattoo* for his friend, the legendary Italian actor Anna Magnani. She toyed with the idea of playing Serafina, but decided that her English was not up to a sustained stage role. Magnani did play the role in the 1955 film opposite Burt Lancaster as Alvaro, but the role in the 1951 Broadway production was played by another of Williams's close friends, Maureen Stapleton, with Eli Wallach as Alvaro. Both play and film, directed by Daniel Mann, were successful, with the Broadway production running more than 300 performances. A fitting celebration of the relationship that inspired it, part of the film was shot in the backyard of Williams and Merlo's house in Key West.

## Romantics in the Real World: *Camino Real*

*Camino Real* (1953) was a deeply meaningful play for Williams, a bohemian *cri de coeur*, more self-revelatory than anything he had yet written. While *The Glass Menagerie* drew directly on his family, and *Battle of Angels* and *A Streetcar Named Desire* reflected some of his important values and conflicts, *Camino* was, as he said, "nothing more nor less than my conception of the time and world that I live in" (P1: 743). He described it in an interview as "a prayer for the wild of heart kept in cages" (C: 32) and thought of it as a representation of the plight of the romantic bohemian in the mid-twentieth century, with its oppressive political, social, and moral institutions and codes.

This important play was 8 years in the making, and it underwent many changes along the way. It began during Williams's trip to Mexico in 1945, with what he called his "Were-wolf" play, "Cabeza de Lobo," which was focused on the arrival of a young man in a Mexican village, where he encounters a werewolf and lifts the veil of a girl named Esmeralda, traces of which survive in *Camino Real*. In January of 1946, Williams was back in New Orleans, shaping this germ into a one-act play called *Ten Blocks on the Camino Real*. In an unpublished foreword to the play, he explained that he had been inspired by a train ride through Mexico, where he witnessed the "blue dusk in the village . . . like the essential myth of a poem" (Parker 1998: 45), the street people, the inscription "Kilroy was here" written on a wall, and two characters resembling Jacques Casanova and Marguerite Gautier (Camille) on the train.

Toward the end of the month, Williams told James Laughlin, his publisher at New Directions, that he would soon send him a manuscript of the play, which included Oliver Winemiller, the male prostitute from his story "One Arm" (1948), as protagonist, as well as Proust's homosexual masochist, the Baron de Charlus, and Don Quixote as characters. At the end of February, he sent a version to Audrey Wood and received a not very enthusiastic reply. Thirty years later in his *Memoirs*, he wrote that she had called him on the phone and said stridently, "about that play you sent me . . . put it away, don't let anybody see it." He said that "her phone call may have prevented me from making a very, very beautiful play out of *Camino Real* instead of the striking but flawed piece which it finally turned into several years later" (M: 101). At the time he had written to Donald Windham that "Audrey thinks the best scene is 'too coarse'" (1980: 184). He took her objections to the play's "coarseness" to heart, for when he wrote to her 2 weeks later about the revised script, he said the only good scene was the one at the Gypsy's (Block 12 in *Camino Real*), saying "I don't see anything objectionably coarse in that," and suggesting that he could eliminate the Baron and the references to the notorious Casanova and Camille, calling them simply "'Actor & Actress' or 'He and She'" (L2: 45).

As Williams worked to erase the traces of sexually transgressive characters like the courtesan Camille, the homosexual masochist

Baron de Charlus, and the libertine Casanova, he thought of building up the character of the young man, who was now no longer the prostitute Oliver Winemiller, but the iconic American wanderer, Kilroy. He explained that "in writing about him I wanted to catch the atmosphere of the world he lived in, bars, stations, cheap hotel-rooms. An atmosphere of the American comic-strip transposed into a sort of rough, colloquial poetry. Comic-strip bar-room idyll, the common young transient's affair with longing and disappointment, a very rough sort of tenderness mixed with cynicism" (L2: 45). While he saw from his agent's reaction that he might not be able to reflect the world of transgressive sexuality as directly as he had hoped, in writing of this world, Williams was evoking the atmosphere of the gay subculture where he spent time during his mysterious disappearances from both the respectable bourgeois world in which he had been brought up and the professional theatrical circle, and he was remembering the bohemian hand-to-mouth life he had lived for the 3 years before his success with *The Glass Menagerie*.

Despite this temporary loss of confidence, Williams completed the one-act *Ten Blocks on the Camino Real* with the characters of Marguerite, Casanova, and the Baron intact, and published it in *American Blues*, a collection of his one-act plays, in 1948. Elia Kazan found it there and used the scene at the Gypsy's (Block VII in *Ten Blocks*) for an acting exercise at Actors Studio in the fall of 1949, which he invited Williams to see. Excited by the performance of Eli Wallach as Kilroy, Williams hoped to interest Kazan in directing the play on Broadway along with another of his one-acts, and some progress was made on this in 1951, but the deal fell apart. In the spring of 1952, the project was reimagined, with Williams revising the play into the full-length *Camino Real* and Cheryl Crawford taking over as producer. They still hoped to get Kazan to direct, but were also considering José Quintero, whose groundbreaking production of *Summer and Smoke* had opened in April at the Circle in the Square Theatre, and the British director Peter Brook. In June, Williams went to Paris to work with Kazan on the script, and both he and Crawford were committed to the project by the middle of July.

In developing the play to full length, Williams concentrated on the Casanova–Camille story, which was to bother Kazan, who thought the focus should be on Kilroy, throughout the production process. In July, Williams explained to Kazan that "what I am saying in their story is really a very clear and simple thing, that after passion, after the carneval (which means 'farewell to flesh') there is something else, and even something that can be more important, and we've got to believe in it" (L2: 438). As a whole, he said the play was "a poetic search for a way to live romantically, with 'honor,' in our times, royally under real conditions," and insisted that "there is very deeply and earnestly an affirmative sort of mysticism in this work" (L2: 438). This affirmation was something they worked hard to realize in production, but, judging from the critical response, they failed to do.

One of the reasons the production failed to convey the romanticism, honor, mysticism, and affirmative outlook that Williams tried to express in the play was the set, designed by his old friend from the University of Iowa days, Lemuel Ayers. They had first offered the play to Jo Mielziner, who expressed reservations about it, and then wrote to Williams that he would like to do it, suggesting that they might use an abstract set that suggested a sort of bear pit or a labyrinth in which Kilroy was trapped. Williams wrote back warning him that the designer would have to have a real enthusiasm and "emotional alliance" with the play, and expressed reservations about the bear pit idea, saying the set should have "the visual atmosphere of a romantic mystery" and the "haunting loveliness of one of those lonely-looking plazas and colonnades in a Chirico [painting]" (L2: 452). Mielziner drew some fluid, imagistic sketches around the concept of a staircase leading to nowhere, but Cheryl Crawford, ever mindful of economy, balked at his fee, and Lemuel Ayers was hired instead. His set was the opposite of Mielziner's idea, a heavily realistic depiction of the scene as described in the stage directions, with the wealthy side of the Camino Real centered on the Siete Mares hotel and the "Skid Row" side anchored by the Ritz Men Only, the Bucket of Blood Cantina, and the pawn shop. Upstage was a flight of steps to the archway leading to Terra Incognita, and to the right of that the Gypsy's balcony where her daughter Esmeralda made her appearance. The set created a familiar visual reality that provided some comfort to the audience, but it worked against the concept of romantic fantasy that Williams had hoped for in the production.

The set was also decidedly not beautiful, but rather hellish or nightmarish, which was in keeping with the style that Kazan had derived for the production from the Mexican artist José Guadalupe Posada's images of the Day of the Dead. This aesthetic shift is also evident in Williams's revision of the play as he developed it into the full-length *Camino Real* throughout 1952. The one-act version, set clearly in a "small tropical port of the Americas", is to have "the grace and mystery and sadness: that peculiar dreamlike feeling that emanates from such squares in Mexico" (1948: 43). In revising the play, Williams reimagined it in the context of the film *Casablanca* and his personal experience of North Africa during a miserable trip there in the company of Jane and Paul Bowles and Frank Merlo in 1949 (Murphy 2011: 83–5). The new set, with its "*confusing, but somehow harmonious, resemblance to such widely scattered ports as Tangiers, Havana, Vera Cruz, Casablanca, Shanghai, New Orleans*" (P1: 749), reflects the universalizing tendency in his revisions. From *Casablanca*, he drew the contrasting wealth and poverty of the city and its existential prison-house metaphor of waiting for escape. More specifically, he introduced the oppressive political order that begins in the Survivor scene and looms threateningly throughout the play in the character of Gutman (based on *Casablanca*'s Sydney Greenstreet), the soldiers, and the Streetcleaners, and the Fugitivo, an analog to the plane to Lisbon in the film, which is an objective correlative for everyone's dream of escape.

At the same time as he was darkening the existential metaphor of the play, Williams also developed the Casanova–Camille story line in which Marguerite (Camille) represents a cynical despair and self-interest in opposition to Jacques' hopefulness that the genuine love that he has come to feel for her will ultimately triumph. Marguerite compares them to "a pair of captive hawks caught in the same cage" (807) who have merely grown used to each other, and says that what they feel "in whatever is left of our hearts" is like "the sort of violets that could grow on the moon, or in the crevices of those far away mountains" (807). While Marguerite believes that "tenderness, the violets in the mountains–can't break the rocks!" (808), Jacques insists that they "can break the rocks if you believe in them and allow them to grow!" (808). At the end of the play, Williams has Don Quixote speak the "curtain line," which affirms the possibility of love overcoming cynicism and self-interest: "*The violets in the mountains have broken the rocks!*" (842). The final result of these revisions is that the spirit of romantic affirmation, which has the last word, is in deep conflict with the existential reality of the Camino Real. The crucial work of a production is to develop the dynamics of the conflict but not tip the balance too far toward the dark side so that the romantic affirmation will ring true.

The original production did not do this, partly because of the set and Kazan's Day of Death concept, which influenced not only the design, but also the dance movement of the street people that was choreographed by Anna Sokolow. The production may also have failed to achieve this balance because it was important to Kazan, trained in The Method, to see a clear arc or "spine" to the play's action, something that was not evident in the series of scenes or "blocks" that Williams wrote for *Camino Real*. His proposal, explained at length in a letter he wrote to Williams on 17 November 1952, was to develop the character Kilroy, whom he saw as the play's protagonist, so that he was present throughout the play, and not just at the beginning and the end (Murphy 1992: 70–4). Williams at first balked at what he saw as overreaching and interfering on the part of the director, and exploded in a meeting with Kazan and Crawford, but eventually yielded to a chastened and conciliatory Kazan, revising the script to weave Kilroy throughout the action by giving him the patsy role and developing his relationship with Jacques. This emphasis on Kilroy, his frantic effort to escape, and his disillusionment with love in the person of the Gypsy's daughter Esmeralda, naturally de-emphasized Jacques and Marguerite and their romantic affirmation. Kilroy has his own affirmative ending, in his acceptance of Don Quixote's advice: "*Don't! Pity! Your! Self!*" (841) and his final determination to join up with him and go "*on* from –*here!*" (841), but they represent a stoic endurance rather than a triumph of love and tenderness.

Williams's perception of interference also resulted in a fight with Molly Kazan, who had been his staunch supporter since she had gotten him a much-needed cash prize from the Group Theatre in 1939. She had persuaded her husband to direct *A Streetcar Named Desire*, and on the whole, she admired *Camino Real*, but she had serious reservations about its ability to reach an audience. Molly offended Williams by sending out a "circular" to the production team with her criticism, and he wrote to his friend Paul Bowles that she was "the self-appointed scourge of Bohemia" (L2: 461), but the core suggestions in her rather verbose letter were appropriate for the production if it was to succeed with a Broadway audience. Essentially, she told him that he needed to make the play's meaning clearer to the audience, to cut 45 minutes from the script, and to create a First-Act climax that would carry Kilroy over to the next Act. The latter two suggestions reiterated her husband's, items that Williams fully entered into, making the "curtain" at the end of *Camino Real*'s First Act (Block 6) one of the most emphatic in all of his plays, as Kilroy and Esmeralda are pursued up and down the aisles of the theatre with a great deal of action and noise until Esmeralda is caught and dragged inside the Gypsy's and Kilroy is caught by Gutman and made to put on the patsy outfit that he wears in Act 2. Williams was less cooperative about explaining the play's meaning to the audience, much to his regret when he found himself writing a new Prologue and Block One in which he tried to do just that, after the play had opened to general confusion among audiences and critics.

When the play opened on 17 March 1953, it began with the Survivor scene, Block 2 in the published text, in which a ragged, sun-blackened young man, dying from thirst, stumbles into the public square and thrusts his hands into the fountain, only to find that it has gone dry. The prostitute Rosita tells him there is plenty to drink in the luxury hotel Siete Mares and shoves him toward it. The hotel proprietor Gutman whistles, and a soldier comes out and shoots the Survivor, who drags himself back to the fountain like *"a dying pariah dog in a starving country"* (758). Gutman explains that martial law has sometimes to be called upon to protect the Siete Mares, built over the only perpetual spring in Tierra Caliente. A character called The Dreamer puts his arm around the Survivor and utters the word *"Hermano"* (brother), which causes the guards to pull guns and put up barriers because, as Gutman says, the word is "a wanton incitement to riot" (763). As the Survivor dies in the arms of La Madrecita, Gutman calls for a diversion, and the Gypsy obliges by announcing a fiesta for that night when "the moon will restore the virginity of my daughter" (763).

Kazan was concerned that an audience would see this opening scene and take the whole play for a political allegory about oppressive government, when government is just one element of the more universal oppression of the romantic spirit that Williams is exposing in the play. He worried that the specific situation of this Block would undermine the more symbolic techniques in subsequent Blocks that focus on what Williams called the "legendary figures"—Casanova, Marguerite, Baron de Charlus, Lord Byron, Don Quixote—and it did in fact prove problematic for audiences, as they had to shift gears immediately for the second scene (Block 3), in which Kilroy was introduced. This scene has more of the "comic-strip transposed into a sort of rough, colloquial poetry" that Williams had described to Audrey Wood back in 1945. Kilroy arrives at the end of Block 2 with his golden boxing gloves strung over his shoulder, carrying a duffle bag, and wearing his jewel-studded "Champ" belt, and changes the inscription chalked on the wall from "Kilroy is coming" to "Kilroy is here." He says that he's just gotten off a ship and spends the first part of Block 3 asking the questions that the audience presumably shares, "What *is* this place? What kind of a hassle have I got myself into?" (768), and is constantly frustrated in his attempt to find the answer. Robbed of his money, he witnesses the Survivor's corpse being carted away by the Streetcleaners and decides to pawn his Champ belt rather than his golden gloves or the "silver framed photo of my One True Woman" (769). This scene sets up the empathy that Kazan had hoped to establish between the audience and Kilroy, as they both recognize the harshness of this world, Kilroy's desperate circumstances, and his need to find out where he is and how to get out.

This scene is followed by the appearance of the Baron de Charlus in Block 4. Williams gives the Baron the sexually transgressive desires that he has in Marcel Proust's *À la recherche du temps perdu*, as he reserves a room in the Ritz Men Only for himself and "a possible guest," requiring "an iron bed with no mattress and a considerable length of stout knotted rope. No! Chains this evening, metal chains. I've been very bad, I have a lot to atone for" (770). He picks up Lobo (wolf), a survival from the werewolf version of the play, "*a wild-looking young man of startling beauty*" (770). When Kilroy, who has pawned his belt, says that he is glad to meet "a normal American. In a clean white suit," the Baron replies "My suit is pale yellow. My nationality is French, and my normality has been often subject to question" (772). The Baron tells Kilroy about the "Bird Circuit," the bars of the Camino's gay subculture whose names are a coded reference to the gay bars of Greenwich Village in the 1950s. After the Baron disappears through the arch leading to Terra Incognita, there is an outcry, and Kilroy goes to help. He is sent plummeting backward through the arch, and tells Jacques Casanova, "I tried to interfere, but what's th' use?" (774). The last that is seen of the Baron is his corpse, doubled up in the Streetcleaners barrel.

The Baron is the third overtly gay character to appear in a Williams play, and like Queen in *Not About Nightingales*, who is scalded to death because he is not "man enough" to withstand the torture of the Klondike, and Allan Grey in *A Streetcar Named Desire*, who kills himself after Blanche reveals her disgust for him, the Baron meets an end that is linked to his homosexuality. But he is just one of the romantic nonconformists who is destroyed by the harsh reality of the Camino Real. In Block 5, Kilroy meets Jacques, who tells him that the Streetcleaners take the bodies of people like the Baron to a Laboratory where "the individual becomes an undistinguished member of a collectivist state" (775), any unique body parts placed in a museum whose proceeds go to the maintenance of the military police. Kilroy and Jacques pronounce themselves "buddies under the skin . . . travelers born . . . always looking for something . . . satisfied by nothing" (776), a good description of Tennessee Williams as well. They agree, however, that they aren't ready to enter the arch to the Terra Incognita quite yet.

In Block 6, the final scene in Act 1, Esmeralda is introduced, trying to escape from the Gypsy's establishment, and Kilroy tries to escape the patsy role that Gutman is forcing him into. Kilroy runs up and down the aisle, asking the audience where the bus station is and running for the Exit signs, while Esmeralda tries to hide among the street people. After Kilroy's dramatic leap from a theatre box, both are caught, and Kilroy puts on the clown outfit of the Patsy, establishing the idea that there is no way out of the Camino Real except through death or the Terra Incognita. In Block 7, Jacques tells Kilroy that he knew he would be confined in some way: "you have a spark of anarchy in your spirit and that's not to˙ be tolerated. Nothing wild or honest is tolerated here!" (784). Marguerite is introduced along with her story as Camille, "the sentimental whore, the courtesan who made the mistake of love" (785). When the hotel guests object to their presence, Jacques tells Marguerite, "you must learn how to carry the banner of Bohemia into the enemy camp," and she replies, "Bohemia has no banner. It survives by discretion" (787). When Jacques' remittances are cut off and it is revealed that Marguerite has escaped from a tuberculosis sanatorium, they are shown to share the same "desperation" (792) as Kilroy.

Lord Byron appears in Block 8, representing the romantic and the poet. As he tells the story of the poet Shelley's cremation, he says that "the burning was *pure!*–as a man's burning should be" (794), and he tells Jacques that a poet's vocation is to "purify [the heart] and lift it above its ordinary level" (795). He confesses that his own vocation has been lost, "obscured by vulgar plaudits" (796) and a luxurious life. "The metal point's gone from my pen, there's nothing left but the feather" (793), and he is determined to go to Athens and fight for freedom. This corruption of his artistic vocation was something that Williams himself was feeling in the wake of his success and financial prosperity with *Menagerie* and *Streetcar*. For the first time, he had experienced prolonged writer's block, and it had taken him a year to write the full-length version of *Camino Real*. In what is probably the central thematic statement of the play, Lord Byron's words as he passes through the arch to the Terra Incognita, "*Make voyages!–Attempt them!*–there's nothing else" (797), Williams referenced the poem "Voyages" by his beloved Hart Crane. Lord Byron is the only character in the play to venture through the arch into the Terra Incognita and not be brought back. His fate is uncertain, but what is important is that he make the voyage.

Of course the historical Lord Byron was killed in Greece, fighting in the war of independence from the Ottoman Empire.

After the Lord Byron scene, Williams concentrates on the Jacques and Marguerite story, beginning with the chaotic Fugitivo scene, in which Marguerite betrays Jacques, stealing his papers in her desperation to escape from the Camino Real. Despite the betrayal, Jacques continues to believe in the ultimate efficacy of his love. Even when he is crowned as the King of the Cuckolds by the street people, he declares himself to be a "GREAT LOVER! The greatest lover wears the longest horns on the Camino! GREAT! LOVER!" (810). He and Kilroy seal their brotherhood, as Kilroy removes Jacques' horns and Jacques removes Kilroy's patsy outfit, and Kilroy pawns his gold gloves, the symbol of his identity, in order to finance his escape. But Kilroy is declared the Chosen Hero of the fiesta by Esmeralda, and his escape is cut short by the scene at the Gypsy's, in which he ends up giving all his money for the chance to "lift the veil" of Esmeralda. Although he expresses skepticism on the basis of his prior experience with Gypsies' daughters, in their brief encounter, they convince each other with their repeated statements of "I am sincere" (826). Immediately afterwards, Kilroy, "tired, and full of regret," remarks that "it wasn't much to give my golden gloves for" (827).

Counteracting this disillusionment, Blocks 13 and 14 deepen Kilroy's relationships with Jacques and Marguerite, as he sympathizes with Jacques after his eviction from the Siete Mares and descent to the Ritz Men Only, and shares a moment of empathy with Marguerite after she returns from an assignation in the bazaar, showing her the picture of his One True Woman, and speaks about the importance of waking next to the person you love and feeling that "warmness beside you. . . . It has to be some one you're used to. And that you. *KNOW LOVES* you!" (833). Kilroy reveals that he has left his wife because his weak heart meant he couldn't box any more, and "why should a beautiful girl tie up with a broken-down champ?—The earth still turning and her obliged to turn with it, not out—of dark into light but out of light into dark" (834). Pounced on by the Streetcleaners, Kilroy dies fighting them. There is a good deal of personal resonance in Williams's representation of Kilroy, from the playful connections between the Champ belt and his success in the theatre and the golden gloves and his writing talent, to his anxiety about his relationship with Frank Merlo, about which he was insecure during the time he was writing the full-length version of the play, to his perennial anxiety over what he thought was his weak heart and imminent demise. Kilroy's heart, "as big as the head of a baby" (836), is also found to be pure gold.

In the final Block, Kilroy pawns his golden heart for things to give Esmeralda after he hears her saying that she wants to dream of the chosen hero, "the *only* one. *Kilroy! He* was *sincere!*" (838). When he brings the "loot," she mistakes him for a cat and falls asleep, while he has the contents of a slop jar thrown on him from the Gypsy's establishment and he proclaims himself "stewed, screwed and tattooed on the Camino Real!" (840). Kilroy's experience is played off against Esmeralda's prayer, the speech that Williams wrote at Kazan's prompting to add a prayer in which she asks God to protect the dying race of romantics, eccentrics, rebels, Bohemians, freaks, queers, artists, wanderers, loafers, drifters, old maids, rebels and other nonconformists. In the play, Esmeralda prays for "all con men and hustlers and pitch men who hawk their hearts on the street, all two-time losers who're likely to lose once more" (839).

Williams hoped for the romantic ideals of honor, endurance, and love to leave the play's final impression on the minds of the audience. Unfortunately, this proved not to be the case for the original production, as the critics reacted vehemently against what they perceived to be the play's obscurity and deep pessimism. Even Williams's friend and most loyal supporter among the critics, Brooks Atkinson of the *New York Times*, pronounced it a "shock to realize that Mr. Williams' conception of the world is so steeped in corruption," writing that "his characters blundering through the malign world he has created for them are caught in a web of corruption, cruelty, disease and death, doomed by the viciousness of human beings, too weak and indolent to escape from the contamination of their kind" (1953: 2,1). John Mason Brown wrote that, "on the evidence supplied by 'Camino Real' it would be safe to say that few writers, even in these times when many authors' sole faith is their belief in man's baseness and meanness, have held the human race in lower esteem that Mr. Williams or found the world less worthy of habitation. . . . The world through which Mr. Williams guides us is a sorry mixture of Gehenna, the Kabash seen (and inhaled) at noon, the 'Inferno' as written by Mickey Spillane, and 'Paradise Lost' in a translation by Sartre. . . . In his cosmos man is finished and unworthy of redemption" (1953: 28–30). Dismayed by the wholesale misinterpretation of his intended meaning, Williams engaged in an exchange of letters with Atkinson and with the respected critic for the *New York Herald Tribune*, Walter Kerr, who had complained that Williams was "hopelessly mired in his new love–symbolism" (March 1953), in which he tried to explain the play's meaning to them. After Kerr wrote that, while the theme of the play became clear to him "after an intolerable amount of post-mortem speculation," it was "something which your audience in the theater does not grasp at all–not in any sense" (April 1953), Williams took the extraordinary step of writing two new scenes for the play, the Prologue and Block 1 in the published version, that would help to explain its meaning and to guide the audience through it, as well as revising the ending.

The Prologue has Don Quixote and Sancho Panza entering the Square and Quixote saying that he has wandered far from the country of his youth and the values of nobility, truth, valor, and *devoir* (duty). Sancho reads from a map that they have left the Ca*mi*no Re*al* (royal road) behind and have come to the beginning of the Ca*mi*no Re*al* (real road): "turn back, Traveler, for the spring of humanity has gone dry in this place . . . there are no birds in the country except wild birds that are tamed and kept in . . . *Cages!*" (751). This establishes the location of the play and its core symbolism for the audience. When Sancho leaves to go back to La Mancha, the expressionistic fantasy of the play is established as Quixote goes to sleep, saying "my dream will be a pageant, a masque in which old meanings will be remembered and possibly new ones discovered" (752). When he wakes from his dream, he says, he will choose someone new to accompany him in place of Sancho, which prepares for Kilroy's joining him at the end of the play. In Block One, Prudence and Olympe, characters from Dumas' *La dame aux camélias* who did not appear in the original Broadway version, give the background of Marguerite Gautier from Dumas' novel, making clear who Marguerite is and what her state is as the play begins.

Williams revised Esmeralda's prayer so that it refers to the individual characters in the play—Kilroy, Marguerite, Jacques, Lord Byron, and Don Quixote—who all have lost their way on the Camino Real but found it again in their pursuit of a romantic ideal, ending with the hope that "sometime and somewhere, let there be something to mean the word *honor* again!" (839). This hope sets the stage for the appearance of Don Quixote, who urges Kilroy not to pity himself as they prepare to go through the arch, like Lord Byron entering the Terra Incognita. In revising, Williams gave the curtain line, "*The violets in the mountains have broken the rocks!*" (842) to Don Quixote rather than to Marguerite, who originally spoke it, establishing the power of love as a general thematic statement for the play. Elia and Molly Kazan might have taken some satisfaction in the fact that Williams was doing what they had asked him to do months before, but it was too late to save the production, which closed after 60 performances. *Camino Real* lost money for its investors, weakening the powerful position Williams had achieved in the Broadway theatre world with *Menagerie* and *Streetcar*. The combined critical and financial failure of *Camino Real* was something he had not faced since *Battle of Angels*, and the fact that it occurred with the play that was his most revealing self-expression to date affected him deeply.

# CHAPTER 7
## *CAT ON A HOT TIN ROOF* (1951–1955)

---

Like the other major plays of the 1950s, *Cat on a Hot Tin Roof* dramatizes fundamental personal issues that Williams was struggling with as he wrote it. He referred to it as "a synthesis of all my life" (L2: 558). As was often the case, the play began with a short story. "Three Players of a Summer Game" was begun in the summer of 1951, while Williams was in Venice and Rome, and he finished the first draft at the end of July. In his journal, he expressed his disappointment with the completed story at the beginning of October, pronouncing it "dull, dull" (N: 537), and he was not better pleased when he picked it up in the following April, finding the writing "stiff" (N: 549). It was published in the *New Yorker* later that year, however, and is recognized as one of his best stories. His discomfort with it may have something to do with the fact that the story marks the beginning of his attempt to work creatively with the metaphor of the closet, expressing the intense conflict he was feeling about living the closeted lifestyle that was necessary to a gay playwright who sought success in the Broadway theatre of the 1950s, a lifestyle that extended into his work.

In "Three Players," the metaphor of the closet is applied to a heterosexual couple, Brick Pollitt and Isabel Grey, who not only are engaged in an affair that transgresses the norms of their small Southern town, but also have administered a fatal dose of morphine to Isabel's husband, who was dying of brain cancer. Williams describes them as coming out of the Victorian house where this has occurred as "out of the mysteries of a walled place, with the buoyant air of persons just released from a suffocating enclosure, as if they had spent the fierce day bound in a closet" (CS: 303). They escape onto a large lawn "of smooth emerald that flickers fierily at some points and rests under violet shadows in others" (303). The lawn becomes what contemporary queer theorists call a queer space, where boundaries are crossed and social norms are destabilized throughout the story, as Brick's alcoholism causes him to talk loudly about his personal affairs and to engage in drunken antics on the lawn, at one point stripping off his clothes and playing under the sprinkler to the scandal of the neighbors, who still have to maintain a deferential attitude toward him as a wealthy plantation owner.

The threat of chaos in this space is imperfectly controlled by the croquet game which provides the third metaphor of the story, the attempt to impose an artificial order on both the "unbearably hot and bright" (308) reality of what goes on in the house and the always threatening chaos of Brick's alcoholic performances on the lawn. Brick explains to the house painters that croquet is the perfect game for a drinker because it "takes concentration and precision" (313) and thus is an incentive to control his drinking, but while he is explaining this, he passes out on the lawn. Brick's conflict with drink is figured as the agon of a hero. He describes it as analogous to the fight of a matador with a bull. This battle is enmeshed in his battle with his wife Margaret. Brick began drinking 2 years after he married her, and the relationship is described with a vampire metaphor: "It was as though she had her lips fastened to some invisible wound in his body through which drained out of him and flowed into her the assurance and vitality that he had owned before marriage" (306). What's more, she has taken away what Brick euphemistically refers to as his "self respect," by emasculating him: "I could feel it being cut off me" (312). At the end of the story, Brick's attempt to conquer his alcoholism has failed, and Margaret has wrested him away from Isabel, driving him through the streets of the town in his own Pierce Arrow car, "exactly the way that some ancient conqueror, such as Caesar or Alexander the Great or Hannibal, might have led in chains through a capital city the prince of a state newly conquered" (325).

There is a transgressive element in Margaret as well as in Brick and Isabel, for as she takes on greater power in her marriage, she is also described with many of the 1950s' markers of lesbianism. Her feminine prettiness is replaced by "a firm and rough-textured sort of handsomeness" (306). She stops being quiet and dainty, lets her dirty fingernails show through the nail enamel, cuts her hair short, and develops "a booming laugh that she might have stolen from Brick while he was drunk" (306). At the end of the story, as she drives Brick through the town, she handles his Pierce Arrow "with a wonderful male assurance, her bare arms brown and muscular as a Negro field hand's" (324). Thus the defeat, capture, and display of Brick is not simply the defeat of a transgressive element by the normative power structure, but the ascendence of one transgressor over another. Margaret has publicly rejected the heteronormative role of the Southern Belle and the submissive wife, and she is able to display her newfound power openly in the town.

*Cat on a Hot Tin Roof* begins with the agon between Brick and Margaret. The battle with alcohol is already lost. Williams describes Brick as having *"the charm of that cool air of detachment that people have who have given up the struggle"* (P1: 885), and Maggie tells him that, "now that you've lost the game, not lost but just quit playing, you have that rare sort of charm that usually only happens in very old or hopelessly sick people, the charm of the defeated.–You look so cool, so cool, so enviably cool" (892). Williams originally thought of the play as, like the story, about "a vital, strong woman dominating a weak man and achieving her will" (L2: 554). The center of the narrative has been shifted from the lawn to the house, and from Brick's love affair to his marriage. Set entirely in the bedroom, the play offers no hope of the kind of relief from the closet that the lawn represents in the story. Although the character of Brick remains essentially the same, Maggie's character has been changed and developed considerably from the story. She no longer has any lesbian markers, and she is desperately attracted to her husband Brick, who refuses to sleep with her. The most important change is that the suggestion of homosexuality has been transferred from Margaret to Brick, and the heterosexual affair to a deep male friendship with Skipper, which clearly involved homoerotic feelings on Skipper's part, and perhaps on Brick's.

Williams had worked on the script in the summer and fall of 1953, but not made much progress, writing in his journal that he was troubled by "a real confusion that seems to exist, nothing carried through to completion but written over and over, as if a panicky hen running circles" (595). In the spring, he told Audrey Wood the play had thrown him into a "terrible state of depression last summer in Europe, I couldn't seem to get a grip on it." Nonetheless he thought it had "a terrible sort of truthfulness about it, and the tightest structure of anything I have done" (L2: 525). The play took on new life toward the end of March, 1954, coinciding with the visit of Edward "Skipper" McNally, an actor and friend of Williams and Elia Kazan's, to Key West. Williams wrote to Kazan that "Skipper was here and should have had him a ball. For some reason this year the Island is over-run by beautiful nymphos, really attractive ones, who almost rape the men in public let alone what they may do in private. . . . Won't take no for an answer if they can possibly get any other. I think Skipper was scared. He left mighty quick" (L2: 524). The image of Skipper being scared away by aggressively sexual women likely contributed to the new subtext in the play, what Williams referred to in his journal on 3 April as "the intrusion of the homosexual theme" (N: 631). Replacing Brick's heterosexual affair with a homosexual attraction brought the play somewhat out of the aesthetic closet where it had been languishing, and possibly confusing Williams, making the play truer to his experience and what he really wanted to write about. In the context of Brick's relationship with Skipper, Maggie's brief heterosexual affair with him is what defines the "normal" in the play, and Brick's behavior becomes transgressive.

At the center of Brick's character is an ambiguity, or "mystery," as Williams preferred to call it. While it is clear from the play that there was an erotic element to Skipper's love for Brick, the nature of Brick's feeling for Skipper is veiled. Williams was taken to task by critic Walter Kerr for evading the truth about this, and he responded by writing the long stage direction in Act 2, when Brick and Big Daddy are discussing his relationship with Skipper. Here he says that "*the thing they're discussing, timidly and painfully on the side of Big Daddy, fiercely, violently on Brick's side, is the inadmissible thing that Skipper died to disavow between them. The fact that if it existed it had to be disavowed to 'keep face' in the world they lived in, may be at the heart of the 'mendacity' that Brick drinks to kill his disgust with. It may be the root of his collapse"* (945). But he also draws back from a clear statement of Brick's homosexuality:

> *The bird that I hope to catch in the net of this play is not the solution of one man's psychological problem. . . . Some mystery should be left in the revelation of character in a play, just as a great deal of mystery is always left in the revelation of character in life, even in one's own character to himself. This does not absolve the playwright of his duty to observe and probe as clearly and deeply as he* legitimately *can: but it should steer him away from "pat" conclusions, facile definitions which make a play just a play, not a snare for the truth of human experience.* (945).

To Kazan, who was to direct the play, he was more frank. At the end of November 1954, he wrote to answer Kazan's question about Brick's drinking: "Why does a man drink: in quotes, 'drink.' There's two reasons, separate or together. 1. He's scared shitless of something. 2. He can't face the truth about something" (L2: 555). Showing the evidence of some Freudian reading, he said he had come to the conclusion that "Brick <u>did</u> love Skipper, 'the one great good thing in his life which was true.' He identified Skipper with sports, the romantic world of adolescence which he couldn't go past. Further: to reverse my original (somewhat tentative) premise, I now believe that, in the deeper sense, not the literal sense, Brick <u>is</u> a homosexual with a heterosexual adjustment" (L2: 555–6). He identified Marlon Brando as a mutual acquaintance who he thought was similar to Brick, noting that such people were usually undersexed and sought attachments to things like pets or sports in preference to sexual relationships: "They have deep attachments, idealistic, romantic: sublimated loves! They are terrible Puritans." If the mask was "ripped off, suddenly, roughly," he wrote, "that's quite enough to blast the whole Mechanism, the whole adjustment, knock the world out from under their feet, and leave them no alternative but–owning up to the truth or retreat into something like liquor" (L2: 556).

Included in Williams's letter was the first version of the dialogue in Act 2 when Big Daddy gets Brick to tell about Skipper's confessional phone call, on which Brick hung up, and responds that "we have tracked down the lie with which you're disgusted and which you are drinking to kill your disgust with, Brick. You been passing the buck. This disgust with mendacity is disgust with yourself. *You!*–dug the grave of your friend and kicked him in it!–before you'd face truth with him" (951). In the play, however, Williams has Brick say that this is "*His* truth, not *mine!*" (951), and Big Daddy agrees, leaving the door open to the interpretation of Brick's character on the part of actors, directors, audiences, or critics that he is not gay. The important thing is that Brick, like Blanche DuBois with her husband Allan, has committed an act of cruelty that resulted in the death of a gay man, and that he has retreated into a life of mendacity, whether it be the life of the closet in which he denies his own feelings as well as Skipper's or simply the denial of responsibility for his friend's death.

The issue of mendacity is also central to the second agon that Williams developed in the play through the introduction of Big Daddy, the battle with death. In creating Big Daddy, and the Pollitt family, Williams had reached back to his experience in 1935, when, while staying with his grandparents in Memphis, he had visited the Perry family, owners of a large plantation in Tunica County, Mississippi. He wrote to his mother that it was his "opportunity to study the life on a Mississippi plantation" (L1: 79). Tipped into an early draft of the *Cat* script is a newspaper article explaining that G. D. Perry was originally manager of a plantation that he was now buying from two men who lived in Memphis, making his total land holdings 14,800 acres. The article notes that Perry and his wife have "nine fine children" and is accompanied by a picture of the family, who are very large people with short necks (Murphy 1992, 97–8). It is clear that Williams made good use of his research in creating the Pollitt family, their plantation of 28,000 acres, Big Daddy, Jack Straw and Peter Ochello, and the no-neck monsters. Big Daddy's character is also informed by Williams's own fear of death, which he often dated to his abdominal surgery in 1946. In July of 1955, he wrote to Kenneth Tynan about the "shadow of death" that had hung over him since then: "My recent history dates from that occasion . . . and I think it has an interesting bearing on all my work since then, romantic pessimism, preoccupation with mortality, Etc. Of course it only became explicit, something I finally dared to deal with directly, in 'Big Daddy' in 'Cat'" (N: 574).

Williams wrote to Kazan that Big Daddy "strikes the keynote of the play. A terrible black anger and ferocity, a rock-bottom honesty. Only against this background can his moments of tenderness, of longing, move us deeply. This is a play about good bastards and good bitches. I mean it exposes the startling co-existence of good and evil, the shocking <u>duality</u> of the single heart" (L2: 551–2). Big Daddy's battle in the play is against death, or rather, the knowledge of his impending death, which the family and the medical establishment are attempting to keep from him by lying about it. Together he and Brick represent the struggle against mendacity that is the play's central theme. This is something that Williams emphasized constantly during the play's writing and production. While trying to get Kazan to accept the job of directing, he wrote that the play "does that thing which is the pure aim of art, the highest pure aim of art, which is to catch and illuminate truly and passionately the true, true quality of human existence" (L2: 549). As they came to the end of the rehearsal period, he praised Kazan for doing one of his "greatest jobs" on the production, adding that "this play is maybe not a great play, maybe not even a very good play, but a terribly, terribly, terribly true play about truth, human truth" (L2: 567). The core of the play is the painful emergence from what Brick calls the system of mendacity into a recognition of truth by both Brick and Big Daddy through each other's agency.

While Big Daddy forces Brick to face the truth about his relationship with Skipper mostly out of a desire to help his son, Brick's immediate motive for telling Big Daddy the truth about his cancer is revenge. Before he tells him, "*he has already decided, without knowing that he has made this decision, that he is going to tell his father that he is dying of cancer. Only this could even the score between them: one inadmissible thing for another*" (949). While he is apologetic once the deed is done, he insists that "we've been friends . . . —And being friends is telling each other the truth" (953). Linking them together, he says, "mendacity is a system that we live in. Liquor is one way out an' death's the other" (953). This facing of the stark truth changes Big Daddy's view of the system of mendacity itself. At first, he had tried to get Brick to see that mendacity is a necessary part of life: "*I've* lived with mendacity!–Why can't *you* live with it? Hell, you *got* to live with it, there's nothing *else* to *live* with except mendacity, is there?" (942). It is when Brick tells him that the alternative is drinking that Big Daddy becomes determined to get to the truth of his relationship with Skipper. When Big Daddy is faced with the truth of his own imminent mortality, he completely rejects the system that has conspired to keep it from him: "CHRIST– DAMN!–ALL–LYING SONS OF–LYING BITCHES! . . . . Lying! Dying! Liars!" (954). These lines, which close Act 2, were meant to be Big Daddy's final words in the play, until Kazan persuaded Williams to bring Big Daddy back in the third act. They express the play's theme as emphatically as it could be expressed.

The issue of the changes in Act 3 has been discussed a great deal since Williams published the play with two versions of the third Act, one from a version of the script that preceded the production process and one from the prompt-book of the Broadway production, which he called the "Broadway Version." He also published a "Note of Explanation" in which, while praising Kazan's work with him on the play, he pointed out the danger of the influence "of a powerful and highly imaginative director upon a play" (977). He explained that Kazan had asked him to make major changes in Act 3, which included bringing Big Daddy back into the scene, making Maggie a more sympathetic character, and indicating that Brick's character has undergone some change as a result of his facing the truth with Big Daddy. He wrote that he agreed with the suggestion about Maggie wholeheartedly, but not with the others, and particularly that he felt "the moral paralysis of Brick was a root thing in his tragedy, and to show a dramatic progression would obscure the meaning of that tragedy in him" (978). He had rewritten the Act, he said, because he had wanted Kazan to direct, but that he was including the earlier version so that "the reader can, if he wishes, make up his own mind about it" (978).

In the earlier version, Act 3 consists of the family meeting, in which Brick's brother Gooper, his wife Mae, and Maggie close in like vultures on Big Mama, hoping to get control of the estate once Big Daddy is dead, while Brick remains detached in an alcoholic haze. This completes the tight three-Act structure that Williams was proud of achieving in the play from the beginning. As he told Audrey Wood, the Acts told the story completely: "First, Brick and his wife. Second, Brick and Big Daddy. Third, The family conference. . . . I thought at least structurally the play was just right, I liked there being no time lapse between the acts, one flowing directly into the others, and it all taking place in the exact time that it occupies in the theatre" (L2: 543). In this version, Maggie makes her announcement that she is pregnant when Big Mama says that Big Daddy's fondest dream would be to pass on the estate to a grandson who was as much like Brick as Brick is like Big Daddy. This is met with skepticism by Mae and Gooper and interrupted by Big Daddy's cries of pain and rage, and the other characters' activity around getting him his morphine shot. The play ends with Maggie putting Brick's pillow on the bed, locking up his liquor and throwing his crutch off the balcony, and saying "Brick, I used to think that you were stronger than me and I didn't want to be overpowered by you. But now, since you've taken to liquor—you know what?—I guess it's bad, but now I'm stronger than you and I can love you more truly!" (974–5). She says that tonight they are going to make the lie about the pregnancy true because what is needed with "weak, beautiful people" like Brick is someone to "take hold of you.—Gently, gently, with love!" (976), and Brick, echoing Big Daddy's earlier line when Big Mama says she loves him (as well as Hemingway's *The Sun Also Rises*), says "Wouldn't it be funny if that was true!" (976).

In the "Broadway Version," Big Daddy returns after the revelation to Big Mama of his illness and while Gooper is trying to convince her to accept his plan for the estate. Big Daddy tells the controversial "elephant story," a joke that refers to male sexual potency and was later censored out of the production and replaced by some lines about the odor of mendacity in the room. More importantly, it is Big Daddy to whom Maggie makes her claim to be pregnant, an "announcement of life beginning" (1001), as a birthday gift, and he responds, "*Uh-huh, this girl has life in her body, that's no lie!*" 1002). In doing so, he endorses the power of vitality in Maggie herself rather than the truth of her pregnancy claim, and Brick supports her, saying "truth is something desperate, an' she's got it" (1004). After Gooper and Mae leave, calling them liars, Maggie takes the pillow from Brick as he *"watches her with growing admiration*" (1005) and puts it on the bed, then takes all the bottles from the bar and throws them off the balcony, telling Brick, "I told a lie to Big Daddy, but we can make that lie come true" (1005). Brick expresses his admiration, and Maggie says that weak, beautiful people like Brick need "someone to take hold of you–gently, with love, and hand your life back to you, like something gold you let go of–and I can! I'm determined to do it–and nothing's more determined than a cat on a tin roof–is there? Is there, baby?" (1005). In this version, Brick does not respond.

Because the Broadway production was a big commercial hit, running for 694 performances, Williams has been accused of selling out to Kazan's desire to make the play more commercial in making the changes, something that both vehemently denied. In fact, Kazan and Williams were simply following their usual method of working together, in which Williams gave the director an early version of the script and Kazan made suggestions for changes. This time, Williams was doubtful about the changes. On the one hand, he wrote to Kazan at the beginning of November 1954, "I am as happy as you are that our discussions have led to a way of high-lighting the good in Maggie, the indestructible spirit of Big Daddy, so that the final effect of the play is not negative, this is a forward step, a step toward a <u>larger</u> truth which will add immeasurably to the play's power of communication or scope of communication" (L2: 552). On the other, he complained to Audrey Wood at the end of the month that the new ending had an echo of *Tea and Sympathy*, Robert Anderson's play about a woman who sets out to "cure" a young student of his homosexual desires, which Kazan had just directed on Broadway: "Here is another case of a woman giving a man back his manhood, while in the original conception it was about a vital, strong woman dominating a weak man and achieving her will" (L2: 554).

Something else happened during the play's development process that made Williams particularly sensitive to the charges of rewriting his plays to make them more commercial. The influential critic Eric Bentley published an essay in his volume *The Dramatic Event* which suggested that the influence of Kazan's aesthetic vision during the production of *A Streetcar Named Desire* had been so great that he was virtually the play's co-author. Kazan immediately protested, saying that Tennessee Williams had written every word of his play, and Williams wrote a letter intended for the *New York Times* in which he said that Bentley had told "an out-and-out lie," insisting "there isn't a line in 'Streetcar' that I didn't write . . . the interpretation of the play couldn't have been more exactly what the author had in mind when he wrote it" (L2: 560). Nevertheless, the suggestion had done its work, undermining Williams's trust in his director and making him hyper-aware of any perception of interference with his aesthetic vision. To make matters worse, Bentley's review of *Cat* reiterated his charge and emphasized Kazan's influence in the last Act where he wrote, "the script is resolutely non-committal, the production strains for commitment to some sort for edifying conclusion," and worst of all, he called it "the outward form of that *Tea and Sympathy* scene without its content" (4 April 1955: 22).

Immediately after the production, Williams wrote candidly to the sympathetic *New York Times* critic Brooks Atkinson that he planned to publish both versions of the Third Act, and "confidentially, I do mean confidentially, I still much prefer the original. It was harder and purer: a blacker play but one that cut closer to the bone of the truth I believe. I doubt that it would have had the chance of success that the present version has and since I had so desperate a need of success, and reassurance about my work, I think all in all Kazan was quite right in persuading me to shape Act III about the return of Big Daddy" (L2: 569). As time went on, he came to see the help that Kazan had given him more and more as Bentley did, as interference with his artistic vision. In 1972, he said in an interview, "I didn't resent his making me change it so much, but it was like a deep psychic violation, I was very disturbed after that experience with *Cat*. In fact, I couldn't write for several months after that" (C: 217). The experience also altered the relationship between Williams and Kazan, who was to direct just one more of his plays, *Sweet Bird of Youth*, before they parted company as artistic collaborators, although they remained friends throughout Williams's lifetime.

In his autobiography, Kazan has indicated that Williams's sense of violation had some validity, for he was determined to execute his aesthetic vision, which differed from Williams's in this production. The original conception of the play was a tightly constructed family tragedy, complete with the classical dramatic unities of time, place, and action. The set Williams described in his "Notes for the Designer" was very much in the style that Mielziner had been developing in collaboration with him and Kazan for a decade, a Victorian house, "with a touch of the Far East," bearing the influence of Jack Straw and Peter Ochello, the "pair of old bachelors who shared this room all their lives together" (880). It was to combine functional realism with abstraction, with the two dominant items on the set a huge bed, the site of the agon between Maggie and Brick, and a "monumental monstrosity" of an entertainment center and bar, the "very complete and compact little shrine to virtually all the comforts and illusions behind which we hide from such things as the characters in the play are faced with" (881). He also indicated that the set should be "far less realistic than I have so far implied" (881) and that the set should be roofed by the sky, with an abstract suggestion of the stars and moon and the walls "should dissolve mysteriously into air" (881), a signature Mielziner effect.

In conceiving of the design for the play, Kazan and Mielziner agreed that it should be even more abstract than Williams suggested. Kazan wrote that he and the designer "had read the play in the same way; we saw its great merit was its brilliant rhetoric and its theatricality. Jo didn't see the play as realistic any more than I did" (1988: 542). Taking the design in a more abstract direction, Mielziner described the set as "a stage within the stage. It would be steeply raked toward the audience with one corner actually jutting out over the footlights. In its final form it turned out to be a sort of thrust stage" (1965: 183). The set consisted of two rectangular platforms, a larger and a smaller one, with corners at the front of the stage to make a diamond shape facing the audience. The ceiling was a similar diamond shape looming over the room with the corner at upstage center. A scrim representing the rear wall of the bedroom could have the images of closed blinds projected on it, or, lighted from behind, could show the activity on the lawn outside the room. The furniture was minimal, including the bed, the entertainment center, a daybed, and another chair and bench. Otherwise the set was bare. As Kazan wrote, "on that setting there was only one way for any human to conduct himself: 'out front' it's called. Dear Tennessee was stuck with my vision, like it or not" (1988: 543).

Williams did not like it. Although he had approved the design when he saw the drawings, he was not prepared for the dramatically abstract construction that he saw. He wrote in his journal that when he arrived in Philadelphia for the first previews of the play, he found the set "a meaningless piece of chi chi–no atmosphere, no relation to the play" (N: 667). To Kazan he wrote, "you know, of course that the first view of the setting gave me a horrible, almost death-dealing, blow this afternoon. . . . I have never had a play that had to get by without visual atmosphere which fitted it, and I am terrified that this may be the first and last time! I have no one to blame but myself as I saw the sketches, but somehow I had always thought, well, Jo is a genius, and Gadg [Kazan] is a genius, and they know what they are doing" (L2: 567). There is a good proportion of pre-production jitters in Williams's worries about the set, but it was also the concrete representation of Kazan's aesthetic vision of the play, which he simply did not share.

To make matters worse, Eric Bentley confronted Williams with the issue of mendacity in his own treatment of homosexuality in the play. "*Cat on a Hot Tin Roof* was heralded by some as the play in which homosexuality was at last to be presented without evasion," he wrote. "But the miracle has still not happened" (11 April 1955: 28). In the spirit of the 1950s' pathologizing of homosexuality, and with *Tea and Sympathy* clearly in the background, he said "one does not of course demand that he 'cure' the boy, only that he present him: he should tell the audience, even if he does not tell the boy himself, whether a 'cure' is possible, and, if not, whether homosexuality is something this individual can accept as the truth about himself. At present, one can only agree with the father that the story is fatally incomplete" (28). Besides winning the Pulitzer Prize for best play, *Cat on a Hot Tin Roof* was nominated for Tony Awards for best direction and best scene design and was an enormous commercial and critical success. Many consider it Williams's best play. The questions of which is the better Third Act and of Williams's treatment of homosexuality remain hotly contested critical issues. Perhaps with the goading of Bentley's and Walter Kerr's criticism of his evasion, the subject of homosexuality was to preoccupy Williams for the next few years, resulting in some of his best work.

# CHAPTER 8
## SUDDENLY LAST SUMMER AND SWEET BIRD OF YOUTH (1953–1959)

### "This hideous story": Suddenly Last Summer

If *Cat on a Hot Tin Roof* is a play about truth, *Suddenly Last Summer* takes it to a new level. One of the most frank representations of erotic desire among Tennessee Williams's plays, it has its roots in his experience as far back as the late 1930s, but only came together after he had written *Camino Real*, particularly after his trip to Barcelona in July 1953. Some of its major motifs date back to the early 1940s, when he expressed himself much more openly about sexuality in fiction than in drama. The short story "Desire and the Black Masseur," finished in 1946 and published semiprivately by James Laughlin in the collection *One Arm* (1948), dealt so openly with cannibalism, atonement, and sadomasochism that Williams stipulated that the book must not be displayed for sale in any bookstores, and a special request was tipped into early copies asking that the collection be sold "by personal solicitation and subscription rather than by general display. We are particularly anxious that the book should not be displayed in windows or on open tables" (L2: 212).

By the summer of 1957, when he was undergoing psychoanalysis daily with Dr Lawrence Kubie, Williams was in a position psychologically to revisit these themes in dramatic terms. He told an interviewer, "I think if this analysis works, it will open some doors for me," adding "I don't think I'll ever be a bland, comfortable sort of writer. . . . I think I'll always be a protestant, an outraged romantic, or a Puritan, shocked by things that are reflected in my own character. I don't think I'm more virtuous than the people in my plays that shock me. I'm just as bad or worse" (C: 50–1). The immediate experience on which he was drawing for the play was his 1953 trip to Barcelona, when he spent time at the beach club San Sebastiano and in the company of Franz Neuner, who served as entree to "the interesting society here" (N: 573). On his first afternoon there, he reported in his journal on "an affair in my Cabana with someone procured by Franz. Had a Paella on the beach, a good swim in a salt water pool" (N: 573). Later during the trip, he resorted to one of the numerous "beach whores" (N: 577) and spent time with a friend of Paul Bowles's, with whom he frequented not only the beach but also the "bordellos of Barachina" (N: 579), smoking kif while walking along the streets. Returning there in 1954, he brought his friend Maria Britneva with him and was still using the services of Franz Neuner and availing himself of the "Eros" of the beach (N: 649). At the end of the trip, however, he wrote that "sex has been a bit disappointing here, especially at San Sebastiano. My appeal, even to the hustlers, seems to have suffered a decline this summer. . . . Middle age" (N: 651).

In *Suddenly Last Summer*, Sebastian Venable, whose sole occupation was traveling and writing a single poem in the summer of every year, was using his mother Violet to "make contacts for him" in the "smart, fashionable places" (P2: 140) they visited. After she suffered a stroke, he brought his cousin Catherine with him to Cabeza de Lobo instead, but he made her attract attention in a much grosser way, by wearing a bathing suit that she says was indecent, because "I was PROCURING for him" (140). Williams did not descend this far, but he did feel that he was making use of Maria Britneva in a similar way. On the one hand, he found her "a charming companion, like one of those dear little girl friends of my childhood or Rose" (N: 587). On the other, he only wanted her around when he needed her. During the first Barcelona trip, he wrote, "Can't make up my mind to send for Maria. She's really so expensive and there's quite enough society here now. But I feel guilty because I said I would ask her to join me. . . . Well, I'm too selfish to be aware of much but myself and my own little quotidinal variations of mood or circumstance" (N: 575).

Sebastian descends to making use of the "bands of homeless young people that lived on the free beach like scavenger dogs" (141), as Williams had descended to the "beach whores." In Barcelona, Williams observed a band of "black-plucked-sparrow children shrilling about for bread and making percussive serenades with flattened out tin cans" (L2: 492). In the play, these became both the victims and the agents of retribution against Sebastian, "a band of frightfully thin and dark naked children that looked like a flock of plucked birds" who made "gobbling noises with their little black mouths" (142). According to Catherine's narrative, they pursued Sebastian and devoured him, a fitting end for one who spoke of people as "items on a menu": "fed up with dark ones, famished for light ones: that's how he talked about people" (118). Williams had used exactly these terms in 1948, writing to Donald Windham that he was planning to go to Florence, because he was "getting an appetite for blonds as the Roman gentry are all sort of dusky types" (Williams 1980: 215).

As Catherine describes the scene, Sebastian, who had been taking little white pills for his heart throughout the afternoon, was pursued by the band of children and started up the "steep street with a hand stuck in his jacket where I knew he was having a pain in his chest from his palpitations. . . . But he walked faster and faster, in panic, but the faster he walked the louder and closer it got!" (146). In a nightmare situation, he finally started to run, and they all "screamed at once and seemed to fly in the air, they outran him so quickly . . . he screamed just once before this flock of black plucked little birds that pursued him . . . overtook him halfway up the white hill" (146–7). When Catherine and the people she called to help found his body, they saw that the children "had *devoured* parts of him" and his body looked like "a big white-paper-wrapped bunch of red roses that had been *torn, thrown, crushed!*–against that blazing white wall" (147). This scene is informed by the terror that Williams was feeling during panic attacks that had become frequent and acute in the early 1950s. In September of 1954, having moved on from Barcelona and Rome to Taormina, Sicily, he wrote in his journal about his experience after he had separated from his companion that night. Finding that the nightclub and bar on the street had closed, he began to walk more quickly:

My chest felt constricted. I breathed hard and fast. I wanted to break into a run but didn't have the breath to. The street was empty. Its length seemed to stretch forever. Every step built up my panic and I seemed to be going further rather than closer to my hotel. Twice or three times I had to stop for breath. . . . Even after I reached the main square, in sight of Hotel Temio, my sanctuary, the panic persisted. In fact reached its climax when I was half way up the gradient, about 50 yds. in length, to hotel gates. . . . Now in my room, the seconal is taking effect (my second today) and I have my liquor and I am quite calm and comfortable. But someday, I fear, one of these panics will kill me. And not at all kindly or agreeably, to say the least. Was anyone ever so scared of death as I am? So craven? I do wonder. (I had my first affair in Taormina, today on a little island near beach. That was when I took my first seconal.) (N: 655)

The terror that Williams was feeling also reflected his chronic worry about his sanity, his fear that he would suffer the same fate as his sister Rose. In *Suddenly Last Summer*, this is conflated in the figure of Catherine who is based on Rose as well as on Maria Britneva. According to his biographer Donald Spoto, in the summer of 1957, during his analysis and while he was writing the play, Williams had visited Rose, whom he had placed in Stony Lodge, a private mental health facility in Ossining, New York, "with a frequency that astonished even the administrators" (1986: 243). Rose, her lobotomy, and the mental facilities where she had lived since she was confined to the Missouri state mental hospital in 1937 are central to Catherine's character, her story about Sebastian, and Violet Venable's determination to "*cut this hideous story out of her brain!*" (147).

In December of 1939, when he was visiting St Louis at Christmas, Williams reported in his journal that he was driving to Farmington to see Rose the next day, writing "I'm getting broken in gradually to the place" (N: 177). He clearly was not prepared for what he would meet the next day, however, when the visit with Rose was "horrible, horrible! Her talk was so obscene—she laughed and spoke continual obscenities–Mother insisted I go in, though I dreaded it and wanted to stay outside. We talked to the Doctor afterwards–a cold, unsympathetic young man–he said her condition was hopeless that we could only expect a progressive deterioration" (N: 177). He called it "a horrible ordeal. Especially since I fear that end for myself," adding "everything seems ugly and useless now—hideously smirched—After all her naked subconscious is no uglier than the concealed thoughts of others—And is sex ugly? Not essentially—not from a cosmic viewpoint. But when it is divorced from reason—it looks like slime" (N: 177). Williams had had a great deal more experience with sex by the time he wrote the play.

Rose's lobotomy had ended the kind of "obscene" talk he alluded to, but as Dr Cukrowicz warns Violet, there is a possibility that "the person will always be limited afterwards, relieved of acute disturbances but—*limited*" (113). This describes Rose's condition, for although she could be described as "peaceful" (113), the word Violet uses to describe the potential results of the lobotomy, she was never again able to live independently. Violet's determination to "*cut this hideous story out of her brain*" (147) is a reflection of Edwina Williams's desire to curtail Rose's obscenities, a desire that her son may secretly have shared at some level. There was a suggestion in Rose's ramblings that her father had molested her, something that has not been substantiated, but that forms the parallel of the "hideous story" that Violet wants to stop. In June, 1953, concerned that his mother was about to move Rose from the small farm where she was being cared for, Williams wrote her that "I am convinced, from all evidence, that these state institutions are perfect nightmares—'Snake pits'" (L2: 482) and that she must be moved elsewhere. He eventually had her moved to Stony Lodge where he could visit when he was in New York.

The nexus of sadomasochism, cannibalism, and religious atonement, major motifs in *Suddenly Last Summer*, developed from their use in "Desire and the Black Masseur." The short story's protagonist, Anthony Burns, has an instinct "for being included in things that swallowed him up" (CS: 205). He feels most secure at the movies "where the darkness absorbed him gently so that he was like a particle of food dissolving in a big hot mouth" (205). His discovery of his particular erotic desire comes when he gets a forceful massage and responds sexually to the pain. This begins a symbiotic sadomasochistic relationship between him and the masseur which escalates until Burns lies in the masseur's room, a mass of splintered bones. Williams links the "pleasure in pain" that Anthony experiences with the religious impulse toward atonement for sins, describing the scene in the church across the street where the congregation was "involved in a massive atonement": "Suffer, suffer, suffer! The preacher shouted. Our Lord was nailed on a cross for the sins of the world! . . . He was The Rose of the World as He bled on the cross!" (210). In response, the congregation runs out into the street "in a crazed procession with clothes torn open. The sins of the world are all forgiven! they shouted" (211). In a veiled allusion to the Christian sacrament of the Eucharist, Williams has Burns whisper to the masseur, "you know what you have to do now?" and the masseur begins "to devour the body of Burns" (211). When he is finished, he places the "bare white bones, left over from Burns' atonement" in a sack and drops it into a lake, and then goes to a new city, "serenely conscious of fate bringing toward him another, to suffer atonement as it had been suffered by Burns" (211–12).

The theme of guilt and atonement preoccupied Williams in the late 1950s, coming to its full development in *The Night of the Iguana* (1961). In *Suddenly Last Summer*, which Williams insisted was not realistic, but "a moral fable of our times" (C: 52), he said in a 1974 interview that the metaphor of cannibalism is meant to suggest that man "feeds upon his fellow creatures, without the excuse of animals. Animals actually do it for survival, out of hunger. Man, however, is doing it out of, I think, a religious capacity. I use that metaphor to express my repulsion with this characteristic of man, the way people use each other without conscience" (C: 274). This metaphor is central to Catherine's narrative about Sebastian, one of the competing "truths" about him that is presented in the play, the other being Violet's narrative of him as a chaste ascetic and visionary artist.

Catherine, who is injected with a drug that she insists "makes you tell the truth because it shuts something off that might make you able not to" (121), presents Sebastian as a selfish egotist and sexual predator, the story of his making use of the boys on the beach, eventually refusing to give them the bread they beg, and then being pursued and devoured by them as by a flock of birds, "a true story of our time and the world we live in" (122–3). To Violet, however,

Sebastian is defined by his art: "Sebastian was a poet! That's what I meant when I said his life was his work because the work of a poet is the life of a poet and–vice versa, the life of a poet is the work of a poet" (102). She believes that he led a celibate, chaste life because she was "the only one in his life that satisfied the demands he made of people" (110) for good looks and youthfulness, a claim that is undermined by Catherine's insistence that he used Violet to "procure" for him by making connections with the "interesting people" in the fashionable places where they traveled. By Violet's own account, Sebastian tried and failed to live as an ascetic when he spent a few weeks in a monastery, but soon left and booked the two of them into luxury hotels in Cairo and Paris. Nevertheless, suggesting an allusion to St Sebastian, famously shot with arrows and then clubbed to death for his efforts to convert other soldiers to Christianity, she insists that he is a "benefactor," which is "the role of a victim, Doctor, a sacrificial victim, yes, they want your blood, Doctor, they want your blood on the altar of their *outraged, outrageous* egos!" (112).

The religious element is introduced directly into the play with Sebastian's search for God. His Darwinian vision of the world is presented vividly in the garden he has created, "*more like a tropical jungle, or forest, in the prehistoric age of giant fern-forests when living creatures had flippers turning to limbs and scales to skin. The colors of this jungle-garden are violent . . . there are massive tree-flowers that suggest organs of a body, torn out, still glistening with undried blood; there are harsh cries and sibilant hissings and thrashing sounds in the garden as if it were inhabited by beasts, serpents and birds, all of savage nature*" (101). Dr Cukrowicz describes it as "a well-groomed jungle" (102). In his search for God, Sebastian seeks out the cruel Darwinian struggle on the Galapagos Islands, as the newly hatched sea turtles make their "desperate flight to the sea," trying to escape "the flesh-eating birds that made the sky almost as black as the beach" (105). Watching the grim spectacle of the baby turtles being flipped over and torn apart by the birds, Sebastian guesses that "only a hundredth of one per cent of their number would escape to the sea" (106). He decides that in this spectacle of nature he has seen the face of God. As Violet explains, "he meant that God shows a savage face to people and shouts some fierce things at them, it's all we see or hear of Him." (107). In a 1975 interview, Williams explained that "these people were total sybarites, creatures with no social conscience whatsoever, and consequently they're godless. They would conceive of God as being the predatory birds killing the newly hatched turtles. They would think that was the face of God" (C: 287). On the contrary, he said, "God exists in our understanding of each other, and in our acts based upon our understanding. This is what the Doctor does at the end, when he accepts the girl's story" (C: 287). This certainly suggests that the audience too should accept Catherine's story and thus her version of Sebastian's "truth."

It is clear that Sebastian is the person Catherine describes, a selfish, egotistical man who callously uses others in pursuit of his own pleasure. As Williams said in 1971, "he is completely enslaved by his baser nature and this is what destroys him. His death is a ritualistic death, symbolic" (C: 210). He is obviously not the chaste, saintly benefactor whom Violet describes. But there is an element of truth in her account. He does seem to have been a poet whose art was his life and whose life was his art. As Williams said, "when he fails, when he is unable to write his poem that summer, then he is completely lost" (C: 210). This theme, the most important of all to Williams, would be developed more fully in *Sweet Bird of Youth*, which Williams had begun in 1956, and would continue to revise until its production in 1959.

With the recent failure of *Orpheus Descending*, which critics and audiences found too violent for their taste, Williams and Audrey Wood decided that *Suddenly Last Summer* should be tried Off-Broadway rather than risk a full-blown Broadway production. In a pre-production interview, he said that "the total effect, I feel, is not distasteful; but it does involve material that will arouse some controversy" (Gelb 1957). Suggesting the way critics should approach it, he said that it involved "a shockingly violent occurrence" with a "symbolic" significance (Gelb 1957). The play premiered on 7 January 1958 in a bill called *Garden District*, along with *Something Unspoken*, a short one-act play about a covert emotional power struggle in which a domineering wealthy club woman confesses her love to her mousy secretary.

Most of the critics missed the point of *Something Unspoken* and dismissed it, but acknowledged, as one Chicago critic wrote, that

"Suddenly Last Summer is the experience you'll carry with you, perhaps dazedly, possibly even in a state of shock" (Dettmer 1959: 28). Another said that it was "a dazzling display of Williams' power to spellbind an audience even with a static play" (Harris 1959: 38). George Oppenheimer wrote that Williams had accomplished the impossible "in making palatable a gross and abhorrent story" (1958: 7C). The play was not without its detractors, however. In London, Kenneth Tynan complained that we do not see Sebastian "with Mr. Williams's eyes, in which all aesthetes are sacred. It is one thing to sympathize with a man who has been garrotted by the old umbilical cord. It is quite another when we are asked to see in his death (as Mr. Williams clearly wants us to) a modern re-enactment of the martyrdom of St. Sebastian" (1958). Clement Crisp rejected the play's claims to tragedy, writing that "Mr. Williams has evoked a torrid atmosphere steaming with suffering, greed and jealously, but has not succeeded in purging us with the pity and terror that he has inspired . . . his horrifying tale can point no moral, illuminate no dark corners in our conscience" (1958: 2).

## "The enemy, time": *Sweet Bird of Youth*

At the same time that he was writing *Suddenly Last Summer*, Williams was working on *Sweet Bird of Youth*, another play with the collapse of art, youth, and morality at its core. It had begun in two separate story lines, one about a young gigolo who uses his older patron, originally a middle-aged man, to help him go back to his home town and win back the girlfriend of his youth and the other about a corrupt political boss and his mistress. In keeping with the closet aesthetic of the mid-1950s, as Williams revised the play, the middle-aged gay man evolved into a woman, Alexandra del Lago, the Princess Kosmonopolis. He tried to put the focus on the young man, Chance Wayne, and his girlfriend Heavenly, the daughter of Boss Finley, but the Princess so captured his imagination that the play ended up with two strong Acts, Acts 1 and 3, which focus on the Princess and Chance, and a weak Act 2, which focuses on Boss Finley's determination to have

Chance castrated for having giving Heavenly the venereal disease that resulted in her hysterectomy. Unaware of Heavenly's operation, Chance brings the Princess back to Gulfport, Mississippi in the hope of winning Heavenly back with a show of his newfound prosperity by driving around town in the Princess's Cadillac and conspicuously showing everyone the Studio contract she has given him. This ends in disaster when a heckler at the Boss's political rally shouts out the truth about the operation and preparations are made for the thugs in his service to kidnap Chance from the hotel and take him aboard the Boss's boat to meet his fate.

Amidst the melodramatic events of the plot, the play's main interest is in the relationship between the Princess and Chance. In these characters, Williams has split the figure of the artist and "degenerate" that is Sebastian in two. Both Chance and the Princess have a desperate ambition to succeed at the art of acting, but there is a big difference in motivation and talent. Chance is chiefly motivated by the desire to win Heavenly back and to impress the people of the town, who think him a failure, that he has made good. Williams makes it clear that Chance has little talent, having placed fourth in a high school drama contest. Chance has determined never to come in second in any contest, "especially not now that Heavenly was my–" (P2: 206). Now 29 years old, he has gone through the typical career of a good-looking young man with a little talent, singing in choruses and getting occasional nonspeaking film roles, but has chiefly made his way as a gigolo. To get the money he needs from the Princess, he first makes a bungled attempt at blackmail, threatening to reveal her having smuggled hashish into the country, and then, at her direction, has sex with her and is paid for it. When Heavenly's sympathetic Aunt Nonnie admonishes him for living "on nothing but wild dreams now," he responds "isn't life a wild dream? I never heard a better description of it" (204), and washes down a pill with a swig from his flask. The people in his home town refer to him as a "criminal degenerate" (161).

The Princess, who as Alexandra del Lago was a great movie star, sizes Chance up for exactly what he is, and makes a clear if brutal distinction between them. She tells Chance that he has "gone past something you couldn't afford to go past; your time, your youth, you've passed it. It's all you had, and you've had it" (233). Chance agrees with her that "the age of some people can only be calculated by the level of–level of–rot in them. And by that measure I'm ancient" (235). On the other hand, the Princess insists that her greater talent gives her greater latitude in human behavior than he has, essentially a license to behave badly. She may have become a monster after the fading of her career, but she still has the "outcrying heart of an–artist" (232). In her defense, she tells Chance, "we are two monsters, but with this difference between us. Out of the passion and torment of my existence I have created a thing that I can unveil, a sculpture, almost heroic, that I can unveil, which is true" (233). She has, in other words, created art, while he only dreams of success. Finding out that the comeback film that she had thought disastrous has actually led the critics to find more power and more depth in her acting, she prepares to drop Chance and head straight to a rehabilitation clinic, but she does offer to take him to the next town to escape from Boss Finley's henchmen.

Both characters achieve some level of redemption, Chance because he really does believe in the value of love and the Princess because she has the endurance to go on with her art despite the fact that she knows she is "dead, as old Egypt" (235). Chance insists that the difference between him and Boss Finley is that "he was just called down from the hills to preach hate. I was born here to make love" and tells the Boss's son to "tell him about that difference between him and me, and ask him which he thinks has more right to stay here" (219). He refuses to go with the Princess, choosing instead to face his fate. Williams gives Chance the play's last words: "I don't ask for your pity, but just for your understanding–not even that–no. Just for your recognition of me in you, and enemy, time, in us all" (236). It is the Princess, however, who emerges as the play's more vivid character, probably because she expresses things that Williams was experiencing intensely during the mid-1950s, the time of the play's composition, primarily the fading of his artistic powers due to the consumption of alcohol and drugs and the increasing recurrence of panic attacks.

From the early 1950s onward, Williams's dependence on alcohol and drugs increased greatly. Entries in his journal for early 1954 give a sense of their dominance over his life. On 18 January, for example, he wrote, "Woke up feeling light-headed. Couldn't finish my coffee, had to wash a 'pinkie' [Seconal] down with a martini and only wrote 2 pages. The day is fair. I suppose I'll keep drinking and take the sun on the beach. I feel weak and silly" (N: 629). In March, he consulted a physician about the edema he was experiencing in his feet and was told that it was early peripheral neuritis caused by "a toxic condition induced partly by liquor" (631). Like the Princess, who carries an oxygen tank with her to ward off panic attacks, Williams lived in constant anxiety that would often elevate into an attack. In February of 1954, he wrote that "each night there is panic or a threat of it" (N: 629), noting, "Panic twice today, both times assuaged by a seconal and bourbon. But the cardiac neurosis is in full flower again and looms as a fearful spectre. After all, what threatens life, threatens everything that is" (N: 629). In July, he wrote, "I can't recover any nervous stability until I am able to work freely again, and I can't work freely until I recover a nervous stability . . . it is true that I go through these cycles repeatedly, constantly, but now the downward curve is fiercely relentless and the little upturns are very little indeed, relatively insignificant, little circles inside a great descending arc which is still descending" (N: 647). This journal entry ends with a quotation from Rilke: "Someday, emerging at last from this terrifying vision, may I burst into jubilant praise to assenting angels!", a more elaborate expression of Williams's perennial slogan, "En Avant!"

Williams's determination to go on with his writing, no matter what, informs the Princess's determination at the end of *Sweet Bird of Youth*. As he makes it clear in the stage directions, "*to indicate she is going on to further triumph would be to falsify her future. She makes this instinctive admission to herself when she sits down by Chance on the bed, facing the audience. Both are faced with castration, and in her heart she knows it*" (235). She agrees with Chance that the passing of time is relentless, but "we've got to go on" (236). The difference is that, like Sebastian Venable and Brick Pollitt, those other figures who were crowned with a laurel wreath that was "given too early, without enough effort to earn it" (177), Chance gives up the struggle, while the Princess, tenaciously clinging to her art, goes on, a reflection of Williams's own tenacious struggle to battle his demons and continue to write. As the Princess says, "You can't retire with the outcrying heart of an artist still crying out, in your body, in your nerves, in your what? Heart?" (172).

*Sweet Bird of Youth* also reflects Williams's continued concern with the search for God. While Boss Finley claims to have been called by God to come out of the hills to preach racial hatred, he is opposed in the play by the Heckler, whose ambition is to break up Finley's "Voice of God" speech. He says he opposes the Boss because he doesn't believe him. "I believe that the silence of God, the absolute speechlessness of Him is a long, long and awful thing that the whole world is lost because of. I think it's yet to be broken to any man, living or any yet lived on earth,–no exceptions, and least of all Boss Finley" (223). This was the major thread that would be taken up in *Night of the Iguana*.

With *Sweet Bird of Youth*, Williams began the practice of trying out his plays at regional theatres before attempting a Broadway production. It opened on 16 April 1956 at the Studio M Playhouse in Coral Gables, Florida, directed by George Keathley, who was to direct several of his later plays as well. Audrey Wood, Cheryl Crawford, and Elia Kazan came to Florida to see the production and advised Williams on revisions, which he made during the next 2 years, while he was also working on *Suddenly Last Summer*, *Orpheus Descending*, and his "serious comedy" about marriage, *Period of Adjustment*. He finished a draft in the spring of 1958, and a production was organized in the fall, with Crawford producing, Kazan directing, Jo Mielziner designing, and Paul Newman and Geraldine Page playing the roles of Chance and the Princess. The movie rights were sold to MGM before the play was produced in New York, opening on 10 March 1959. As they had with *Cat on a Hot Tin Roof*, Kazan and Mielziner edged the play away from realism and further toward presentational staging than was already suggested in the script. Both Chance and the Princess addressed the audience directly, and the design was similar to that of *Cat*, with three platforms, minimal furniture, a cyclorama used for projections, and a large screen used to project Boss Finley's speech in Act 2, a novel effect in 1959. Through the use of spotlights, the lighting emphasized the play's theatricality and also was used in a cinematic way, to help carry the play's narrative thread (Murphy

1992: 147–9). This was to be the last production that Williams and Kazan would do together, and Kazan's last Broadway play, as he moved on from serving playwrights to concentrate on his film career, and later fiction. Although not as critically or commercially successful as *Streetcar* or *Cat* had been, *Sweet Bird of Youth* ran for 375 performances on Broadway.

# CHAPTER 9
## THE NIGHT OF THE IGUANA
## (1940–1948 AND 1959–1961)

In January of 1961, Williams wrote to producer Cheryl Crawford that *The Night of the Iguana* would be his last play (Spoto 1986: 271). Many of his critics think it should have been his last play. It certainly was his last critical and commercial success, running for 316 performances on Broadway and winning a New York Drama Critics Circle Award and a Tony nomination for Best Play. Williams said several times in interviews that, like *Suddenly Last Summer*, it is "more a dramatic poem than a play" (C: 85) and that, from the point of view of his "own personal satisfaction," it was his most important. He spoke of it as a "summation" of what he had derived from his life experience (C: 100). In a newspaper article just prior to the New York opening, he wrote about the trip to Mexico in the summer of 1940 that had provided the base experience for the play, and explained that during that summer he had "discovered that it was life that I truly longed for, but that all which is most valuable in life is escaping from the narrow cubicle of one's self to a sort of veranda between the sky and the still water beach (allegorically speaking) and to a hammock beside another beleaguered being, someone else who is in exile from the place and time of his heart's fulfillment" (NSE: 128).

Williams was referring to his experience at the Costa Verde hotel, where he arrived in September 1940 after a long bus journey from Mexico City during which he was suffering from chills, fever, and heart palpitations. In his opinion, "it was a desperate period in my life, but it's during such times that we are most alive and they are the times that we remember most vividly, and a writer draws out of vivid and desperate intervals in his life the most necessary impulse or drive toward his work, which is the transmutation of experience into some significant piece of creation, just as an oyster transforms, or covers over, the irritating grain of sand in his shell to a pearl, white or black, of lesser or greater value" (NSE: 125). His first deep love affair, with Kip Kiernan, had just ended, and he had fled Manhattan for Mexico seeking some kind of peace, which he found in a daily routine of writing, swimming, and spending the evenings talking and drinking rum cocoas with Gordon Sager, a young writer from St Louis whom he had met and had a brief affair with in New York the previous summer. He worked on *Stairs to the Roof* and the short story that would become "The Night of the Iguana," but the experience was much more important as it formed the basis for the four main characters of the play he would write 20 years later, the Rev T. Lawrence Shannon, Hannah Jelkes, Jonathan Coffin ("Nonno"), and Maxine Faulk. In the play, their interaction dramatizes the major themes that had developed in Williams's work in the 20 years between the Mexico trip and his writing it: the search for God; the values that should drive relationships between people; the struggle with sexual desire and psychic upheaval; the ultimate prospect of aging and death. He once described the play's theme as "how to live with dignity after despair" (Peck 1961: X5).

Many of those who knew Williams well, from Audrey Wood onward, have noted the autobiographical nature of the major characters and their interconnection (Hannah-Nonno-Shannon). In fact, while it is a compelling realistic drama at one level, at another *The Night of the Iguana* is, like *Camino Real*, a kind of monodrama in which aspects of Williams's psyche or character that were in constant conflict fight it out on stage. The most notable conflict is the debate between Shannon, who is desperately fighting his religious doubt, his "spook" (the specter of mental illness), his alcoholism, and his insistent sexual desire for underage girls, and Hannah, who has battled her "blue devils" (the term Williams used for his own depression), but has mostly moved beyond desperation to embrace endurance and fleeting communication between people as a substitute for God. Maxine and Nonno also express aspects of Williams. Maxine dramatizes with stark simplicity the loneliness and compulsive sexual behavior in a bid to assuage these feelings, feelings that Williams experienced during periods of the 1940s and 1950s, and Nonno, "a minor league poet with a major league spirit" (P2: 379) who is facing death, expresses Williams's own fears about his dimming creative talent and what he perennially believed to be his imminent death.

Besides the expression of aspects of William's own experience, the characters are also based on external figures. "Nonno" was what Frank Merlo called Williams's beloved grandfather, the Rev Walter Dakin, who lived and traveled with Williams and Merlo for long periods of time before his death in 1955. Williams said that he was "such a joy to be with, he was, not the rough sort of man, but gentle and sensitive, like Nonno in *Night of the Iguana*, who he was of course" (C: 153). Shannon is partly based on Williams's companion at the Costa Verde, Gordon Sager, whom he remembered as constantly threatening to take "the long swim to China" (NSE: 128) and nearly killing them both and the man who shared his car with them on the drive back to Texas. At the end of Sager's foolhardy drive through the mountains, Williams "was all through with my death wish and knew that it was life that I longed for, on any terms that were offered" (NSE: 128). Williams said that Maxine was partly based on his bohemian landlady in Santa Monica during his stint at MGM, whom his friend David Greggory described as "a remarkable, well-preserved woman, and very freewheeling. She always had a couple of young male admirers courting her" (Spoto 1986: 106). Hannah Jelkes, the spinster artist who is prone to mental illness, of course owes something to Rose Williams, although it is her hard-won battles with the blue devils and her discovery of the therapeutic power of art that links her more closely to Tennessee, who hoped he would escape his sister's fate through the same stratagems. While each of the characters faces what Hannah calls "*inside* disturbances" (358), which Williams knew intimately, enacting his own inner conflicts on the stage, they are also fully developed and compelling characters in a realistic if stylized series of human interactions.

The first form of "The Night of the Iguana," the short story of that title written during Williams's trip to Mexico, was first published in 1948. He said on several occasions that the story is not connected to the play except by the Mexican background, and, although its protagonist is named Miss Jelkes, she is quite different from the

Hannah of the play. She is essentially a voyeur, eavesdropping on the conversation of the two male characters, an older and a younger writer. The conversations are intense, as the younger writer seems to be trying to decide whether to stay with the older writer or go back to his wife. In its strange ending, the older writer tries to rape Miss Jelkes, who has schemed to get the room next to the one the writers share, and after ejaculating prematurely, he breaks down in sobs. Miss Jelkes goes back to her room, thinking that, as the iguana tied beneath the veranda had been cut loose, "in some equally mysterious way the strangling rope of her loneliness had also been severed by what had happened tonight on this barren rock above the moaning waters" (CS: 245). While she lacks Hannah's identifying qualities of spirituality, carefully controlled calm, and compassion, Miss Jelkes does have some of her characteristics. She is an artist who has had a breakdown, still has bouts of "neurasthenia," and takes barbiturates for her nerves. The iguana functions as it does in the play, as the objective correlative for characters who are "at the end of their rope," but in composing the play, Williams switched the strange sexual encounter to Hannah's past with the stories of the man in the Nantucket movie theatre and the Australian underwear salesman and made her encounter with Shannon a meaningful if momentary release from their loneliness for both of them.

Like *Sweet Bird of Youth*, the play version of *The Night of the Iguana* developed through a process of productions and revisions. It was first produced as a long one-act play at the Spoleto Festival in July 1959. According to Brian Parker, it was at this point that Williams changed the gay characters, since he and his director, Frank Corsaro, agreed that "the time was not yet ripe to put that version's open homosexuality on stage" (Parker 2004: 61). It was also at this time that Williams revised the play to focus on his experiences of traveling with his elderly grandfather. Later revisions included aspects of his 3-month trip to Asia in the fall of 1959, during which he had suffered from his "spook" and had met a drunken Australian tour guide from whom he got "a lot of material" for the play (Parker 2004: 66).

The first production of the full-length play was in August 1960 at the Cocoanut Grove Theatre in Miami, directed by Corsaro and produced by Charles Bowden and Violla Rubber. With many revisions, this was the production that eventually reached Broadway on 28 December 1961, after an 8-week tour of Rochester, Detroit, and Chicago. Williams originally wanted Katharine Hepburn to play Hannah, and they wrote back and forth several times, with her warming to the part as she recognized her affinity for it. She agreed to play the role for 6 months, but negotiations with Bowden broke down, and Margaret Leighton was cast instead. Patrick O'Neal, in his first major role, was cast as Shannon, and Alan Webb as Nonno. All gave excellent, critically acclaimed performances, with Leighton winning the Tony award for Best Actress. The fly in the ointment was Bette Davis, the production's Maxine, who behaved like a movie star rather than an actor, and fought with the Method-trained Frank Corsaro throughout the tryout phase. Williams wrote in his *Memoirs* that Davis announced in Chicago she would not take any more direction from Corsaro and that "he must be returned at once to New York and that goddam Actors' Studio, which had spawned him" (M: 182–3). Williams claimed that he and Bowden took over the direction of the play, although Corsaro's name remained on the program. In April, Shelley Winters replaced Bette Davis.

Williams also had a very difficult time personally during the production. He was not in good shape, having been bitten on the ankles by his dog while they were in Detroit. Corsaro said that "he was rewriting furiously and delivering new script every day, which was hard on the actors, and he had a strange lack of perspective about how the play might gather focus and momentum. His working habits were not helped by his reliance on pills and shots from a quack doctor, and his resulting nervousness didn't help the cast" (Spoto 1986: 274). Margaret Leighton said that, "with the amount of his writing that was rewritten, altered, replaced, taken out, or put in again, you could have made another play" (Parker 2004: 57). She said that he rewrote something every day, with the changes given to the actors around noon: "We used to go to the theatre in the afternoon and work on it, and it went in at that night's performance. And this went on for eight weeks, and he was there every minute of the day. All the time" (Parker 2004: 57).

The staging of *The Night of the Iguana* reflects an aesthetic that is realistic, but ultimately poetic. Williams wrote that "the truth of life is dream-like: and that is the over-all concept and aim of this play. It must be poetically allusive: that is the key-note to the style of performance: and yet the style of performance should not be 'stylized,' in the common sense of the term" (Parker 2004: 83–4). He wrote to Bette Davis that "if there is any one thing for all the cast to remember it is the primary aim of the play: the making of 'poetic reality' in which everything occurs with the ease and the spontaneity of occurrences in life, no matter how long and carefully the play has been planned and written with that objective in mind" (Williams 1990: 177). Unlike the description of the set in *Suddenly Last Summer*, the description of the jungle in this play is a realistic description of the *"rather rustic and very Bohemian hotel, the Costa Verde,"* and its surrounding *"jungle-covered hilltop"* above the *"morning beach"* of Puerto Barrio as it was in 1940, *"among the world's wildest and loveliest populated places"* (328).

The staging departs from realism in the hotel rooms or "cubicles," each of which *"appears as a little interior stage, the curtains giving a misty effect to their dim inside lighting"* (328). Williams wrote that the cubicles "are like numbered cells in a prison, or a poetically softened dream of a prison: they are symbols of each individual's separation from others; but this alleghorical [sic] meaning should be treated romantically, with a visual beauty. The cells are too narrow for comfort: the occupants of them come out on the verandah to look down at the sea which is limited only by the horizon and the sky, but is oblivious of their own living, human conditions" (Parker 2004: 83). At times during the play, the cubicles are lit separately, revealing consciously theatrical images, as when Hannah appears during Act 3, wearing a Kabuki robe and holding *"a gold-lacquered Japanese fan motionless but open in one hand; the other hand touches the netting at the cubicle door as if she were checking an impulse to rush to Shannon's defense. Her attitude has the style of a Kabuki dancer's pose"* (396). Most of the play's symbolic import is contained within its realism, however. Williams said of the cubicles, for example, that they express the play's main import, of "people trying to reach each other" (C: 86). "Each one has his separate cubicle but they meet on the veranda outside the cubicles, at least Hannah and Larry Shannon meet on the veranda outside their cubicles, which is of course an allegorical touch of what people must try to do . . . they must try to find a common ground on which they can meet because the only truly satisfying moments in life are those in which you are in contact, and I don't mean just physical contact, I mean in deep, a deeper contact than physical, with some other human being" (C: 86–7).

Williams makes the symbolism of the iguana explicit in Shannon's lines, "See? The iguana? At the end of its rope? Trying to go on past the end of its goddam rope? Like *you*! Like *me*! Like Grampa with his last poem!" (421). The most obvious symbolism is in the Germans, the Fahrenkopfs ("travel heads") who troop through the scene at various points, singing German marching songs, exulting over radio reports of the Nazi triumph, drinking and behaving callously toward the suffering of the other characters. Shannon describes them as "fiends out of hell with the . . . voices of . . . angels," and Hannah sees them expressing "the logic of contradictions" (408). The critic Annette Saddik identifies them as the antithesis of Hannah's ethereal, saintly, and androgynous quality. These grotesque figures are based on a party of Germans who were at the hotel during Williams's Mexico trip: "ecstatic over the early successes of the Luftwaffe over the R.A.F. When they were not gamboling euphorically on the beach, they were listening to the radio reports on the battle for Britain and their imminent conquest of it, and the entire democratic world" (NSE: 127). What is interesting about the figures in the play is that their grotesqueness lies in the juxtaposition of their coarseness and their beauty. They are *pink and gold like baroque cupids in various sizes— Rubensesque, splendidly physical*" (333–4), but they are spiritually ugly, an objective correlative for the larger contradictions that Shannon must face in his image of God. Williams said in an interview that they "offer a vivid counterpoint—as world conquerors—to the world-conquered protagonists of the play" (Peck 1961: X5). He compared them to Stanley Kowalski, except that "instead of one Blanche DuBois, I have three in 'Iguana.' But with the mutations in the Blanche-architecture that correspond to the length of time that's passed since I

141

conceived of our world and time as a place of mortal combat between the Blanches and the Stanleys" (X5).

While each of the major characters is strongly delineated, they all represent what Williams called "captives: rope-enders" (Parker 2004: 83). The simplest of them, Maxine, is "*a stout, swarthy woman in her middle forties–affable and rapaciously lusty*" (329). She tries to compensate for her fundamental loneliness, which has been deepened by the recent loss of her husband Fred, through casual sex with the beach boys she employs. She admits that this is unsatisfying and is desperate to replace Fred with Shannon. When Shannon appears on the scene, her "*whole concentration shifts abruptly to him. She freezes and blazes with it like an exposed power line*" (359). At the end of the play, she is willing to compromise her dignity to get Shannon, who she knows is only staying with her because he despairs of any other solution. Nevertheless, she accepts the situation, and "*her face wears a faint smile which is suggestive of those cool, impersonal, all-comprehending smiles on the carved heads of Egyptian or Oriental dieties*" [*sic*] (426).

Nonno, the poet who is trying to find a way to accept his coming death, is almost equally straightforward as a "rope-ender." He has insisted that Hannah take him to Mexico in order to be near the ocean, "the cradle of life" (348). In his name, Jonathan Coffin, is not only the implication of death, but also the inheritance of the Williams family, particularly Tennessee's father, Cornelius Coffin Williams, who had died in 1957. Nonno's struggle to write the poem he knows is his last is informed by Williams's struggle to write what he thought might be his last play, each of them trying to articulate an acceptance of the cycle of life and the inevitability of death. The poem Nonno composes, expressing the calmness with which the orange tree faces the natural process of death and decay, was actually composed during Williams's 1940 trip to Mexico, when he was facing his own intimations of mortality, and revised for the play (CP: 259). After Hannah tells him that he has written his loveliest poem, Nonno prays, giving "thanks and praise," and dies, an image of calm acceptance and dignity in death that Williams associated with his own grandfather and aspired to reach through his own artistic creation.

It is Shannon whose spiritual and psychological state most mirrors Williams's as he was writing the play. He first appears *"panting, sweating and wild-eyed."* His *"nervous state is terribly apparent; he is a young man who has cracked up before and is going to crack up again–perhaps repeatedly"* (330). This describes Williams in 1940 and in 1961 as well. In his journal shortly after he arrived at the Costa Verde in September 1940, he wrote, "this is the period after heart-break and it is full of the dullness and tedium of a mind that no longer particularly cares for existence. Yet is desperate to continue, to survive, to fight the way through a mind that fears breaking because of its constant neuroses. But must & will <u>not</u>." He confessed to being lonely and wretched and that "life is merely endurance. Cannot relax. Cannot sit still. But no activity diverts me very much, not even swimming," believing "never, never in all my life will I know the meaning of peace" (N: 215). Shannon tells Maxine that he "can't go on. I got to rest here a while" (331). When Maxine asks if he's "going to pieces," he responds, "No! Gone! Gone!" (332), and he proceeds to demonstrate that he is *"on the verge of hysteria"* (346) and has overdrawn his *"emotional reserve"* (376). Threatened by Maxine with the "Casa de Locos" (400) where he has been before, he realizes that he has to "fight this panic" (400), taking advantage of Hannah's kindness to help him through it.

Although the immediate cause of Shannon's panic is fear of the loss of his job at Blake's Tours – from whence there is nowhere lower to go in the travel business – because he has had sex with a 16-year-old girl on the tour, his panic has a much deeper cause. Like Sebastian Venable, he is engaged in a search for God, and it has led to his rejection of traditional Christianity and his preaching of a sermon against the "senile delinquent" that he believes is its image of God: "He's represented like a bad-tempered childish old, old, sick, peevish man" (369). Although he is an Episcopal priest, Shannon ascribes this image to all of Christianity: "All our theologies do it—accuse God of being a cruel, senile delinquent, blaming the world and brutally punishing all he created for his own faults in construction" (369). After preaching a sermon that reflected this belief, he has been locked out of his church and "put in a nice little private asylum to recuperate from a complete nervous breakdown as they preferred to regard it" (369).

143

He sees the tours he has conducted since then as a means of collecting evidence for his own view of God and hopes to go back to the church and preach "the gospel of God as Lightning and Thunder . . . and also stray dogs vivisected . . . his oblivious majesty" (370). Unlike Sebastian, however, Shannon is, according to Williams, "a man who is very much concerned with what is going on in society . . . this is a person whose great redeeming virtue is that he has a true and deep social conscience" (C: 80). Shannon's "deep awareness of social inequities, the starvation and the misery . . . of the places he's conducted tours through" (C: 81) is vividly reflected in the story he tells of the starving people picking particles of food from a heap of human waste. Nevertheless, he at first desires to return to the Church, and he uses his clerical garb as a symbol of dignity and respectability in which he takes refuge when confronted with his sexual misdeeds.

Shannon's sexual acting-out is in direct conflict with his desire for the kind of respectability that is conferred by the Church, as he has explained to Fred Faulk in rather simplistic Freudian terms that are paraphrased by Maxine, who overheard the conversation. When his mother caught him masturbating as a child, she punished him "because it made God mad as much as it did Mama, and she had to punish you for it so God wouldn't punish you for it harder than she would" (390). Shannon had told Fred that he loved both God and his mother, so he stopped, but "got back at God by preaching atheistical sermons" and "at Mama by starting to lay young girls" (390). This acting out is reflected in his having sex with a young Sunday School teacher, which resulted in his being locked out of his church, and with young Charlotte, which results in his being fired from Blake's tours.

As in *Suddenly Last Summer* and "Desire and the Black Masseur," the issue of atonement is related to Shannon's sexual transgressions, but it is also connected to Williams's presentation of him as a Christ figure. Hannah takes him to task for his histrionic suffering: "Who wouldn't like to suffer and atone for the sins of himself and the world if it could be done in a hammock with ropes instead of nails, on a hill that's so much lovelier than Golgotha, the Place of the Skull"

(402). She insists that there is something voluptuous in his self-inflicted penance and that he is indulging himself in his "Passion Play performance" (403). His internal drama is played out through the objective correlative of the gold cross he wears, a symbol of his priesthood that he has recently redeemed from a pawn shop. Shannon recognizes the justness of her description and pulls at the chain of the cross during his panic, cutting into his neck until Hannah removes it for him. It is significant that he gives the cross to Hannah at the end of the play, having made his decision to stay with Maxine, which enables Hannah either to journey on or to go back home. Learning from Hannah's gentler form of spirituality, in "a little act of grace" (426), he "plays God" at the end of their evening together on the veranda by freeing the iguana, "one of God's creatures at the end of the rope" (426). Thus, he enacts a much more humane image of the deity than the "senile delinquent" he had rebelled against earlier in his life.

Hannah is the least realistic of the characters, which is fitting for someone who is based more on an aspirational ideal for Williams than lived experience. He wrote that "she is close to what the Zen Buddhists call a state of 'satori'–a state of being that combines living sentience with the peace of non-sentient nature, if I understand it rightly" (Parker 2004: 84). In a 1961 interview, he said that he meant her "almost as a definition of what I think is most beautiful spiritually in a person and still believable" (C: 83). In the stage directions, he emphasizes the idealized nature of Hannah by describing her as "*ethereal, almost ghostly. She suggests a Gothic cathedral image of a medieval saint . . . totally feminine and yet androgynous-looking–almost timeless*" (338).

Hannah is squeamish about physical contact and sees sex only as an effort at communication. Like Val Xavier, she is a bohemian artist wanderer, but unlike him, she has passed through her periods with the "blue devil" (409) of depression and despair and reached a state of calm undisturbed by sexual desire and nonjudgmental about the desire of others unless it is "unkind, violent" (418). She finds a home in her grandfather, disputing Shannon's criticism that a bird shouldn't nest in a "falling-down tree" (413) with the insistence that permanence is not the ultimate consideration in building a home, and that when her grandfather dies, she will probably go on with her travels alone. Hannah's version of religion includes compassion, human kindness, the desire of "decent" people to "help each other all that they can" (386) and "broken gates between people so they can reach each other, even if it's just for one night only . . . a little understanding exchanged between them, a wanting to help each other through nights like this" (408–9). Its sacrament is the poppyseed tea she administers to Shannon, herself, and Nonno to help them through the difficult night, bitter but ultimately soothing.

Hannah is not all saint and ministering angel, however. She exhibits a hard-headed practicality and toughness which Williams increasingly found essential to the artist's survival. She "performs" her role as artist, much as Shannon attempts to perform the role of minister, and with no greater success, at least during the action of the play. She wears "an artist's smock–picturesquely dabbed with paint–wide Byronic collar and flowing silk tie" (353) as she sells her wares. Shannon recognizes her as a "fantastic cool hustler" (371), and Williams writes that she in her artist's smock and Shannon in his clerical garb *are like two actors in a play which is about to fold on the road, preparing gravely for a performance which may be the last one*" (366). She insists that she is "not a weak person" and it is credible that she would go through with her plan to walk to town and sell her paintings in the plaza if Maxine doesn't allow her to stay at the Costa Verde on credit. She also has no compunction about doing business with the Nazis if she can persuade them to buy her paintings.

Williams wrote that the three "rope-enders," Nonno, Shannon, and Hannah, are all, like the iguana, set free at the end of the play: Nonno by the completion of his poem and acceptance of death, Shannon "by facing and accepting the truth of his nature and Hannah by her unwanted, unsought release from her hopeless attachment to the old poet whose life is all spent" (Parker 2004: 83). With Hannah's help, Shannon has found a rest from the internal struggle between the spiritual and physical drives that has led to his distraught state and is prepared to give up the Church and "live off la patrona for the rest of my life" (423). In his confession to Maxine that he can get himself down the hill, but not back up, and her promise, "I'll get you back up the hill" lies the dynamic of their probable future together. Hannah has expressed confidence in her ability to go on alone after Nonno is gone, but with her final line, "Oh, God, can't we stop now? Finally? Please let us. It's so quiet here, now" (427) intrudes a note of doubt. With Nonno's death comes the end of the "home" they have built for each other. Although she is well prepared to turn strangers into companions, and sometimes friends, her lot will be a lonely one, even with its occasional "broken gates between people."

The critical response to *The Night of the Iguana* was a harbinger of the difficult two decades that would follow for Williams. Like most of his earlier plays, it opened on Broadway to a positive press. It had a good run of 316 performances, was recognized with awards, was sold to a movie studio for a good sum, and was made into a successful film that was nominated for four Oscars and numerous other awards. But among the mostly positive reviews were various signs that the critics were growing tired of Williams's themes and techniques. Robert Brustein, for example, compared the play positively to the "unmelodious banalities" of *Period of Adjustment* and the "strident masochistic dissonances of *Sweet Bird of Youth*," giving the rather grudging praise that "his new materials are handled with relative sincerity, the dialogue has a wistful, graceful, humorous warmth, the characters are almost recognizable as human beings, and the atmosphere is lush and fruity without being outrageously unreal." Nevertheless, he complained that "the play seems tired, unadventurous, and self-derivative" and that it is "very short on plot, pattern, or theme" (Brustein 1962: 20). The *Boston Globe*'s Kevin Kelly wrote that the play "reverberates with dead echoes, with haunting poetic words and repetitive ideas that have remained unchanged from 'The Glass Menagerie' to 'Period of Adjustment,'" and complained about Williams's "obsession with the theme of loneliness" (Kelly 1962: 61).

The long period of the Williams's mostly kind treatment by the critics was about to end, and with it his dominance of Broadway. Fortunately, he had been pursuing Off-Broadway and other alternative venues for several years. He told an interviewer in 1961 that he was thinking of giving up Broadway, where "the playwright always has to have a smash, as if he were carrying a pass in football. I don't want to have all that money riding on me any more. There's much less tension off Broadway" (Peck 1961: X5). Off-Broadway, regional, and foreign theatres were soon to be the only ones available to him.

# CHAPTER 10
## THE LATER PLAYS (1961–1983)

### "Stoned Age"

There is no doubt that, after the success of *The Night of the Iguana*, the years from 1961 to 1969 were among the worst of Williams's life, both professionally and personally. The familiar narrative of these years depicts a swift downward spiral that includes his deep depression after the death of Frank Merlo in 1963, his increasing impairment by alcohol and drugs, and his devastating series of failures on the Broadway stage: *The Milk Train Doesn't Stop Here Anymore* (1963/ 69 performances), *Slapstick Tragedy* (1966/ 7 performances), *Out Cry* (1967/ 12 performances), and *The Seven Descents of Myrtle* (*Kingdom of Earth*) (1968/ 29 performances).

Williams's alcohol and drug ingestion became notorious during these years. In the early 1950s, he had begun taking Seconal, a barbiturate, first to sleep, and then to relieve anxiety throughout the day. By the mid-1950s, he was washing down four or five tablets with alcohol every day. During the 1960s, he was prescribed a variety of amphetamines and barbiturates to help him get energized to write and then to try to relax. Besides Seconal, among the drugs he mentioned casually in letters or interviews were Miltowns, the ubiquitous "downers" of the 1960s, Doriden, Nembutal, Reserpine, and Mellaril, and the "uppers" Dexamyl and Reactivan. The worst of these was Doriden, a drug (since removed from the market) which caused symptoms similar to drunkenness as well as hallucinations and paranoid-like delusions. He built up such a resistance to it that, according to biographer Donald Spoto, he was taking a potentially lethal dose daily by 1966. He became incoherent, flew into hysterical rages, and was unsteady on his feet, sometimes falling down spontaneously. In 1964, he rather ironically told Paul Bowles that he had quit smoking because he was worried about lung cancer, and was restricting himself to drink and pills, which included a fifth (4/5 quart) of Bourbon or Vodka daily and "to pep up, I take half a Dexamyl, and when I find it's necessary to smooth things over I take one and a half Seconals. And when I suffer from acute insomnia, which is also often, I take up to four sleeping pills" (Spoto 1986: 292).

In addition to these drugs prescribed by various physicians, in 1964, Williams came under the care of the notorious Hollywood "Dr Feel Good," Max Jacobson, who supplied him with concoctions of amphetamines that he taught him to inject. With his building tolerance for the substances, these injections became stronger throughout the decade. In 1965, he explained his writing ritual to an interviewer: "I begin with two cups of coffee, rather strong coffee. And then I go to my bedroom and I give myself an injection to pick me up. . . . I give myself one c. c. of whatever the thing is, the formula—I don't know what it is. I just know that immediately after it I feel like a living being! Then I can go to my table and work" (C: 114). In 1966, he mentioned adding a martini to the mix. The result of this behavior was perhaps inevitable, and in September of 1969, after he was called to a crisis in Key West, Williams's brother Dakin brought him to St Louis and had him committed to the psychiatric unit of Barnes Hospital. Williams claimed that the treatment he was given there was completely "cold turkey," so that his alcohol and drugs were removed all at once, a dangerous process. He suffered three seizures and two cardiac episodes that he referred to ever after as heart attacks during his withdrawal. He blamed Dakin for this and cut him out of his will, although he did acknowledge later on that his confinement in Barnes from September to December of 1969 had certainly saved his life.

This period that Williams called his "Stoned Age" was marked by a series of devastating attacks by critics, not only on his work, but also on him personally. It was inaugurated by the response to *The Milk Train Doesn't Stop Here Anymore* in 1963. The tenor of this can be seen in Richard Gilman's *Commonweal* review, entitled with a snide allusion to Joseph Conrad's *Heart of Darkness*, "Mistuh Williams, He Dead." In the review, he wrote that Williams "has had it. . . . There is no point looking for another rebirth," and asked, "Why, rather than be banal and hysterical and absurd, doesn't he keep quiet? Why doesn't he simply stop writing"? (1963: 515). He concluded that, "in using the stage not to solve his dilemmas esthetically but to exhibit them in their inchoate form, he is bringing about the permanent death of his art, intruding himself into the space it should occupy and thus drawing the sickness it is meant to heal more airlessly and irrevocably around him" (517). To a man who was always obsessed with his mortality and the failure of his creative powers, announcing his demise as a writer was cruelly devastating. He was to read such things over and over during the 1960s, but it was probably the response to the last of his new plays in the decade, *In the Bar of a Tokyo Hotel*, in May of 1969, that precipitated his final emotional crisis. The critical response to the play was vicious, personal, and mean-spirited, with critics trying to make their reputations by skewering the eminent playwright who was clearly at the low point of his professional career.

The most devastating to Williams was Stefan Kanfer's review in *Life* Magazine, which compared him to a white dwarf, or "star that merely shrank and faded," writing that "an astronomer would be derelict in his duty to history if he did not record their extinction." Of Williams he wrote that "we are still receiving his messages, but it is now obvious that they come from a cinder" (1969: 10). According to Spoto, Williams broke down and wept after reading the review, and refused to leave his hotel room for 3 days while he worked on *The Frosted Glass Coffin*, with its references to death, senility, and breakdown (Spoto 1986: 311). Reading this review in *Life* was bad enough, but the magazine chose to make its attack on Williams the central piece of a full-page advertisement in the *New York Times*, which featured the words "Come to Life!" in huge letters, a picture of Williams, and the following text:

> **Played out?** "Tennessee Williams has suffered an infantile regression from which there seems no exit. . . . Almost free of incident or drama . . . nothing about *In the Bar of a Tokyo Hotel* deserves its production."
>
> That's the kind of play it is, and that's the kind of play it gets in this week's Life.

> From a theatre review that predicts the demise of one of America's major playwrights to a news-breaking story that unseats a Supreme Court judge, we call a bad play when we see it.
>
> And it's that kind of strong stuff on Life's pages that gets us a major play from 36.5 million adults. Every week. (Display Ad 1969: 96).

After nearly a decade of failure and negative reviews, this was hardly the daring statement that the magazine pretended it was, but it was a horrific culmination of rejection for Williams. It is not surprising that it precipitated 3 months of desperately aimless behavior, during which he moved restlessly among Tokyo, New York, St Louis, San Francisco, Miami, New Orleans, and Key West, ending with his hospital confinement.

This is a nightmare narrative indeed, but it doesn't tell the whole story of the 1960s. The narrative that emerges from Williams's letters to Maria Britneva gives the other side of the dark downward spiral, a playwright who was working almost every day, traveling a good deal with the aid of hired assistants or friends, constantly looking forward to productions of his new plays and revivals of his old ones, and receiving a number of honors. The astonishing thing is that Williams was able to continue working during this period and that he produced a substantial body of drama. In this work, he continually revisited his perennial themes—the family, sexuality, the relationship between madness and creativity, the social and existential condition of the artist, the bohemian and the misfit—but he did so in terms of an experimental approach to theatre that he had never entered into so freely. Although not as well crafted as the earlier plays, these works are often startlingly original and revealing.

After his hospitalization, Williams by no means gave up drinking or taking drugs, but was much more careful about it. His work from the 1970s shows the same interest in new forms of theatre that had developed in the 1960s, and for the most part is far less referential, more imagistic, more what he called "plastic," more immediately symbolic than his earlier work, with less concern for plot or craft. In 1972, he said, "I've certainly grown less naturalist, in the Sixties very much less.

I think that I'm growing into a more direct form, one that fits people and societies going a bit mad, you know? I believe that a new form, if I continue to work in the theater, will come out of it. . . . I'm very interested in the presentational form of theater, where everything is very free and different, where you have total license" (C: 218). He took the trouble at times to divorce himself from the dominant new form in the 1960s, the so-called theatre of the absurd, saying it "can't appeal to me. I can't really work in the theater of the absurd. I can work in fantasy–in romantic fantasy–and I can work in very far-out plays. But I could never just make a joke out of human existence" (C: 118). During this period, he worked as compulsively as ever, and with his diminished powers of concentration and craft, worked longer on particular plays, revising them for years. The most conspicuous of these is *The Two-Character Play*, also called *Out Cry*, on which he worked for more than 10 years, referring to it as "my last long play" (Williams 1990: 202), and considering it his summary statement as an artist.

## The Artist Plays

### Compulsion and Fear: The Two-Character Play

The *Two-Character Play* uses Williams's perception of his own condition as an artist working in the commercial theatre as an exemplum for the universal condition of the contemporary artist. Central to its thematic import was the feeling that he had been abandoned by his audience and was being targeted by increasingly hostile and vicious critics. In 1973, he described the play as "a history of what I went through in the Sixties transmuted into the predicament of a brother and a sister," but called it "my most beautiful play since *Streetcar*." He said, "I've never stopped working on it. I think it's a major work. I don't know whether or not it will be *received* as one. It is a *cri de coeur*, but then all creative work, all *life*, in a sense, is a *cri de coeur*. But the critics will say I am excessively personal and I pity myself" (C: 239).

The play was begun in the mid-1960s. Williams wrote to Maria Britneva in 1966 that he had "completed" it in October of that year (Williams 1990: 194). It was first produced in London in 1967 (as *The*

*Two-Character Play*), directed by James Roose-Evans, and Williams said that he had written ten versions of the script by 1974 (Philp 1974). Most important was what he called the "Bangkok version," written during a visit to Thailand in 1970, which served as a basis for the 1971 Chicago production (as *Out Cry*) directed by George Keathley. He preferred this to the much-revised version for the 1973 Broadway production (as *Out Cry*) directed by Peter Glenville. Williams had great hopes for a major production of the play with actors he admired. He was very anxious to get Paul Scofield and Margaret Leighton or Angela Lansbury, or Geraldine Page and Rip Torn to do it. In the end, he settled for performers who did well in the play, Peter Wyngarde and Mary Ure in London, Donald Madden (his favorite) and Eileen Herlie in Chicago, and Michael York and Cara Duff-McCormick in New York. Peter Wyngarde recalled that, for the 1967 production, "Tennessee was at all the rehearsals, with his wretched companion of the time [Bill Glavin] bullying him. But Tennessee was gone [drunk or stoned], out of it, completely. He could offer nothing approaching directorial advice" (Williams 1990: 195). He was in much better shape for the 1971 and 1973 productions, even holding publicity interviews before the premieres, although he insisted he had little creative involvement with the 1973 production.

In 1970, Williams described *The Two-Character Play* as "'a play within a play within a play.' Its two characters are a brother and sister, Felice and Claire [sic], and the setting is an empty theater in a cold, distant place 'that could be the North Pole'" (C: 164). In an interview before the Chicago production, he called the play "an allegory about human anxiety. They talk about the two of them performing a play. He insists it's necessary; she insists it's impossible. This creates a tension between them. . . . They love each other very deeply. The play doesn't say they'd been to bed. I had a feeling they had. You know the brother and sister relationship is quite different from any other" (Campbell 1971: 5A). In his Notes to the play written in 1970, he wrote that "there may be no apparent sexuality in *The Two Character Play* and yet it is actually the *Liebestod* of the two characters from whom the title derives" (Williams 2009: 211). He wrote on the title page of the first draft that it was written "from the state of lunacy . . . it is the story of the last six to seven years of the 1960s. The play is about disorientation–these people are lost as I am. They are two sides of one person" (Spoto 1986: 297). Peter Wyngarde said that Felice was "the most harrowing part I have ever done. To convey the madness within the madness, like Chinese boxes, and yet to appear to be saner than Clare: we both came out after the show with hoops of steel around our heads. Because it is so near the bone, it's a terribly depressing piece to play in" (Williams 1990: 195).

The play's situation is that the ironically named Felice ("luck," "happiness"), a playwright and actor, and his sister Clare ("light," "purity"), his leading lady, find themselves deserted by the rest of their company in a cold and desolate "state theatre of a state unknown" (T5: 313). The company has deserted them and left a cablegram that Felice reads: "Your sister and you are–*insane*!–Having received no pay since–. . . . We've borrowed and begged enough money to return to–" (321). The set is the backstage, at the same time an image of the play's monodrama and its referentiality: "*It must not only suggest the disordered images of a mind approaching collapse but also, correspondingly, the phantasmagoria of the nightmarish world that all of us live in at present, not just the subjective but the true world with all its dismaying shapes and shadows*" (308). The set is dominated by the pedestaled statue of a giant "*which has a sinister look*" (308) and the Victorian house surrounded by sunflowers that will be used in the play-within-the-play. As the frame play begins, the audience is filing in, and Felice has determined that he and Clare will perform in the one play for two actors in their repertory, the "Two-Character Play" that is based on their family. During the performance, the audience gradually walks out in disgust, leaving them finally alone, and they find that they are locked in the cold theatre. To escape this reality, they endeavor to get "lost in the play" again and return to its final scene as the frame play ends. In the frame play and the play-within-the-play, Williams sets up two metaphors of entrapment or confinement. The first is the playwright or actor trapped in the theatre, compelled to perform despite the rejection by fellow theatre artists and the audience, and the cruelty of the critics. In the end, Clare remarks, "so it's a prison, this last theatre of ours. . . . I've always suspected that theatres are prisons for players" (364) and Felice responds, "Finally, yes. And for writers of plays" (364).

The second metaphor is that of the house, the objective correlative for the family in the play-within-the-play. In this play, Clare and Felice have become agoraphobic, trapped in the Victorian house surrounded by the Blakean sunflowers and exhibiting the astrological signs of their father's mysticism. It is, Felice says, "a small house and we've lived in it always" (326). Clare complains that she has to sleep in the "death chamber," where, as she tells it the first time, their father has killed their mother and then himself. She later attempts to change this narrative as part of her attempts to escape from the house. First, as an effort to "go out calling" (336), she tells a minister on the telephone that her father did not kill her mother. She says it was a "housebreaker who murdered our parents, but I think *we* are suspected. My brother Felice and I are surrounded by so much suspicion and malice that we almost never, we hardly ever, dare to go out of the house" (337). In another scheme to get out, Felice suggests that they go to Grossman's market, where their credit has been cut off, and tell Mr Grossman that they will soon be receiving their father's life insurance because what they saw was their mother with the revolver killing their father and then herself. Clare objects that this is "the absolute opposite of the truth" (344). In the final scene, Clare says, "we won't stay in so much now. I'm sure they'll believe that Mother shot Father and then herself, that we saw it happen. We can believe it ourselves, and then the insurance company will come through with the policy payment" (369).

Besides having immobilized them and confined them in the house in which this horrible act is the dominant reality, the shooting hangs over the action as an act that Felice and Clare are destined to re-enact. Felice hides a revolver on the set at the beginning of the play, and when they go back into the play-within-the-play at the end, he touches Clare's hand, indicating a new line in the script, and says, "Clare, didn't you tell me that yesterday or last night or today you came across a box of cartridges for Father's revolver?" (355). Although she denies it, he picks up the revolver, "which she's always hated and dreaded, so much that she refuses to remember that it exists in the play" (355). He says, "now I remove the blank cartridges and insert the real ones as calmly as if I were removing dead flowers from a vase and putting in fresh ones" (356), but his hand shakes so that the revolver falls to the floor, and Clare laughs. Felice places the revolver on the table between them. Clare insists that he "come out of the play" (357), and they try and fail to escape from the locked theatre in which they are confined. As they once more try to get "lost in the play," Felice hides the revolver under a cushion. After Clare distracts him with the sight of a giant sunflower "that's grown as tall as the house," she retrieves the revolver and aims it at him. He says harshly, "*Do it while you still can!*," and she cries out, "*I can't!*" (369), dropping the revolver to the floor. Felice picks up the revolver, points it at Clare, and "*tries very hard to pull the trigger: he cannot*" (370). On each of their faces "*is a tender admission of defeat*" (370). The play ends with their embrace and the stage goes dark.

In the play-within-the-play, the house represents a complex, contradictory nexus of confinement, destruction, thwarted mysticism, and the protective comfort of family. Confinement is the thing both characters dread. It is what Felice calls "a prohibited word," noting that, "when a word can't be used, when it's prohibited its silence increases its size. It gets larger and larger till it's so enormous that no house can hold it" (338). It is the family's confinement in the house that has led to the mutual self-destruction of the parents, a drive that is revisited on Clare and Felice. Yet the house, ironically shielded by the transcendent image of the sunflowers, is impossible for any of them to leave except through death. Blake's poem "Ah! Sun-flower" provides the play with a subtext of aspiration thwarted: "Where the Youth pined away with desire,/ And the pale Virgin shrouded in snow:/ Arise from their graves and aspire,/ Where my Sun-flower wishes to go." When Felice tries to go alone to Grossman's market, he finds that he can "move not a step further. Impossible without her. No, I can't leave her alone. I feel so exposed, so cold" (353). The house is alive: "Behind me I feel the house. It seems to be breathing a faint, warm breath on my back. I feel it the way you feel a loved person standing close behind you. . . . The house is so old, so faded, so warm that, yes, it seems to be breathing. It seems to be whispering to me: 'You can't go away. Give up. Come in and stay.' Such a *gentle* command! And what do I do? Naturally I obey" (353).

When Felice complains to Clare that the house has become a prison, she responds, "I know it's a prison, too, but it's one that isn't strange to us" (354). When Clare asks Felice if he hates her, he responds, "Of course I do if I *love* you, and I think that I do" (363). Caught in this nexus of love and hatred, they are compelled to remain in the house and to repeat over and over in their art the same story of compulsive mutual self-destruction in which it confines them. The play itself is mirrored in this image. As Clare says, "it never seems to end but just to stop, and it always seems to stop just short of something important when you suddenly say: 'the performance is over'" (360). Felice replies that "it's possible for a play to have no ending in the usual sense of an ending, in order to make a point about nothing really ending" (360). But Clare reminds him that there is always the ending of death, saying "I didn't know you believed in life everlasting," and reminding him, "things do end, they do actually have to" (360). Williams wrote in his Notes to the play that "in both the total play and the play within it, two desperately gallant but hopelessly deviant beings, find themselves, in the end, with no escape but self-destruction, which fails them, too" (Williams 2009: 212).

Both the metaphor of the cold, empty, locked theatre and the metaphor of the house are related to Williams's view of the compulsiveness of the artist. In his case, there was the daily compulsion to write and the compulsion to return again and again to his family, particularly his relationship with his sister Rose, in his work. There was also the compulsion to work in the theatre, and, despite his disavowals in the 1970s, to succeed on Broadway, regardless of the increasing toll that was taken by repeated failure and rejection by critics and audiences. The compulsion is related to the theme of fear, panic, and anxiety that Williams identified as central to the play, "the fierce little man with the drum inside the rib cage," as Felice describes it. Compared to fear which has grown into panic, no "other emotion a living, feeling creature is capable of having, not even love or hate, is comparable in—what?—force?—magnitude?" (309). In a sense the play is about the struggle between compulsion and fear: the compulsion to escape the house (the family, the past) and the fear of being without it; the compulsion to write about it and the fear of the self-destruction it creates; the compulsion to create one's art and the fear of destruction by audiences and critics. Perhaps more fundamentally, it represents the artist's divided self, *"disordered images of a mind approaching collapse"* (308). The love/hate emotion that Felice feels for Clare represents a desire for unity and integrity of consciousness that is thwarted by the awareness of the division between male and female, mind and body, writer and actor, animus and anima that are as necessary to the creation of Williams's art as they are detrimental to the maintenance of sanity.

Williams was never happy with the productions of *The Two-Character Play* and *Out Cry*. At the 1967 London production, he admitted, he was "in no condition to notice much going on. I behaved abominably" (C: 290). While he was pleased with the acting of Michael York, he said that the 1973 New York production "didn't have the kind of visceral outcry, the compulsion, which this play requires" (Philp 1974). He complained that director Peter Glenville hadn't given him the chance to revise the script as he wanted to, and "arbitrarily took out whatever he thought he wanted from all the versions" (C: 289). He thought the staging was a far too literal rendering of the play's symbolic import: "I had a number of references to sunflowers in the script; they had these huge projections of sunflowers on the back wall. They weren't necessary, unfortunately. . . . Everything had to be literally shown. If they were in prison, there had to be bars, or trapped figures projected in huge size on the cyclorama of the set" (C: 289).

The response to the play was perhaps predictable. As Williams rather shrewdly said in a 1971 interview, "I don't have an audience. I had one, but I lost it. I lost it back in the mid'60s. Yes, I know that" (Marks 1971: E1). In 1967, London critic Herbert Kretzmer confessed, "I understand very little of it," suggesting that "it would need a psychoanalyst–and preferably Tennessee Williams' own–to offer a rational interpretation of the enigmas that litter the stage like pieces of an elaborate jigsaw" ("Williams' Play Foggy" 1967: C5). W. A. Darlington wrote in the *London Daily Telegraph*, "I could make no sense of The Two Character Play; and long before the end had stopped trying to" ("Williams Drama Baffles" 1967: 54). There was a similar response in Chicago, where one critic complained that "'Out Cry' is so intensely autobiographical that it asks an audience to come into the theatre with a knowledge of its playwright that it cannot possibly be expected to have" and another called it "a seriocomedy leaning in the direction of comic elegy that ultimately reminds one of a vine-melon left too long in the sun to ripen" (Terry 1971: G59). On the other hand, the *grande dame* of Chicago critics, Claudia Cassidy, who is so often given credit for saving *The Glass Menagerie* back in 1944, wrote that *Out Cry* "proves beyond a doubt that Tennessee Williams can still write a beautiful, terrible, magical, haunting play" (Terry 1971: G59–G60).

In New York, given the play's import, some critics were clearly somewhat chastened by the callous personal treatment the playwright had been afforded in 1969 and its contribution to his recent emotional ordeal. Edwin Wilson wrote in the *Wall Street Journal* that "it is a matter of public record that Williams has been battling a number of private and public ghosts in recent years. He has undergone serious doubts about his work and in his personal life he has encountered problems which led to a breakdown. He has since recovered to the point where he is once more functioning well–completing this play and a full length autobiography to be published soon." Nonetheless, Wilson concluded in his review that "for all the play's incandescence and poetic excitement it does not fulfill its promise." In that case, he asked, why bother with the play? His answer was that "we bother partly because it is Tennessee Williams and he is a writer of proven talent. He seems to have recovered some of his former powers and it would be good for him to recover them all. In a broader sense, however, we bother because his loss is our loss and this is due to the plight of the serious play on Broadway" (Wilson 1973: 24).

The subject of the artist, and particularly the artist whose condition mirrored Williams's, was one that he explored many times as he experimented with theatrical techniques and dramatic form in the last two decades of his career. In her essay in this volume, Felicia Londré discusses his treatment of the artist in *In the Bar of a Tokyo Hotel* and *Vieux Carré* (1977) as well as *The Two-Character Play*. Two other plays that are important to the discussion are *The Gnädiges Fräulein*, a one-act play that was first produced along with *The Mutilated* as *Slapstick*

*Tragedy* in 1966, and *Clothes for a Summer Hotel* (1980), Williams's "ghost play" about Scott and Zelda Fitzgerald which was his last play produced on Broadway.

## Grotesque Metaphor: *The Gnädiges Fräulein*

*The Gnädiges Fräulein* was one of Williams's self-described "far-out plays," a fantastic metaphor for the condition of the artist. It is set in the "Cocaloony Key," a bizarre representation of Key West, with its proud claim that everything there is "southernmost." Williams describes the set as "a totally unrealistic arrangement of porch, assorted props, steps, yard, and picket fence. The main playing area, the porch, should be to the front, with maybe the yard displaced to upstage left–as if Picasso had designed it" (T7: 217). In a Preface, he wrote that *Slapstick Tragedy* was not theatre of the absurd, but "short, fantastic works whose content is a dislocated and wildly idiomatic sort of tragedy . . . the style of the plays is akin to vaudeville, burlesque and slapstick, with a dash of pop art thrown in" (Williams 2009: 148).

The Gnädiges Fräulein is a once "talented young soubrette" (247), complete with the scrapbook of clippings to prove it, who began her career in Middle Europe and has fallen on such evil days that she now lives in a boarding house on the Key with an open dormitory for transients where she manages to earn her keep by competing with the cocaloonies, disgusting sea birds that Williams describes as "a sort of giant pelican" (218), for the waste fish discarded when the fishing fleet comes in. Her career has been a downward spiral from performing before royalty in Europe to serving "as a B-girl at the Square Roof and Conch Gardens" (238) on the Key, to finally making use of her unique talent for mere survival. At one point in her career, she had "astonished her audience" (247) by catching the fish thrown to the act's trained seal in her own jaws. This became her popular signature until the seal took its revenge by clouting her in the jaw, and the act dissolved. Now she uses this skill to compete with the cocaloonies. She has to provide three fish a day to her landlady in order to hold her place in the dormitory "and one fish more to keep the wolf from the door" (239).

The landlady, Molly, describes the battle against the cocaloonies as the Gnädiges Fräulein's agon for survival: "now that the cocaloonies have turned against her, will she have guts enough to fight the good fight or will she retire from the fish-docks like she did from show business, under pressure!?" (239).

During the course of the play, the Gnädiges Fräulein has first one eye then the other pecked out by the birds, and is stripped of her clothing. At the end of the play, she has a bloody bandage around her head and "*all of her costume has now been torn away: she appears in flesh-colored tights, streaked and dabbled with blood. Patches of her fuzzy light orange hair have been torn away*" (260), yet when the whistle signaling the return of a fishing-boat sounds, she assumes the starting position of a competitive runner and "*starts a wild, blind dash for the fish-docks*" (262). When she is allowed to sing, "*she is transfigured as a saint under torture*" (245). Williams resisted being identified with the theatre of the absurd, but this play makes use of its grotesque metaphor in an absurdist way. In the plight of the Gnädiges Fräulein may be seen the plight of the playwright, or the artist generally, who receives applause from the audience for vulgarizing his or her art, and continues to do so in order to hold onto popular success. The competition of show business does its damage, and the audience loses interest as the novelty wears off, resulting in a diminishing career, and finally, a struggle for survival, in the arts and in life. Yet, Williams, suggests, there is something in the artist that cannot be snuffed out with the ending of popular success.

The grotesquely Promethean image of the Gnädiges Fräulein at the end of the play, blinded, bloodied, and stripped naked by the birds, but still in the fray, making the most of her talents in order to survive, suggests that there is a possibility for heroism even in this final state. In the guise of its "slapstick tragedy," the play is the darkest image of the artist's condition that Williams created. It is his own nightmarish image of himself in the mid-1960s, his audience gone, his creative abilities severely impaired, and himself the target of merciless critics, but it rises to a more general image of the condition of the artist in the commercial theatre where art is treated as mere amusement for the audience and commodity for the producer, and there is no mercy from the competition or the critics.

## "Ghost play": *Clothes for a Summer Hotel*

*Clothes for a Summer Hotel* dramatizes the situation of Zelda Fitzgerald, who was best known as the subject of her husband's fiction, but struggled compulsively to achieve her own artistic identity through painting, through her writing, some of which was literally appropriated by her husband and published under his name, and through an ill-fated attempt to become a professional ballet dancer at the age of 26, an experience that she wrote about in her novel, *Save Me the Waltz*. In his "ghost play," Williams has Scott visiting Zelda at the sanitarium where she was to die in a fire 8 years after his death. In the play, her life is lived in anticipation of destruction, her fate suggested in the classical imagery of mythic figures associated with fire: Cassandra, the salamander, and the phoenix. Zelda's compulsion for artistic expression is figured grotesquely in the play, as the middle-aged mental patient practices her ballet, but her drive for artistic creation is treated with respect. The alternative, Williams makes it clear, is madness. As Zelda says, "between the first wail of an infant and the last gasp of the dying–it's all an arranged pattern of–submission to what's been prescribed for us unless we escape into madness or into acts of creation . . . The latter option was denied me, Scott. . . . Look at what was left me!" (T8: 274).

At the end of the play, Zelda claims her own identity, telling Scott, "I'm not your book! Anymore! *I can't be your book anymore! Write yourself a new book!*" (280). As Thomas Adler has suggested, there is a striking parallel between Fitzgerald's appropriation of Zelda for his work, which the character Ernest Hemingway calls "Zelda and Zelda and more Zelda" (268), and Williams's appropriation of his sister Rose in his work. He calls it "a play of guilt, spawned by the author's betrayal of the person closest to him" (Adler 1997: 176). But Hemingway also tells Scott, "you know as well as I know that every goddam character an honest writer creates is part of himself. Don't you?" (269). To Williams, the characters who were most deeply based on Rose—Laura, Alma, Catherine, Clare, Zelda—were also most deeply himself. It is true that Williams wrote in his *Memoirs* that, while his relationship with his sister was "quite unsullied by any carnal knowledge . . . our love was, and is, the deepest in our lives" (M: 119–20), and noted with apparent approval that "some perceptive critic of the theatre made the observation that the true theme of my work is 'incest'" (119). But to understand Williams's art, it is perhaps more important to remember that he spoke of Clare and Felice as one character and thought of Rose as his soul, or Jungian anima. As Scott Fitzgerald says in *Clothes for a Summer Hotel*, the writer has "multiple selves" as well as "dual genders" (269).

*Clothes for a Summer Hotel* was the last play Williams had produced on Broadway. The production was heralded as a comeback for both the playwright and director José Quintero, who had also struggled with alcoholism, and with great hopes of Geraldine Page, the animating genius of *Summer and Smoke* and *Sweet Bird of Youth*. Williams was simply not up to the task of cutting his script, however, and the 3-hour Washington production was panned for its "excessively wordy but unrevealing narrative" (Paul 1980: 132). Despite Quintero's herculean efforts to help Williams cut 45 minutes from the script, the play opened to negative reviews in New York on 26 March 1980, and despite a $20,000 infusion of cash from Williams, it closed after 15 performances.

## Bohemians and Misfits

With his increasing sense of marginalization in the theatre and victimization by critics during this period, Williams intensified his treatment of the marginalized figures in whom he had always been interested, the figures he called the bohemians and misfits. One strand of his creative work led to the grotesque, an aesthetic in his later plays that is examined at length by Annette Saddik in her essay in this volume. In the plays she writes about – *Kingdom of Earth/ Seven Descents of Myrtle* (1968), *A Cavalier for Milady* (c. 1976), and *A House Not Meant to Stand* (1982) – there are numerous misfits, and these characters abound in the later plays generally. Whether his treatment of them is in the experimental mode of *The Gnädiges Fräulein* or *The Red Devil Battery Sign* (1976) or in the more realistic mode of *Vieux*

*Carré* (1977) or *A Lovely Sunday for Crève Coeur* (1979), the vision the later plays express is distinct from the sympathy and sentiment of earlier plays like *Fugitive Kind* and *The Glass Menagerie*.

## "The wayward and deformed": *The Mutilated*

The later plays tend toward that mix of emotions and aesthetics that Williams designated as "slapstick tragedy," a balance of the humorous and the monstrous that underlies the aesthetic of the grotesque as well. Like *The Gnädiges Fräulein*, the other one-act play that makes up the play *Slapstick Tragedy*, *The Mutilated* certainly belongs to this category. This slight play is important among Williams's later efforts because, like *Small Craft Warnings* (1972) and *A Lovely Sunday for Crève Coeur*, it takes the existential condition of the misfit as the subject of the play, using its dramatic form to bring some resolution to the human situation of being marginalized, alone and lost in both a social and a spiritual sense, a condition Williams was acutely aware of in the last two decades of his life.

*The Mutilated* has what Williams refers to as a "nonrealistic style" (P2: 584), "the set as delicate as Japanese line drawings" (584). This abstract set is combined with Brechtian techniques to present the action of the play as a moral exemplum, a Christmas story. The play takes place over Christmas, and the action is framed in a Brechtian way with a verse commentary that is "set to music and sung (probably *a capella*) as 'rounds' by a band of carollers" (584). Williams notes that the carollers should include all the characters in the play, including those who have just acted the scene, and be signaled by a pitch pipe. This technique provides a Brechtian alienation effect, distancing the actors from their roles, and prodding the audience to reflect on the characters and their situation rather than become emotionally involved with them. The opening verses suggest a sympathy for the marginalized in keeping with the Christmas season: "I think the strange, the crazed, the queer/ Will have their holiday this year/ And for a while, A little while,/ There will be pity for the wild" (585). In keeping with this hope for respite, "the mutilated will/ Be touched

165

by hands that nearly heal,/ At night the agonized will feel/ A comfort that is nearly real" (585).

The "mutilated" of the play include Trinket Dugan, who feels herself to have been physically mutilated by a mastectomy, and has had her entire life taken over by this obsession. Her erstwhile friend Celeste, an alcoholic, kleptomaniac prostitute who has just been bailed out of jail by a brother who will not allow her to come to Christmas dinner, confesses, "we all have our mutilations, some from birth, some from long before birth, and some from later in life, and some stay with us forever" (590). In a grotesque affinity with the *Gnädiges Fräulein*, Celeste at one time made her living as the "bird girl," called "the world's greatest freak attraction" (589). In reality, it was just Celeste with chicken feathers glued all over her body with a glue gun that gave her second-degree burns. Speaking of the current bird girl, she suggests the pervasive attitude toward the mutilated that the play brings to the audience's consciousness: "if she was a bird, the humane society would be interested in her situation but since she's a human being, they couldn't care less" (590). Celeste was at one time saved from her desperate life situation by Trinket, who has an income from her father's oil wells, and they were companions for each other until Trinket finally grew angry at Celeste's calling her a *mutilated monster* (592). When Celeste asks her to bury the hatchet for Christmas, Trinket replies, "we can't bury the hatchet. We hit each other too hard, and now it's too late to forget it" (591).

While Trinket has gone without love for 3 years because her sense of mutilation makes her fear human contact, particularly sexual contact, she shows great endurance and persistence, major Williams virtues, by showing "*no intention of giving up, not a bit in the world, wouldn't dare to or–care to!*" (600). Taking courage on Christmas Eve, in the Café Boheme she finds the sailor Slim, a young man distinguished by the perfection of physical beauty, "tall, crowned with gold that's so gold it's like his head had caught fire, and I know, I remember the kind of skin that goes with flame-colored hair, it's like snow, it's like sunlight on snow, I remember, I know!" (606). Slim's exterior masks an ugly soul, however, as he exposes his hatred for "freaks" with unusual sexual desires and his intolerance of Trinket's "morbid situation" (612). As Trinket goes to sleep next to Slim, saying, "well, anyhow, I have somebody here with me. Celeste's alone but I'm not, I'm not alone but she is" (614) and Celeste, outside on the stairs, seeks comfort in the idea that "I'm not mutilated. She is" (614), the general ugliness is allayed by the carol's insistence that even these deformed souls deserve mercy:

> I think for some uncertain reason
> Mercy will be shown this season
> To the wayward and deformed,
> To the lonely and misfit.
> A miracle! A miracle!
> The homeless will be housed and warmed. (614)

The play has the resolution of a typical Christmas story when the unkindness that is deforming these souls is purged and a Christmas miracle brings joy. Slim is ejected from the scene after his fellow sailor tells him, "you lack decent human feelings!" (615). Trinket and Celeste make up. Celeste literally sees the comforting vision of the Blessed Virgin that she was promised by an old nun if she "was ever cut off and forgotten by the blood of my blood and was homeless alone in the world" (620), and Trinket finally feels that the pain in her breast is gone. As part of the miracle, the death figure Jack in Black appears with the carollers, putting off "the tolling of a ghostly bell" (621) and allowing Celeste and Trinket to "forget me for a little while" (622). The moral of the tale is a perennial Williams theme, perhaps best expressed in *The Night of the Iguana*, the efficacy of temporary human connections to stave off the existential and emotional terror of being alone, facing death in an indifferent world. It goes further than his other expressions of this idea, however, to suggest that everyone deserves this kind of comfort, most of all the desperate and the marginal who are most unappealing as objects of love and compassion. *Slapstick Tragedy*, which combined *The Mutilated* with *Gnädiges Fräulein*, was produced on Broadway in February, 1966, with Alan Schneider, who understood its aesthetic and had had recent success with the nonrealistic work of Edward Albee and Carson McCullers, directing a talented cast that included Margaret

Leighton, Kate Reid, Zoe Caldwell, and Ralph Waite. It ran for just seven performances, with critics dismissing it as "one of the worst plays yet written by America's once foremost dramatist" (Kelly 1966: A15) and an "artless exercise in the Theatre of the Absurd, for which he is not temperamentally equipped" (A19).

## Fragile Community: *Small Craft Warnings*

*Small Craft Warnings* is in the tradition of the American saloon play, in which a collection of down-and-out characters with illusions about themselves are presided over by a benign figure who protects them from the importunities of the outside world and from facing reality by helping to keep them in an alcoholic haze and in a state of comparative harmony. The most familiar of these is Eugene O'Neill's *The Iceman Cometh*, in which the "pipe dreams" of the social outcasts of Jimmy the Priest's bowery flophouse are ultimately preserved against the insistence by the invader Hickey that they face the reality of their various failures in the world outside the bar. Williams was also undoubtedly familiar with his self-perceived rival William Saroyan's *The Time of Your Life*, which was a major hit by the Theatre Guild and Eddie Dowling in 1940, the first year Williams spent in New York, and perhaps with Philip Barry's *Here Come the Clowns*, which had run the previous season. Like all of these plays, *Small Craft Warnings* is set in a bar that is, in the words of Doc, "a place of refuge for vulnerable human vessels" (P2: 718), presided over by a benign presence, the aptly named Monk, who describes the bar as a community that "takes the place of a family in my life," and says the "confidences and confessions" of the patrons make him feel "not alone" (748). Williams's play differs from the other saloon plays in that it is really about the dissolution of the community, the recognition that, like other refuges for the misfit, it is only temporary, and each of its members must ultimately move on.

The play is "*a somewhat nonrealistic evocation of a bar*" (715), with the fog rolling in on three sides. Like the other saloon plays, it has little plot, the point being the monologues, emphasized with spotlights, that reveal each of the characters. It is the women who provide the vitality in the bar's community. The central character, Leona, is a lonely itinerant hairdresser, a *"large ungainly woman"* and pugnacious, loud-mouthed drunk (719). She has taken in the aging hustler Bill, who provides her with sex, but she pines over her dead brother, the real love of her life. Williams said in an interview that Leona is "a fully integrated woman . . . the first really whole woman I have ever created and my first wholly triumphant character. She is truly devoted to life, however lonely–whether it be with a stud like Bill or some young faggot she takes under her wing because he reminds her of her brother" (C: 216). The other feminine presence in the bar is Violet, played in the original New York production at the Off-Broadway Truck and Warehouse theatre by Candy Darling, an ethereal transsexual member of Andy Warhol's core group of actors. Doc describes Violet as "amorphous . . . more like a possibility than a completed creature" (716). She lives out of a suitcase in a room over an amusement arcade and can't remember when, how, or why she came to be there. Leona describes her as "a water plant, with roots in water, drifting the way it takes her" (763). Besides Bill, who is about to lose his meal ticket in Leona, the men include Steve, a middle-aged short order cook who feels he "has to be satisfied with the Goddam scraps in this world, and Violet's one of those scraps" (729); Doc, who has lost his license to practice because of drunkenness and carries on illicitly performing abortions and delivering babies; and the strangers Quentin, a jaded middle-aged gay man, and Bobby, the young transient he has picked up for the night.

As the characters are launched, willingly or unwillingly, out of the security of the bar, the theme of the play emerges as the ability or inability to embrace life. It is Leona who shows the most vitality, and most values life. She tries unsuccessfully to nurture and browbeat Violet into becoming aware of her own value and to keep Doc from the drunken attempt to deliver a baby, which results in the death of both the mother and the premature infant. She believes that "the one thing you mustn't lose ever" (743) is love, and acts to give "protection" (745) to others. She most values love and beauty, which she sees as embodied in her dead brother, a violinist, insisting, "the companionship and the violin of my brother would be all I had any need for in my lifetime till my death-time" (734). But she doesn't dwell in nostalgia or self-pity.

At the end of the play, having kicked Bill out of her trailer because she perceives his lack of respect for her, she is ready literally to move on with her life, going to a new place to find new companions. Her final monologue expresses her embracing of "Life! Life! I never just said, 'Oh, well,' I've always said 'Life!' to life, like a song to God, too, because I've lived in my lifetime and not been afraid of . . . changes" (751).

Violet has her own form of embracing life by living in the moment, in her limited way, for human contact through sex. Leona gives up being angry with Violet for her groping of Bill when she realizes that her compulsive sexual contact is just "worshipping her idea of God Almighty in her personal church" (763) as her "dirty fingernail hands reach out to hold onto something she hopes can hold her together" (763). In the end, Violet rises to a modicum of self-respect, dismissing Steve because he gives her "no protection and no support" (759) and choosing instead "a temporary, a night" (764) upstairs with Monk, who accepts with grace "the solace of her companionship" (757). Doc, the most troubling of the characters, also moves on after allowing a woman to hemorrhage to death because he "thought of the probable consequences to [him]" (760) and did not call an ambulance for her, and then paid her companion with the 50 dollars he had gotten from an abortion not to remember his name. When Monk warns him of Leona's earlier attempts to keep him from trying to deliver the baby by exposing him, Doc too decides it is time to move on. It is difficult for the audience to agree with Monk that "that old son of a bitch's paid his dues" (760) or to square his bringing of death to life with the "triumphant" embracing of life that Williams saw in Leona.

Equally opposed to Leona's spirit is Quentin, the character who has received the most attention from critics because he is the first gay character to appear in a Williams play after he came out publicly as gay on David Frost's television show in 1970. Nicholas de Jongh wrote that in Quentin, Williams "defines all homosexuals in terms that the homophobes of the 1950s had made their accusatory own" (1992: 70). Quentin has been tagged as a "self-hating homosexual" by critics who write from a gay or queer studies perspective, and he certainly conveys a negative view of his sexuality. In his often-quoted monologue, he says there is "a coarseness, a deadening coarseness, in the experience of most homosexuals. The experiences are quick, and hard, and brutal, and the pattern of them is practically unchanging. Their act of love is like the jabbing of a hypodermic needle to which they're addicted but which is more and more empty of real interest and surprise" (743). Leona explains to Bobby that Quentin wants to pay him despite the lack of satisfaction in their connection because "it's part of his sad routine. It's like doing penance . . . penitence" (741).

These are certainly familiar tropes in Williams's representation of homosexuality, and not favorable ones, but Quentin's homosexuality is not his most important characteristic in the play's thematic terms. What's more important is that Quentin feels that his particular sexual experience has led to his inability to feel surprise, to be "startled by the sense of being alive, of being *myself, living!* Present on earth, in the flesh, yes, for some completely mysterious reason, a single, separate, intensely conscious being, *myself: living!*" (743–4). The one who has not lost this capacity is Bobby, the kid from Iowa who is bowled over by the realization that he has reached the Pacific ocean. Bobby's sexuality is still an open question. John Clum has suggested that Bobby is not homosexual, but "healthily, polymorphously perverse," an example of "carefree bisexuality" (Clum 2000: 164). He is open to Quentin because the older man's hand on his knee was "just a human touch and it seemed natural to me to return it" (746). Bobby's future is likewise open, as he refuses Leona's offer to take Bill's place in her trailer and hits the road on his bicycle again, saying "I've got a lot of new adventures, experiences, to think over alone on my speed iron" (747).

In an interview, Williams said that it was not Quentin's homosexuality that degraded him, but his promiscuity, which he said was "a perversion of the love impulse" (Brockway 2003). It is the hard, impersonal way he pursues sexual experience that has led to both his inability to respond to Bobby's "human touch" and his inability to look at the world with wonder and surprise. As Michael Paller has noted, the play also includes several "self-hating heterosexuals" (Paller 2005: 200), particularly Steve, who refers to Violet as a "pig," a "pitiful scrap," and a "bone thrown to a dog" in his "miserable, cheap life" (729). The patrons of the bar exhibit a broad spectrum of sexuality. What's important is not the gender of those they devise, but the humanity and respect with which they treat them. Williams said in an interview that it was Quentin with whom he identified. He wrote *Confessional*, the one-act play *Small Craft Warnings* is based on, in 1967, at a time when he was under so much that sedation he lacked the capacity to feel surprise and "there seemed to be an increasing sameness and brutality in my personal relations" (C: 228). In his opinion, "the lack of variation and surprise in sexual relations spreads into other areas of sensibility." He felt that Quentin's monologue was "the very *heart* of my life," although "Quentin's sexual aberration was never mine–I would never reject a person because he returned my touch, you know? I *love* being touched" (C: 228).

The production of *Small Craft Warnings* meant a good deal to Williams, and he was not above participating in marketing tricks to get an audience for it. In the original New York production beginning 2 April 1972 at the Truck and Warehouse Theater in Greenwich Village, he played Doc for the first few performances, garnering the reviews and the publicity this Off-Broadway venue would not otherwise have received. Reviews were mixed, but good enough to enable a transfer of the production to a larger uptown theatre in June, where he again played the part of Doc and even participated in after-show talks. Critics and audiences received it better than they had a Williams play in some time. Although there were complaints about padding of the originally one-act play, and its lack of action and motivation, some critics understood what Williams was doing. Clive Barnes noted that the play was in a tradition that used "the bar as a symbol of the transcience [sic] of American society, a resting period outside the punctuation of events and yet at the same time an indication of a world adrift," calling it "a study of people surviving" (Barnes 1972: 50). He thought *Small Craft Warnings* would "survive better than some of the much-touted products of his salad years" (50).

## Memory

In revisiting the "memory play," a genre he had established with *The Glass Menagerie*, in the last decade of his career, Williams returned to the form of his earliest theatrical success as well as to the subject of his youth. As memory plays, *Vieux Carré* (1977) and *Something Cloudy, Something Clear* (1981) form a trilogy with *Menagerie*, based on Williams's experiences in the crucial time between 1938 and 1940 when he was committing himself to the profession of writing and at the same time discovering his sexuality in the context of the bohemian life of New Orleans's French Quarter and the gay subculture of the summer colony of Provincetown, Massachusetts. In December of 1938, thanks to the generosity of his grandmother, he went for the first time to the French Quarter, settling in a boarding house at 722 Toulouse Street, which is the setting for *Vieux Carré*. Soon out of money, he lived a bohemian life, existing as he could by pawning his possessions and working briefly for his landlady, Mrs Anderson, who opened a restaurant, the Quarter Eat Shop, for which Williams coined the slogan "meals for a quarter in the Quarter." He left New Orleans in February of 1939 with the young musician Jim Parrott, with whom he traveled to Los Angeles, and had various adventures, spending an idyllic summer at Big Sur. Returning to St Louis in December, he learned that he had won a $1,000 grant from the Rockefeller Foundation.

What followed was a brief period during which Williams's star seemed to be rapidly rising, as *Battle of Angels* was optioned by the Theatre Guild. A brief love relationship that he would see as one of the most important of his life developed in July, when he went to Provincetown to work on revisions for the play. He met Kip Kiernan, who, with his friend Joe Hazen, was staying in the same building on Captain Jack's Wharf as Williams. With Kip, he fell deeply in love for the first time, and he took great joy in their sexual relationship rather than feeling guilty about it. He told Donald Windham to keep a letter in which he described it, "and be very careful with it. It's only for people like us who have gone beyond shame" (Williams 1980: 10). In the letter, he said confidently, "I know that he loves me!–That nobody ever loved me before so completely. I feel the truth in his body" (10). Kip's behavior showed signs that he was not comfortable with the relationship, however, and when a girlfriend appeared in Provincetown, he told Williams that the relationship was over. Williams physically attacked the girl and wrote in his journal, "I feel that I have never given my love more uselessly in any whore house" (N: 205). He was clearly devastated by the experience, but also dramatized it for himself and others. In his journal, he wrote that he thought "almost continually of K.–Memories–dreams–longings–little hopes and great desolations–Will he ever come back? Can there–will there be someone else?. . . . K. If you ever come back, I'll never let you go. I'll bind you to me with every chain that the ingenuity of mortal love can devise! Hmm. Getting rhetorical again" (207). In early September, he had escaped to Mexico, and he wrote of his depression, "it is bound to get better. It couldn't get worse. The cause–heartbreak over K.–is all but forgotten. The effect will run its course also" (215). *Vieux Carré* is based on the time he spent at 722 Toulouse, while *Something Cloudy, Something Clear* is based on the relationship with Kip.

## From Innocence to Experience: *Vieux Carré*

In writing *Vieux Carré* in the late 1970s, Williams was unabashedly aiming to return to the form of *The Glass Menagerie*, and repeat its success, approaching the subject of his discovery of the bohemian life of the artist and his own sexuality in the New Orleans of 1940 with essentially the same theatrical approach he had taken to the St Louis family life in *Menagerie* 30 years before. The characters and incidents of the play are based on those at 722 Toulouse. Mrs Wire's restaurant is based on the Quarter Eat Shop, and, like Mrs Wire, Williams's landlady, Mrs Anderson, did actually pour boiling water down into the apartment below to break up what she thought was an orgy, ending up in night court. Two old ladies like Miss Carrie and Mary Maude worked in the restaurant along with Williams for their meals. Sky is based on Jim Parrott. The couple based on Jane and Tye lived elsewhere in the Quarter. The identity of Nightingale is not definite, although Williams wrote in his journal soon after his arrival that someone had "moved in the room next door–even a stranger across a wall is comforting to me in this state" (N: 131).

As the events of 1939 are filtered through the Writer's memory, the play is focused on the theme of change, the transformation of the

Writer as he passes from the state of innocence to that of experience and the human cost of this necessary transformation. Although the play's form is similar to that of *Menagerie*, the set has a much different aesthetic, a poetic minimalism replacing the subjective realism of the Mielziner set: "The stage seems bare. Various playing areas may be distinguished by sketchy partitions and doorframes. In the barrenness there should be a poetic evocation of all the cheap rooming houses of the world" (P2: 827). Like Tom in *Menagerie*, the Writer is used as a narrator who addresses the audience directly, simultaneously creating an unmediated connection between him and the audience and distancing it from the action of the play. Describing the house as once alive and occupied in his opening monologue, he says, "in my recollection, it still is, but by shadowy occupants like ghosts" (829). At several points throughout the play, Williams disrupts the fourth wall to spotlight the Writer as he reflects aloud, calling attention to both the play's theatricality and its theme.

The change that takes place in the Writer is emphasized in the narration. As he becomes more experienced, he becomes hardened, self-interested, and less open to emotional connections. As a writer he exploits the people around him, turning them to profit in his work. Mrs Wire berates him for the "shockin' diff'rence between your looks an' manners since when you arrived here an' now, mockin' me with that grin an' that shifty-eyed indifference, evidence you're setting out on a future life of corruption" (875). Nightingale, the tubercular painter with whom the Writer has an affair, says, "you know, you're going to grow into a selfish, callous man," comparing the cataract on his eye to "a shell of calcium" (858) that is growing over his heart. In a spotlight that indicates "*interior reflection*," the Writer recognizes that "there's a price for things, that's something I've learned in the Vieux Carré. For everything that you purchase in this marketplace you pay out of *here!* (*he thumps his chest*). And the cash which is the stuff you use in your work can be overdrawn, depleted, like a reservoir going dry in a long season of drought" (854–5). He realizes the value of this experience, telling Mrs Wire that he ought to pay her tuition for what he has learned in the house, but he also knows that the price he has paid is already great. Toward the end of his stay, Nightingale says, "you used

**175**

to be kind–gentle. In less than four months you've turned your back on that side of your nature, turned rock-hard as the world" (885). The Writer counters, "I had to survive in the world" (885), but he realizes the loss that involves.

The specter of Grand, the image of the Writer's grandmother, the "elderly female saint" (843) derived from Williams's early short story about this time, "The Angel in the Alcove," provides a symbolic focus for the change from innocence to experience. Early in the play, the image provides comfort to the Writer. Having had his first sexual encounter with Nightingale, he wonders "what her attitude was toward such–perversions? Of longing?" (844). He finds peace in her "almost invisible gesture of . . . forgiveness? . . . through understanding?" (844). At the end of the play, when he is described by Nightingale as a "boy with soft skin and stone heart" (886), he feels the influence of Grand dimming: "her image was much fainter than it had ever been before, and I suspected that it would fade more and more as the storm of my father's blood obliterated the tenderness of Grand's" (886). This recognition of his inheritance from the hard-drinking, sexually promiscuous C. C. Williams is another expression of gain and loss for the writer. Williams often equated the Dakin side of his nature with tenderness and kindness and the Williams with callousness, selfishness, and sensuality.

At the end of the play, the Writer professes himself to be "grown into a man, about to take his first step out of this waiting station into the world" (894). As he prepares to go off with Sky, Grand lifts her hand in a valedictory gesture. The ending of the play owes something to Arthur Miller's *After the Fall* (1964), which depicts the action in the "*mind, thought, and memory*" (Miller 1964: 1) of its protagonist Quentin. In Miller's play, the set is literally a representation of Quentin's mind, and the characters come to life as he is visited with thoughts and memories about them. At the end of the play, all of the characters are alive and facing him. At the end of *Vieux Carré*, "*dim spots of light touch each character of the play in a characteristic position*" (900). The Writer says that the people are disappearing as "the earth seems to swallow them up, the walls absorb them like moisture, remain with you only as ghosts; their voices are echoes, fading but remembered . . . this house is empty now" (901). Although it is visually arresting, the effect of the ending is not as powerful as that of *The Glass Menagerie*. The idea of Tom Wingfield being unable to escape the memory of his sister and mother provides forward momentum, with implications both for the play's meaning and for the writer's future work. The ending of *Vieux Carré* is about the death of something. The Writer's work, certainly made possible by the people and the experience that is dramatized in the play, seems to be over, with only the ghosts remaining.

The original Broadway production of *Vieux Carré* opened on 11 May 1977, and closed after six performances. Critics disagreed about the play, but agreed that the production was pretty much a disaster. The "monstrously shabby physical design" (Kerr 1977: 65) by James Tilton was faulted, as was the "appalling" (Kerr 65), "sluggish" (Barnes 1977: 70) direction of Arthur Seidelman. Although the acting was effective, given the poor production, it was difficult for critics and audiences to see anything in the play but what Clive Barnes described as "the journey of a character through a chamber of his past, fondling relics, stumbling Proust-like on cobblestones and tasting the cakes of yesteryear" (1977: 70).

## "Double exposure": *Something Cloudy, Something Clear*

*Something Cloudy, Something Clear* (1981) has even more in common with *After the Fall* than *Vieux Carré* in that it makes conscious use of dramatic form to dramatize the concepts of subjectivity and memory. The difference is that, while Miller physicalizes the mind of Quentin, in this play, Williams is able to dramatize August's subjectivity while avoiding elaborate staging techniques. He indicates that the time is September, 1940 *and* September, 1980, what August refers to as "present and past, yes, a sort of double exposure" (Williams 1995: 38). The set, a ruined shack on the dunes at Provincetown, is referred to as "dreamlike" and suggests "the spectral quality of a time and place from deep in the past: remembered, specifically, from a time forty years later" (x). The action is fluid, with time shifts between 1940 and 1980, and memories of Williams's first girlfriend Hazel Kramer, his long-time partner Frank Merlo, and the actor Tallulah Bankhead intruding from other times as well.

Williams foregrounds the issue of subjectivity when he has August suggest, "perhaps I've transfigured [Kip] in my memory," but after he looks at Kip through the window insisting, "No. I've memorized him exactly as he was" (12). Clare, the lover/sister character who is the other half of Kip, responds, "this is the summer of 1940, August. Let's drop the metaphysics, play it straight, play it not like summer long past but as it was then" (13). In theatrical terms, this makes for several dimensions of reality: the past, 1940 "as it was then" and the dramatization of that past by the actors; the past as it is remembered or "transfigured" by August; the characters from various times who appear only in August's memory; and the present of the play, 1980. Openness to the fluidity of this subjective reality is necessary if the audience is to follow the play, thus making it complicit in August's subjective vision of things. The play's through-line is provided by August's working through a dilemma in the course of the play, the issue of the morality of his relationship with Kip.

The "something cloudy, something clear" of the title refers to the two aspects of August's feeling for Kip—the purely sensual, pragmatic impulse to pursue sex and the romantic impulse to fall in love. August's clear eye is associated with sympathy and forgiveness (20). Clare, who is endowed with two eyes that are "both as clear as the sky" (61), tells August that he loves Kip, "and I hope it's with the clear eye" (25), but she fears the other side of his desire, which is pragmatic and exploitative. August tells Clare that on first meeting them, "I knew you cared for him, Clare, very deeply, didn't want him used," and she responds "I didn't want his body violated, to satisfy yours" (15). It is Kip who proposes that they appeal to August to "keep" them during the winter, hoping to avoid Clare's going back to being the mistress of Bugsy Brodsky. When he becomes aware of what is being proposed, August asks Kip about the sexual nature of the liaisons he's had: "But, Kip, these other demands, you *do* submit to them, don't you" (33). Kip responds, "don't I have to? When I can't–you know–appeal to their better natures if they have them" (33).

Although Kip says that he can see August's better nature "in the eye that's clear" (33), August reminds him that his desire is physical. It is a desire that is figured in the character of the drunken Merchant Seaman August pays to have sex with him. The seaman vomits on the floor of the shack, leaving a pervasive odor. The nature of their relations is made clear in the crass negotiation at the end of Part One, when the Seaman agrees, "so you can fuck me for another fin and a drink" and August agrees, "Yes, I reckon–we've made a deal this time" (56). The cloudy, callous side of August's nature is also exposed in his negotiations with the Fiddlers (based on the Theatre Guild's Lawrence Langner and Armina Marshall) over his play, during which he pragmatically withholds the revisions he has done until he is offered a contract and a regular advance for the play. These transactions prefigure the "cloudy" side of his relations with Kip. As he and Kip talk about the conditions for Kip's spending the night with him, August says, "Kip, we're negotiating for an advantage, aren't we? Like most people, if not all, sometimes?" (65). After they spend the night together, Clare says that Kip looks "like a whipped dog" with a "bruised" look in his eyes (72). August explains, "We had a long discussion of terms. It was a–negotiating table out here–the same as it was between me and the Fiddlers and between you and Bugsy Brodsky" (72). August's moral dilemma comes in the clash between his pragmatic means of satisfying his physical desire and his deep feeling for Kip. As Kip tells Clare, "he had what he thought he wanted, but I don't think it was. . . . He used me like a–" but "I think he's just about as desperate as we are" (74).

There is a generically comic element in the play's moral resolution as August, Clare, and Kip come together for a meal at the end, and there is some reconciliation of the clear and the cloudy elements of August's nature when, Clare having escaped from Bugsy Brodsky, he suggests, "couldn't we all live together? For a while?" (76). Clare agrees, but, "purely, cleanly. I'll not have you use him again like a whore." For the first time, August expresses the integration of the physical and the emotional: "I love him. You know I love him.–Would you permit me to hold him?" (76). Clare says, "The cloudy eye demands something, even now?" and August responds, "I think he'd want to be held, to be caressed?" (77). Clare's response to this suggests both hope and skepticism that the emotional could outstrip the physical: "If that—would suffice" (77). Clare and Kip decide to leave August, but first they have a dinner together and August kisses Clare, telling her that she has "a mouth full of flowers" (84). The play ends with August's tribute to "the lovely ones, youthfully departed long ago" (Kip Kiernan died in 1944 at the age of 26). Of the play, he says, "while this memory lives, the lovely ones remain here, undisfigured, uncorrupted by the years that have removed me from their summer" (85).

*Something Cloudy, Something Clear* was first produced by the Jean Cocteau Repertory Theatre in New York, in August, 1981. Predictably, the critics projected their inability to see what Williams was getting at onto the playwright. Walter Kerr called him "a playwright at sea" (1981: D3), and Michael Feingold complained that he had depicted himself as an "unscrupulous, horny bastard on the make" (1981: 89). In her Introduction to the published text, director Eve Adamson explained the meaning of the play that she had reached for in the production: "It seeks a reconciliation between love and art, life and death, and—to use two phrases which recur in the play—exigencies of desperation and negotiation of terms. The cloudy and the clear" (vi). The key metaphor of the play, she wrote, is double exposure: "two times, two selves, two sensibilities exist simultaneously in August. But also, hovering around and permeating the entire dramatic poem, is the double exposure of Tennessee Williams: the artist and his art, the man and his theatrical persona, immediacy and retrospect, time stopped and time flowing" (vii). It is perhaps the most unsparingly truthful of Williams's memory plays and second only to *The Glass Menagerie* in art and craft. Unfortunately it seems to have reached the theatre at the wrong time for audiences and critics, and a 2001 revival by the New York Art Theater, which literalized many of the images, was not a successful staging of the play. Like many of the later plays, it awaits a production that will do it justice.

# CRITICAL PERSPECTIVES

## All in the Timing: The Meanings of *Streetcar* in 1947 and 1951
*Bruce McConachie*

As Philip C. Kolin and others have noted, several New York critics greeted the premiere of *A Streetcar Named Desire* with decidedly mixed reviews in December of 1947. Most recognized the excellence of Tennessee Williams's play, admired Elia Kazan's directing, and praised Marlon Brando's Stanley, but a majority found Jessica Tandy's Blanche neurotic and unlikeable (Kolin 2000: 1–33). When the film of *Streetcar* based on a shortened and censored version of the play appeared in 1951, however, movie critics applauded Vivien Leigh's nuanced and sympathetic Blanche as well as complimented Kazan and Brando. Because the response to Blanche's actions will necessarily center most spectators' general interpretation of the play, it is important to understand how and why many spectators in 1947 and 1951 probably responded to the two Blanches as they did. In her careful analysis of Tandy's Blanche, Susan Spector concludes that the 1947 premiere of *Streetcar* "left audiences feeling that a madwoman had entered an alien world and, after shaking that world, had been successfully exorcized" (1989: 558). Certainly there were important differences between Tandy and Leigh in the leading role, which help to account for the disparity in their reception.

In assessing this disparity, however, critics need to focus on timing as well. By "timing," I refer both to the nearly 4-year gap between the Broadway opening and the film's premiere and to differences in the initial reception of *Streetcar* in theatre and film venues. The 4-year delay was important because *Streetcar*, like all performance events in American culture in 1947, was produced in the shadow of World War II and some memories of the war years had faded by

1951. More importantly, perhaps, spectators going to the Barrymore Theatre in1947 experienced an intermission between scenes four and five of Williams's play, while movie viewers witnessed the film version of *Streetcar* without a break, as they did with nearly all feature-length movies at that time. I will argue that the intermission led the audience to arrive at certain negative conclusions about Blanche that guided their response to her for the rest of the performance.

Of course there will be some scholars who would deny that such a comparison between theatrical reception and film viewing is possible. If, as some allege, there are significant, even unbridgeable differences between the "live" and "mediated" experiences of an enacted drama, comparing the reception of *Streetcar* on stage to a film of much the same story is a hopelessly "apples-and-oranges" exercise.[1] My first task, then, must be to address what some take to be this larger theoretical problem. To do this, I will use the logic and conclusions of the evolutionary and cognitive sciences, which will also guide my analysis when I examine the still-potent memories of World War II in 1947, the fading of those memories by 1951, and the way spectators make meanings while they are watching a dramatic story unfold on a stage or on a film screen. As in my previous work on performance and cognition, I will deploy a scientific framework that understands all performance events ("mediated" or "un-") as embodied and interactive. Consequently, timing—evolutionary timing, historical timing, and event timing—will be important considerations in each of the three parts of the essay to follow.

I am particularly interested in the dynamic system that underlies the process by which spectators watching dramatic fictions come to understand and evaluate characters. In the mix and clash of the many theories and paradigms that populate the cognitive sciences, dynamic systems theory, also known as the "enaction paradigm," has been gaining adherents. From this perspective, audience members begin judging characters' actions the moment they are mentioned by others and/or the characters step into a scene. Spectators use their individual and cultural memories of people, situations, and locations that are similar to the characters in the fiction to appraise and respond to them, gradually expanding and complicating their evaluations of each. For the most part, memories from outside of the dramatic context lead to initial judgments, while memories and events from within the drama will shape later responses and appraisals as the action unfolds in time. This interaction, involving dramatic events followed by spectatorial perception, memory, and appraisal, is a dynamic one, in that the appraisal formed in the spectator's mind from one cycle of the system is invariably reshaped in the next cycle by a different dramatic action which sparks new memories and appraisals. In most plays and films, a spectator will gradually settle into one or a few general attitudes toward a character and this conclusion (unless overturned by significant narrative developments) will help to determine the spectator's response to the character for the rest of the dramatic action.[2]

Writers, directors, actors and others can work to delay spectatorial conclusions about a character, however, and this is effectively what Jessica Tandy, under the strong directorial hand of Elia Kazan, attempted to do with Blanche in 1947. Kazan and Tandy, relying on the protean possibilities of Williams's script, initially emphasized the negative qualities of Blanche.[3] As we will see, though, Williams gives audiences significant reasons to sympathize with Blanche as well as to dislike her in the first four scenes and the result, for many spectators, was likely the emergence of several possible appraisals of Blanche. The intermission, however, halted this ongoing process, encouraging spectators to bring their judgments together to form some conclusions. As often occurs in social situations, this largely negative first impression left by Blanche shaped audience understanding of Blanche for the rest of the dramatic action. This interruption did not occur in 1951, allowing spectators more time to process their feelings about Blanche. In addition to other factors, then, a change in the historical circumstances of American culture and the elimination of intermissions in the experience of film viewers accounted for the many of the different responses to Blanche DuBois from US audiences in 1947 and 1951.

## Two *Streetcars* in Evolutionary Perspective

A comparison between the two *Streetcars* properly begins by recognizing the changes Hollywood made to Williams's script. At 122 minutes, the film version of *Streetcar* was roughly 20 minutes shorter than the running time of the Broadway performance, minus the two intermissions that the producer built into the event. In addition to trimming some lines and business that did not alter the narrative, script adapter Oscar Saul (under the guidance of Williams) accommodated the demands of the Hollywood censors that they excise all references to homosexuality, avoid overt sexual references or displays from any of the characters, including Stanley's rape of Blanche, and alter the ending to suggest that Stella decides to leave Stanley. The new script implied the sexual orientation of Blanche's first husband through euphemism and, with Kazan's help, provided two strong visual metaphors for Blanche's rape—Stanley's breaking of Blanche's mirror in the bedroom at the climax of their tussle with a broken bottle, followed abruptly by the phallic explosion of a street-cleaning hose. Except for the ending, which involved Stella telling neighbor Eunice that she would never go back to Stanley, Williams was satisfied with the film. "*A Streetcar Named Desire* was a brilliant film until the very end," he said, "when the distortions of the censorial influences made it appear that Stella would no longer live with Stanley" (Kolin 2000: 153). As Kolin points out in his thorough overview of productions of *Streetcar*, however, spectators could recall that Stella had made such a vow before, during the night of the poker game, only "to come down soon after a penitent Stanley shouted her name" (2000: 153). Further, the ending did not fundamentally alter the centrality of Blanche in the narrative arc of the play and the reasons for her eventual destruction.

Of course there were also some obvious differences in the experiences of the theatrical and filmic spectators. In 1947, live actors and an audience occupied the same architectural space, which meant that spectators could interact directly with the performers during the play. This was not the case in 1951. While spectators in 1947 understood that the conventions of theatrical storytelling limited their ability to "travel" to several locations to watch the narrative unfold, film viewers 4 years later probably enjoyed the opening footage at the New Orleans train station and may have noticed the several ways that Kazan opened out and rearranged the Kowalski apartment to facilitate better camera shots. Audience members at the Barrymore Theatre saw *Streetcar* from the vantage point of their own seats in the playhouse. Spectators at movie houses, in contrast, allowed the camera work of the film to provide several angles of vision and to zoom them in for closeups that gave them intimate perceptions of the faces of actors Brando and Leigh as Stanley and Blanche. As we will see, reading facial expressions matters a great deal in assessing the emotions, beliefs, and intentions of dramatic characters.

But did these conventional differences between theatre and film viewing fundamentally alter the experience of enacted drama for each group of spectators? In his *Embodied Visions: Evolution, Emotion, Culture and Film*, Torben Grodal emphasizes the conservative and creative organization of the human mind to argue that, for the most part, the gradual evolutionary construction of our brains allows us to convince ourselves that the images on a film screen can be just as animate and interactive as the images we perceive on a stage full of live actors. Grodal's assertion is in line with the general conclusions of evolutionary scientists, who acknowledge that our brains do not usually engage in new modes of operation when old cognitive practices can be called on to serve similar purposes. Evolution is parsimonious; we process actor/characters on the screen or stage much as we process other people in social situations.[4]

Further, what Grodal calls "visual representationalism" tends to structure much of our response to film viewing. He asserts, "The fundamental architecture of the brain was made at a time when incoming data were essentially true, so that reality status evaluation was a secondary process and the later cultural development of visual (and acoustic) simulations made it necessary to contain the impact of such simulations by higher order cognitive processes" (2009: 185). In other words, the more primitive brains of our ancestors, which continue to undergird much of our present cognition, processed appearances as reality. Before mammals evolved from reptiles, the reptilian brains of our precursors had no way of distinguishing between perceptions of animate beings and inanimate objects (such as film images on celluloid) that could appear to have the same characteristics as live animals. Over the last 2 to 4 million years, however, our hominid ancestors evolved what Grodal calls the capacity for "reality status evaluation" that allows us to distinguish the reality of animate actions from their appearance. Both systems of perception remain potentially active in our brains, however, which explains how people who enjoy horror films can shift back and forth between a belief in the terrifying images they witness and the knowledge that these images are just part of a movie.

In order to compare and contrast audience perceptions of Jessica Tandy and Vivien Leigh in the role of Blanche DuBois in the 1947 and 1951 *Streetcars*, then, I must work within the constraints that visual representationalism imposed on spectatorship. In this regard, the relevant question is the kind of Blanche that spectators experienced when they collapsed the actor and the character together to see and hear a single Tandy/Blanche or a Leigh/Blanche. Posing the research problem in this way rules out of consideration comments in reviews that reflected the workings of higher-order cognitive operations. Although spectators in 1947 and 1951 were certainly able to step back from their immersion in the flow of the drama to think about the artistry of Tandy or Leigh apart from the character she played in the fiction, my focus for the initial comparison must be on the actor/character as a single image moving through the dramatic action. Consequently, insofar as spectators did not invoke the kind of reality checks that would have permitted them to understand *Streetcar* as a fiction constructed by several artists, we may compare the two Blanches.

Surprisingly, perhaps, spectator responses prompted by visual representationalism are not only available in reviews of both productions, but are also predominant. In their theatre and film reporting, most critics followed the general convention of separating commentary on the overall dramatic action from specific paragraphs aimed at evaluating Tandy, Leigh, and the other artists involved in the production. When informing readers about the story of *Streetcar*, both sets of reviewers invariably revealed a great deal about their understanding of Blanche's background, her major character traits, and the reasons for her psychological disintegration. These summaries, which might comprise half of a typical newspaper or magazine review, implied that their journalist-authors were simply relating the character and story of Blanche as written by Tennessee Williams. The dominant conventions of stage and filmic realism reinforced this premise. While watching a play or movie, spectators were rarely encouraged to step back from the realistic appearance of the fiction, evaluate the reality status of what they were perceiving, and consider the acting and directing that went into making the work. Knowing this, reviewers usually addressed readers whom they assumed had already or soon would be immersing themselves in the fiction of the play or film as though it were a reality unfolding before them. Put another way, the critics reinforced visual representationalism, their own and their spectators' most primitive levels of perceptual response.

I will summarize two sets of responses to *Streetcar* in 1947 and 1951—reviews written by the New York newspaper critics after opening night, 3 December 1947, and reviews posted by New York-based film reviewers in newspapers and popular magazines soon after the national release of the film early in September of 1951. By narrowing the field of possible reviews in this way, I am trying to ensure an "apples-to-apples" comparison concerning the 1947 and 1951 critics' experience of Blanche. At mid-century, New York journalists understood that they were writing for both a local and a national audience. Despite the rising importance of Hollywood and other regional centers, New York City remained the cultural capital of the nation, New York critics decided most of the important cultural awards, and many New York writers believed they had a responsibility to uphold high critical standards. Although most reviewers cultivated their idiosyncrasies, these common activities and assumptions led to broadly shared rhetorics and values among the New York critical tribe.

Looking at both *Streetcars* through the eyes of New York spectator-journalists in 1947 and 1951, it is evident that these groups experienced two very different versions of Blanche DuBois. In 1947, most of the nine reviewers identified Blanche as a sexually voracious, decadent Southern woman, who was out of touch with reality. Eight of the nine used the term "prostitute," "nymphomaniac," or a near-synonym of these words to describe her. Howard Barnes, for example, identified Blanche as a "boozy prostitute," while Robert Coleman typed her as a "paranoiac-nymphomaniac." Other phrases for Blanche's promiscuity included "town trollop," "notorious tramp," and "the Hatrack of her Mississippi town." Seven of the nine critics also explained Blanche's actions in the play by referring negatively to her Southern heritage. Four linked her to the Southern affectations and delusions of Amanda Wingfield in *The Glass Menagerie*, which had appeared on Broadway in 1944. According to Richard Watts, Blanche represented "a long line of decadent Southern aristocrats," while for Ward Morehouse, she was simply "the faded, shattered daughter of the South." Most reviewers also found fault with Blanche for her delusions and neurosis. John Chapman noted that Blanche "shuns the reality of what she is and takes gallant and desperate refuge in a magical life she has invented for herself." Less charitably, Louis Kronenberger flayed Blanche as "the most demonically driven kind of liar – the one who lies to the world because she must lie to herself." In sum, most of the reviewers in 1947 saw Blanche as sexually predatory or a lying tramp, whose Southern past had left her deluded and neurotic.[5]

Given the structure of Williams's narrative, most New York critics of the Broadway and Hollywood productions invariably took sides between Blanche and Stanley in their reviews. In 1947, this balance of sympathies among the spectator-journalists tilted sharply toward Stanley. William Hawkins summed up the general preference for Stanley over Blanche in his comment that Stanley, as played by Brando, is "an honest animal who needs no motivation for anything he does other than he wants to do it at that particular time." Five of the nine reviewers expressed variations on this theme, which effectively eliminated Stanley's agency in the climactic rape scene of the play. While none of the reviewers applauded Stanley's rape of Blanche, most ignored it or used euphemisms to evade its implications; the word "rape" occurred in none of the reviews. Complementing this perception of the story, three reviewers also dismissed Blanche as fated and hopeless. For Richard Watts, for instance, *Streetcar* was the story of "a doomed Southern girl." And Richard Barnes called attention to the universal qualities of Blanche's "tragic destiny," her inevitable "degradation" in the midst of "cruelty, kindness, and sheer animal living." For these critics, Blanche, predestined for destruction, was doomed to end up in an institution even before Stanley laid a hand on her.

Even though the rape was treated less overtly on screen than on the stage, most of the eight film critics in 1951 spoke frankly about

Stanley's violence and blamed him for Blanche's destruction. Bosley Crowther in the *New York Times*, for example, linked the "brutal act of rape" to Blanche's "final, unbearable madness" and *New Yorker* critic John McCarten noted that Blanche's "roughneck Polish brother-in-law destroys her poor pretenses and her mind by raping her." Although the critics continued to praise Brando, several of them found his Stanley both more vicious and vulgar than had their theatrical counterparts in 1947, in part due to the closeups of his face. *Life* magazine, in a four-page spread that featured the closeups of Brando and Leigh from the film, ran four images of Brando's Stanley "contorted in expressions of gluttony, childish grief, anger and passion," according to the caption. While a few film reviewers suggested that Leigh/Blanche's situation was hopeless to begin with—Manny Farber in *The Nation* called her "a rotten old Dixie apple fated for squashing"—most believed that Blanche "could still be saved," in the words of *Commonweal* critic Philip T. Hartung. The film critics still referred to Blanche as a decadent Southerner (a "bedraggled magnolia," said the *New Yorker*), but few made much of her sexual appetite, even though two reviewers retained the adjective "nymphomaniac" to describe her. The critics of Vivien Leigh's Blanche understood her as deluded and neurotic, but tended to cite factors beyond her control for this problem. *Saturday Review* critic Hollis Alpert, for example, blamed Blanche's "disturbance" on "the shattering discovery of her young husband's inversion," as homosexuality was often referred to in 1951.[6] Oddly, perhaps, no film reviewers whom I read referred to Leigh's Blanche as a kind of older and updated version of her Scarlet O'Hara from *Gone with the Wind*, which most of them had seen 12 years before.

Although Williams expected a generally compassionate response to his protagonist, few of the 1947 critics cared for her very much. Brooks Atkinson was the most sympathetic to Blanche, concluding his review, "Out of poetic imagination and ordinary compassion, [Williams] has spun a poignant and humane story." Chapman and Morehouse admitted that Blanche's story evoked "pity," but both avoided expressing warm sympathy for her at the end of the play. Kronenberger termed the emotion experienced by spectators "dry pity," suggesting that although the audience recognized Blanche as a victim, they were not shedding any tears for her. Because "there is something a little embarrassing about watching the torment of as helpless a victim of a playwright's brooding imagination as the heroine of [*Streetcar*]," critic Watts said that he found Blanche's downfall "painful rather than pitiful." Hawkins went the furthest in this direction. Commenting on the "unrelenting hopelessness" and "desperate falseness" of Blanche, Hawkins called her "repellent rather than sympathetic." He added, "As the story progresses, one wishes that Blanche would only slip over into recognizable derangement, but the scarring truth is that she never quite does." It is difficult to generalize about the reviewers' emotional response to Blanche in 1947. While most of them recognized her as a victim, her situation evoked as much embarrassment and even disgust as it did pity.

In contrast, the New York film critics were much less confused about their emotional response to Leigh's Blanche in 1951. None wrote about "dry pity" or complained that they felt more repelled than compassionate. Three reviewers used the term "poignant" to describe their general feelings about Blanche's situation, echoing Atkinson's singular response in 1947. The *Newsweek* critic found Blanche "very moving," "a pathetic mixture of feminine grace and dementia." Hartung was the most sympathetic. Williams and Kazan, he said, tell "the story of a woman's loneliness and desperate need for love," which becomes a "study of Blanche's demoralization and the need for charity." If the reviews of 1947 and 1951 are any indication of the response to Blanche among popular audiences in New York, Williams's character had altered considerably during those 4 years.

## *Streetcar* in a Changing American Culture

Spectators always bring cultural memories with them when they go to see a play or film. While such collective memories are never monolithic, some may be widely shared and these invariably shape audience expectations and initial responses in all dramatic presentations. I use the term presentation to emphasize the importance of audience perception over artistic representation in the making of meaning.

As Grodal notes, what spectators perceive often works at the level of visual representationalism, which means that the actions embodied and presented by actor/characters are usually more significant for audiences than the artistry of their representations. Further, how and what spectators perceive in the moment-to-moment unfolding of a drama is generally more important to their meaning construction than is their retrospective analysis after the narrative is complete. Audiences do not normally "read" the visual and auditory signs of a production to sift them for delayed meaning because they experience most of a performance as a series of actions by actor/characters, not as discrete representations. As in other social interactions, audiences always filter what they are seeing and hearing in an ongoing search for meaning. Perception is not a passive conductor of outside images to an inside brain for later synthesis; it is a proactive and highly selective search engine, driven mostly by emotions and memories, that posits gestalts of immediate meanings and works continuously to confirm or alter them. This dynamic process is primarily unconscious, prompted by emotion-charged stimuli and varieties of memory in continuous interaction in our brains, our bodies, and in our immediate environment.[7]

Soon after they settled into their auditorium seats to enjoy *Streetcar* in 1947 and 1951, most spectators in New York City found themselves experiencing a dramatic presentation that touched on values that were linked to several clusters of significance in their memories. I have singled out five of these clusters that, judging from the play, the reviews, and from a general knowledge of postwar US history, appear to have been important in helping New York spectators to generate initial meanings about *Streetcar*: The American South, female sexuality, heterosexual marriage, the moral status of male veterans, and female mental health. Williams introduces all of these clusters in the first scene of *Streetcar* and New York audiences were primed by cultural tradition and recent history to respond to them. As we will see, major similarities and differences among the 1947 and 1951 critics tended to gravitate to these clusters.

From the perspective of postwar New Yorkers, the South of Blanche DuBois was a foreign country. The inheritor of plantation-era Southern traditions and sensibilities, Blanche and her kind probably represented the faded gentility, aristocratic pretenses, and emotional extremes that they associated with Hollywood films and romantic novels about characters who attempted to live by the values of the Old South. As Flannery O'Connor noted about such figures at the time, "[A]nything that comes out of the South is going to be called grotesque by the Northern Reader, unless it is grotesque, in which case it is going to be called realistic" (1961: 40). For Northerners, the most popular US guide to such traditional character-types in the 1940s and early 1950s was W. J. Cash's *The Mind of the South* (1941). As historian John Shelton Reed notes, Cash presented the South as culturally distinctive, resistant to change, willfully individualistic, and extravagantly romantic, all qualities that New York audiences could easily attribute to Williams's Blanche (2003: 15–27).

Cash's analysis led New Yorkers to perceive sharp contrasts when they compared their beliefs about the North and the South. While watching *Streetcar* and judging Blanche's immersion in Southern cultural traditions, most spectators could define themselves as more cosmopolitan, more accepting of progress, more cooperative, and more rational than Blanche. Indeed, in terms of the acting and directing choices of the 1947 and 1951 productions, audiences could easily perceive the two Blanches as more southern than the other major characters. None of the other actors (not even Kim Hunter as sister Stella) attempted a "thick" southern accent, with the consequence that Tandy's and Leigh's Blanches seemed even more isolated from the rest of the characters in the French Quarter of New Orleans and more peculiar to the audience.

Social constraints on expressions of female sexuality, conservative enough in peace time, became more repressive during the war years. Not only were stateside married women expected to remain faithful to their husbands fighting overseas, but it was widely believed that unmarried women should refrain from involving "our boys" in romantic entanglements when they had more serious matters to attend to. Such values were apparent in the restrictions on women who joined the Women's Army Corps and the Women Accepted for Volunteer Emergency Service and on those performing in United Service Organizations troupes. These social norms also played out in

Hollywood films during and after the war, which depicted deceptive, immoral women who had betrayed brave husbands during the fighting (*The Best Years of Our Lives*) and emphasized the combination of heightened sexuality and villainy in the numerous *femme fatales* of film noir. In the popular imagination, attractive women remained potential "bombshells" through the early 1950s.[8]

Although many women experienced some loosening of such restrictions by becoming temporary Rosie the Riveters during the war, postwar society quickly removed most women from such jobs after 1945, in the widespread belief that a woman's "normal" place was in the home. The result of these constraints was what historian Elaine Tyler May has called a domestic version of containment from the mid-1940s into the 1960s: "Within [the home], potentially dangerous social forces of the new age might be tamed, where they could contribute to the secure and fulfilling life to which postwar men and women aspired. Domestic containment was bolstered by a powerful political culture that rewarded its adherents and marginalized its detractors. More than merely a metaphor for the Cold War on the home front, containment aptly describes the way in which public policy, personal behavior, and even political values focused on the home" (1988: 14). The postwar consensus embraced heterosexual marriage and a happy home as the answers to containing the sexual desires of men and women.

Blanche's presence in the Kowalski household, of course, presents a direct threat to the norms of domestic containment. Her decision to move in with her sister and brother-in-law would have reminded many New Yorkers in 1947 of similarly difficult and potentially combustible situations during the war, when a lack of housing forced distant relatives and even strangers to share temporary living quarters. While New Yorkers might have understood the "end of the line" desperation that drove Blanche to New Orleans, many would have had direct or imagined (through filmic depictions) experience of the sexual tensions that could erupt between men and women in such a domestic situation. Consequently, given the widespread desire to return to "normal" gender relations after the war and to begin building a home and family, most would have seen Blanche as a potential home-wrecker and blamed her for the heightened tensions in the household. From this perspective, it is understandable that the male critics in 1947 could not bring themselves to call Stanley's attack on Blanche a "rape." Her presence in the house, her flirting with Stanley, and her apparent sexual availability, from their point of view, had simply caused the poor boy to explode. Domestic containment was no less in force in 1951 than in 1947, but the immediacy of war memories linked to housing and sexuality had likely faded.

The image of Stanley as a heroic veteran was also probably less important in the minds of spectators in 1951 than before. While there is little in Williams's play that comments directly on Stanley's wartime experience, the mere fact of his having served would have elevated him in status in the eyes of most New Yorkers. The popular mythology surrounding "the good war" tended to conflate "our boys"—all veterans were implicitly "boys" regardless of their age—with America itself. The suddenness of the Japanese attack on Pearl Harbor shocked Americans into an image of their enemies and themselves that would stay with them for a generation: treacherous evildoers had violated the trust of innocent, vulnerable Americans. But most also believed that the same good-hearted innocence, coupled with brash toughness and a can-do attitude, became America's best defense in waging a war for democracy and freedom. Hundreds of war films in the 1940s and early 1950s delivered variations on these themes (and none of them showed American soldiers raping local women). In short, if a veteran sexually molested a woman, he must have been driven to it; to think otherwise raised more questions about our boys, the war, and American intentions than most patriots wanted to consider. Consequently, many New York spectators would have understood the sexual tensions between Stanley and Blanche and the eventual rape as a case of "she was asking for it" (McConachie 2003: 56–61).

From the point of view of Cold War spectators after World War II, however, women were not altogether accountable for their actions. Freudian psychiatry, never more popular in the United States than in the two decades after the war, had long warned that women were more vulnerable to psychological problems than men were. Further, postwar psychiatry, especially the Freudian version of "ego psychology" widely practiced in the United States, preached that rebellion against normative social roles could lead women to psychological distress and neurosis; social conformity, in other words, was the key to personal mental health. Again, Cold War Hollywood provided several films that demonstrated the vulnerability of women to psychological disorders (*The Snake Pit* and *The Three Faces of Eve*) and prescribed normative cures for their problems (McConachie 2003: 61–4, 202–3). It would not have mattered to most spectators that circumstances beyond her control had eliminated Blanche's options for a "normal" life. Her presence, her past, and her demands that she had a right to find a place for herself were an affront to the norms of Cold War American life as they were emerging in 1947 and had solidified by 1951.

New York spectators came to watch stage and film versions of *Streetcar* with various ideas, images, and prejudices in their memories about the South, female sexuality, marriage, male veterans, and the psychological vulnerability of women. These expectations helped to shape their perception of the drama, especially in its opening scenes. How individuals in the audience connected the dots among these clusters of themes and applied them to Blanche cannot be known, of course, and may have varied widely. Broadway and Hollywood, after all, had long enchanted many northerners with southern women who shared some of the same traits as those of Blanche DuBois, and these institutions would continue to enthrall American audiences with similar figures throughout the Cold War. While we can say that memorial expectations, in general, worked against a positive evaluation of Blanche, cultural memories alone could not have led most New Yorkers to conclude that she was a tramp or a nymphomaniac.

## Dynamic Processing in 1947 and 1951

How people read the minds of others in social situations and dramatic fictions is more complicated than attributing ideas and images to them that they have learned in the past. Cultural memory can prompt initial stereotyping, as we will see, but this attribution usually fades under the weight of subsequent perceptions and judgments. Assuming that the 1947 critics reflected several of the popular perceptions of

Blanche, what was it about the experience of the performance that specifically led spectators to believe that Tandy/Blanche was neurotic, decadent, and nymphomaniacal? Why might these attributions have changed or at least softened when the critics watched Vivien Leigh in the role 4 years later? An investigation of the dynamics of these processes demands some cognitive knowledge about how people use their perceptions to bridge the divide between themselves and others and also a closer reading of the first three scenes of the play.

Evolution equipped us with numerous strategies to read the minds of other people in social situations. Because our survival often depended upon cooperation, our species learned many ways of reading the emotions, understanding the intentions, and anticipating the actions of other conspecifics. As cognitive psychologist Bertram Malle asserts, there is no single "mindreading module" or unitary "theory of mind" that people use to understand others (2005: 40). Rather, evolution fitted us with a series of overlapping strategies that range from simple observation to complex empathetic engagement to figure out the emotions, beliefs, intentions, and actions of other people. Although I will discuss four of these strategies (projection, stereotyping, trait attribution through narrative, and empathy) in the context of the first four scenes of *Streetcar*, I must emphasize that the process of mindreading is never as sequential and straightforward as my discussion will suggest. People unconsciously jump among various strategies, get stuck in some, and double-back frequently to others as they process incoming stimuli, reach tentative conclusions, and constantly update their results about the dramatic characters they are trying to understand. While many of these stimuli are memories—cultural memories, memories of past dramatic behavior, and memories of interactions that happened maybe 10 seconds ago on the stage or screen—immediate actions and emotions also play important roles. Spectatorial mindreading is a dynamic process that only temporarily stops (but may never finally end) when a dramatic presentation ceases.

As noted in the previous section, our cultural memories about how and why similar people acted in similar situations provide one guide. According to social psychologist Daniel R. Ames, if people perceive a social other to be like them, they will tend to project their own traits onto that person in a first encounter to gain some initial understanding of their beliefs and goals. In contrast, if they perceive the other to be dissimilar to themselves, they will usually draw on stereotyped images from their memories at first. In Ames's summary of this conclusion, "*Perceived similarity governs projection and stereotyping: perceptions of general similarity to a target typically draw a mindreader toward projection and away from stereotyping; perceived dissimilarity does the opposite*" (2005: 164).

This insight has a straightforward application to Scene One of *Streetcar*. Encountering a Blanche DuBois who was quite different from themselves, many New York spectators attempting to read her mind would have jumped initially to stereotypes. Williams shows Blanche under extreme stress in the first scene of the play; she drinks compulsively to quiet her nerves, careens between extremes of affection and combativeness in her initial interactions with Stella, and sinks into depressed memories of death when she recalls the recent parade of funerals at Belle Reve. Given what northern spectators already believed about the South, the suspect status of single women, and about female vulnerability to mental disease, it is not surprising that many New Yorkers at both productions might have initially assumed that her character was a neurotic—another grotesque victim of southern tradition and female weakness.

Yet there are also possibilities for audiences to project some similarity, even sympathy, onto Blanche in this scene. Williams's lines allow Blanche to be played as more physically exhausted than high-strung and antagonistic in her initial encounter with Stella. And after Stanley enters and begins questioning her about her background and intentions, Blanche is initially withdrawn as he is sizing her up. Is she mostly repulsed by his vulgar speech and stripped-to-the-waist physicality or simply unsure of how to proceed in the face of his preening cockiness? The emphasis could go either way in the acting and spectators, too, might read either or both intentions into Blanche's reserve. The end of the scene calls for Blanche to admit to Stanley that her first husband died and to collapse into a chair, defeated. Spectators, especially women who may have found themselves in similar circumstances, might easily have read their own feelings of vulnerability and memories of past defeat into Blanche's situation at the end of Scene One. Scene One of *Streetcar* invited New Yorkers to engage initially in strong anti-Blanche stereotyping in 1947 and 1951, but ended with the possibility of more sympathetic projection for the Blanche in the film than on the stage.

According to Ames and others, the strategies of stereotyping otherness and projecting sameness tend to fade with time. This occurs as well in most social situations, as personal and collective memories give way to immediate observations. Following Scene One of *Streetcar*, many New Yorkers may have stereotyped Blanche as a decadent southerner prone to neurosis, but even in 1947 there would have been little in the first scene to suggest that she was a loose woman or a sexual predator. In an article concerning how people make inferences about the social goals and personality traits of others, authors Stephen Read and Lynn Miller draw on several studies to conclude that "we comprehend other people's minds by creating a coherent narrative or story of their actions, organized around their goals" (Ames 2005: 125). Following this process of narrative creation, the perceiver-creator can ascribe specific traits to the other person. For Read and Miller, ascribed traits are "frame-based [mental] structures that identify the central actions of a sequence of behaviors and the goals of and reasons for that sequence" (133). "X" can term "Y" "helpful," "selfish," or perhaps "immoral," for example, because X has constructed a narrative of Y's past actions that explains them. Likewise, New Yorkers in 1947 could only term Blanche a "nymphomaniac" after they had created a similar kind of narrative built around coherent goals and reasons.

Scene Two, the trunk scene, offered both audiences for *Streetcar* some possibilities to begin constructing Blanche as sexually voracious. The scene begins with Stanley obtusely insisting on his right to a share of the profits from the sale of Belle Reve and then "unpacking" the contents of Blanche's trunk to show his wife how Blanche has squandered their money. Stella, trying to avoid a conflict between her husband and sister, fails to quiet his anger and exits. Then Blanche emerges from the bathroom in a slip and red satin robe and immediately begins to flirt with Stanley, presumably because she heard parts of their argument and seeks to win him over. Spectators who had stereotyped Blanche as a potentially neurotic and decadent Southerner in Scene One, however, might easily read a different motive into this strategy. They may have understood Blanche's flirtation, together with her red-robbed and fresh-from-the-bath, perfumed body, as an attempt to seduce Stanley. Stanley is clearly aroused and accuses her of being a tease, but Blanche soon dresses herself and the erotic atmosphere of the scene momentarily dissipates.

Next, Blanche makes what some spectators probably thought was another provocative move. She sends Stella off to the drugstore to buy her a coke so that she can speak to Stanley alone. Apparently sure that she has the upper hand with Stanley, she continues the flirtation, perhaps as a means of securing her immediate victory and setting up a relationship that will give her long-term control without sexual consequences in the household. Williams is clear later in the play that Blanche has often relied on playful flirtation to control her relations with men. But in the midst of Scene Two the audience could not yet have been sure that controlling Stanley was her intention and some evidently believed that she had gotten rid of her sister in order to have another chance at seducing Stanley. Blanche's stratagem—whether perceived as control or seduction—fails, however, when Stanley rips off the ribbon from the stack of letters from her dead husband and begins to paw through them. Blanche is unnerved, grabs them back, and drops her flirtation.

By this point in the scene, the audience, convinced that there was something psychologically wrong with this faded southern belle, could begin to build a narrative to explain Blanche's behavior. Perhaps the story went something like this: "Older sister loses husband in mysterious circumstances; is unsuccessful in marrying again in her small town and worried about her advancing age, so decides to change her territory and move in with her younger sister, whom she can boss around; older sister is immediately attracted to younger's stud husband and decides to seduce him to wreck their home and steal the husband; husband apparently interested so older sister orders younger sister out of the house to make her move; seduction might have worked, except that older sister is neurotic as well as sexually predatory." This is not Williams's understanding of Blanche's past and her goals, of course, but for some northern spectators who had only watched the first scene and a half of the play, such a narrative probably seemed plausible. The story weaves together many of Blanche's significant actions, grounds them in the actual circumstances of what the audience understood so far about her past and present, and tracks her life in terms of an overall goal—to get a husband—that would have been believable to many of the spectators who created the narrative and perceived it to be true. The story also explains why so many spectators in 1947 (and quite a few in 1951) attributed the trait of nymphomania to Blanche's personality. In fact, to turn the question around, it is difficult to explain why so many spectators believed her to be a sexual predator if they had not created a story much like this one.

From the 1951 reviews, it is apparent that several critics of the film went beyond ascription through stereotyping and constructing narratives and began to empathize with the actor/character of Leigh/Blanche. Empathy is a more complex cognitive process than the use of cultural memories to stereotype and the imagining of stories to ascribe personality traits. Although there are several competing definitions of empathy, some cognitive scientists are now pushing for a unified theory of this cognitive operation.[9] Neurobiologist and phenomenologist Evan Thompson, for example, discusses several stages of empathy. The first, in which empathizers mentally mirror the movements of others, he calls "sensorimotor coupling"; it puts people "in tune" with the emotions of others and provides a foundation for later stages of empathetic engagement. Thompson terms the next stage "imaginary transposition." As the name suggests, imaginary transposition allows the empathizer to attempt to place her or himself into the mind of another. Many psychologists call this operation "perspective-taking" and recognize it as a widespread and mostly unconscious means of mindreading. It differs from simple projection in that the empathizer does not read the emotions and goals of the self into the other, but effectively separates self from other to imagine what the other is thinking and feeling. Nor does perspective-taking necessarily lead to sympathy, the usual result of projection. After getting in tune with the other through sensorimotor coupling and figuring out the other person's intentions and beliefs through perspective-taking, the empathizer may decide that she does not approve of the others' goals.[10] This may have been partly what happened when the critics of *Streetcar* empathized with Tandy or Leigh in the role of Blanche. They took her point of view, judged it as crazy and/or disgusting, and rejected Blanche on the basis of what they believed to be her immediate intentions and long-range goals; imaginary transposition is not always accurate.

Other reviewer perspective-takers, however, probably arrived at a more sympathetic understanding of Blanche's situation at the end of Scene Two. Blanche recovers herself after grabbing back the letters, drops her posing and flirting, and admits her vulnerability to Stanley concerning this part of her past. Blanche then tells Stanley he can have access to all of the papers concerning Belle Reve, reacts with joy to the news of Stella's pregnancy, and jokes with her sister at the end of the scene. Spectators who engaged in imaginary transposition would likely have concluded that this was a very different Blanche than they had witnessed so far. When not exhausted, cross, and defensive from traveling or playing up to a man to win some advantage, Blanche could be humorous and pleasant. After Stella returns, Blanche laughingly admits that she was flirting with her husband, hardly a comment she would make if her intention really had been to seduce Stanley. Nor would Blanche seem morbid, overemotional, or self-dramatizing to an empathizing spectator at the end of Scene Two. In short, this brief look at a nearly normal Blanche might prompt some spectators to question their assumption that Blanche was a neurotic nymphomaniac.

Those same spectators, however, would likely type Blanche as a tramp in Scene Three, the Poker Night, for her flirtation with Mitch. Although she is less forward with him than she had been with Stanley in Scene Two, Blanche shows off her body, finds some sexy music on the radio, and plays the role of coy schoolteacher for Mitch. Spectators already alarmed at Blanche's sexuality would also note that she lies about her age and dims the bedroom light to shade her wrinkles. At this point, those who had put together a narrative about "Blanche the Nymphomaniac" could easily revise it to "Blanche the Tramp." "Having concluded that she cannot seduce and marry Stanley," the new story goes, "this loose woman is now after Mitch."

Of course a spectator-empathizer would come to the same conclusion about Blanche's goals, but, having looked at Blanche's situation from her perspective, her intention of marrying Mitch would be more understandable. Imaginatively standing in her shoes, the viewer might be more forgiving about Blanche's social lies and role-playing.

At the end of Scene Three—after Stanley hits his wife, gets dowsed in the shower, memorably bellows, "STELL-LAHHHHH –," and the two of them embrace and hurry to bed—Blanche and Mitch share some conversation and a cigarette. Blanche, still shaken by the night's events, seeks kindness from him and he diffidently provides it. Their little savior-victim drama at the end of the scene, however, pales in comparison with the violence and sexuality of the previous 10 minutes. Williams contrasts Stanley and Stella's fireworks with the diminuendo of their end-of-the-scene duet partly to suggest that Mitch and Blanche's budding but artificial romance stands little chance in the rough and steamy context of the Quarter.

This ending also suggests a new possibility for Blanche, one that will be developed in Scene Four when she attempts to rescue her pregnant sister from her husband. For spectators who already believed that Blanche was a neurotic nymphomaniac and probably a tramp, however, her *"Don't – don't hang back with the brutes –"* (P1: 511) near the end of the scene could only confirm a goal of hers they had likely suspected earlier in the play: Blanche was a home-wrecker. Her fantasies about Shep Huntleigh, her hysterical call to Western Union, and her insults to Stella earlier in the scene had probably also revived the stereotype of the neurotic Southern belle. Scene Four ends with a victory for Stanley, when Stella embraces him fiercely after Blanche's tirade and Stanley grins at Blanche. As the houselights came up after Scene Four, many spectators must have wondered how this loving couple could ever manage to get rid of Stella's crazy, lying, and predatory sister.

## Conclusion

When the theatrical audience broke for intermission in 1947, those spectators who had stepped back from their immersion in the action of

*Streetcar* had several possible Blanches to consider. Collective memories about the South and female vulnerabilities to mental disease, plus several of Blanche's actions, suggested that she might be a decadent neurotic. Recent memories about sexual complications between men and women during the war, belief in the innocence of US veterans, some knowledge of Blanche's past, and her bossiness toward Stella, together with aspects of her sexualized behavior toward two men, led them to construct a story that turned Blanche into a home-wrecker, a nymphomaniac, and probably a tramp. Sympathetic projection and the imaginary transposition of empathy, however, may have painted more positive images of Blanche for some spectators. From this perspective, Blanche might be a victim of circumstances, deserving of pity. Beyond that, perhaps Blanche was trying to gain some control and direction in her life by using flirtation and role-playing to stabilize her situation in Stella's house and gain the romantic interest of a possible suitor. And maybe she really was attempting to save her sister from a violent husband. All spectators newly engaged by *Streetcar* will struggle to read the mind of Blanche in the first four scenes of the play; 1947 audiences apparently faced several competing and contradictory interpretations of Blanche at the first intermission.

Four years later, film audiences would continue to process their mindreading of Blanche without stopping at the conclusion of the Don't-hang-back-with-the-brutes scene. The general evidence from the 1951 reviews suggests that the later scenes of Williams's story, plus differences in the casting of Blanche and the helpfulness of filmic closeup for mindreading, may have tipped the balance in favor of a more sympathetic understanding of Blanche by the end of the movie. In contrast, many theatregoers in 1947 got stuck in stereotyping and negative trait attribution. Why? Daniel Ames, cited earlier on projection and stereotyping, notes that negative information generally overrides positive attributions when people meet others for the first time: "*Negative social intention information weighs heavily in mindreading: within a mindreading strategy, cues signaling negative social intentions may dominate neutral or positive cues; between mindreading strategies, those strategies that signal negative social intentions may dominate*" (2005: 169). At intermission, 1947 spectators were considering a Blanche whose "negative social intentions" far outweighed the positive ones within the strategies of stereotyping and narrative trait attribution. Further, when balanced against other mindreading strategies, these negative results also counted more than the results of projection and empathy.

While Ames is correct about the valence of negative and positive factors in mindreading, he and others would also insist that mindreading usually occurs on the fly; it is rarely the result of social interactors' or spectators' stepping back from a situation that has occurred for many minutes to weigh the many factors that might affect their assessment. It was certainly possible for audience members to withhold a judgment about Blanche until intermission, just as Brooks Atkinson (and later critics in 1951) delayed their understanding of her until the end of the play. But the dynamic processing of social information does not normally encourage such restraint. Mindreading continuously factors in the results of all strategies as they occur, favoring up-to-the-minute conclusions rather than a measured and postponed response. Further, as Ames states, "negative *moral* information is more attention-grabbing [than other kinds] and is weighed more heavily in [immediate] impressions" (2005: 168). In consequence, when the "second act" of *Streetcar* began in 1947, spectators thought they had already figured out Blanche's beliefs and goals and simply ignored information that did not fit this knowledge. Kazan was wrong to expect that audiences would change their minds about Blanche. A negative first impression will usually stick, regardless of subsequent information. There are probably evolutionary reasons for preferring negative results and speedy social processing. For thousands of years, it was better to suspect the motives of a stranger than to turn away and get a stone-age knife in the back.

When the dramatic action stopped at the end of Scene Four in 1947, it was as if a door had shut on an important social situation that spectators had been invited to watch from a distance. Knowing the door would soon open again, most audiences quickly drew their thoughts and judgments together about each of the major characters, including Blanche. No such door closed for the film audience 4 years later. They continued to process the ongoing interactions and gradually altered what had likely been initially negative conclusions about Blanche early in the movie. Significantly, several reviewers in 1951 referred to Blanche as a neurotic, a morally loose woman, and even a nymphomaniac, but these assessments, made after they had witnessed the complete film, carried less weight in their overall understanding of, and sympathy for, Blanche. The delay of 4 years, the change from Tandy to Leigh in the casting of Blanche, and the mindreading possibilities offered by the film certainly helped to cause this shift in attitude and judgment. But so, too, did the interruption after four scenes in 1947 that momentarily stopped the cognitive processing of Blanche for spectators at the opening of *A Streetcar Named Desire*.[11]

## A Broken Romance: Tennessee Williams and America's Mid-Century Theatre Culture
*John S. Bak*

In a 1970 interview with Don Lee Keith, Tennessee Williams said of himself:

> Some folks have said that the plays of Tennessee Williams are *passé*, that their time has come and gone. Perhaps they're right, certainly if they are talking about plays that have to do with verbal values. But the use of the word *passé* does not bother me much anymore, because after all this time, I finally reached a point where I'm more concerned about survival as a person than I am about survival as a playwright. (C: 159)

Anyone even casually familiar with Williams during the 1960s would have easily seen through his insouciance to the criticism mounting against him. Reviewers of plays such as *The Mutilated*, *The Gnädiges Fräulein*, *In the Bar of a Tokyo Hotel*, *Kingdom of Earth*, and *Out Cry* were so cruel at times that no one as sensitive as Williams was to the reception of his work would have escaped their barbs unscathed. The wounds festered for over a decade, left for friends to dress and critics to peck at.

The Broadway "romance" which had once brought Williams and America together during the 40s and 50s—that is, both their "love affair" *and* the "stories" he wrote that fuelled it—was now breaking them apart. Williams had frequently indicated that he was through composing the "symphonies" Broadway critics and audiences demanded from him and was instead concentrating on his "chamber music" (Rader 1985: 257), those quirky, uncharacteristic plays that he considered his personal *Guignol*. Recent scholars like Annette Saddik, Linda Dorff, and Philip Kolin have begun reclaiming these forgotten or *maudites* plays for the Williams canon, and their consensus is that Williams's career did not end with *Iguana* in 1961, but that a second, more experimental career began just after it with the Noh-inspired play, *The Milk Train Doesn't Stop Here Anymore*. While their respective explanations for the reasons behind Williams's fall in the 60s—and subsequent resurrection as a postmodern playwright—are largely incontestable, another more subtle dimension to the "broken romance" might be adduced.

Once a Progressivist nation in puberty, America was by the 60s a postwar predator in full sexual bloom, finding ample avenues of release for its pentup frustrations through various forms of American media. While Hollywood and the National Broadcasting Company were hardly the *Folies Bergères*, their attitudes toward, and exposure of, sexual content were growing more liberal by the year, for which Williams was in part responsible when his plays moved off the stage and onto the big screen. Largely uninhibited by the same Production Code that policed Hollywood, Broadway was a good 10 or 15 years ahead of the 7th art concerning the treatment of adult content.[12] As such, it became simultaneously the nation's secular church on issues of propriety *and* its prurient closet, where boys could hide their *Playboy*s and girls their clandestine love letters. Williams, who had had a role in expunging Broadway of its own self-censoring Wales-Padlock law, was all too willing to play Svengali to the nation's Trilby, as he helped America to explore publically the dark corners of its libido, and the nation, in return, bestowed upon him its highest literary laurels.

By the early 1960s, though, Hollywood had usurped Broadway's dual role as the nation's moral pedagogue *qua* sex peddler, as Barton Palmer and Robert Bray have cogently argued, and Williams found himself out of a theatre job, though his film career logically was thriving.[13] He could no longer compete with the suggestive sex and gratuitous violence offered on the big and, then later, on the small screens and needed to find a new way to reach the nation on the cusp of its sexual revolution. Williams's former representations of sex and violence had to be taken to new levels, lest his theatre would be labeled derivative of the Hollywood that at one time he had led by the hand, if not by the nose.

Williams, of course, had understood this sea change by the late 1950s. He could not have missed or ignored it; his theatre critics made certain of that. True to his voice, but aware that change was inevitable, Williams gambled on a new style and lost his underclothes in the bet. Yet, the reasons for the change had as much to do with the emergence of a new breed of theatre critics as it did with the quality of Williams's plays or with the evolving tastes of American audiences. If Williams had rightly predicted his audience's difficulty in decoding the esotericism of his new theatre despite its familiarity with the black humor of Europe's absurd playwrights, what he had grossly underestimated was the complete indifference or hostility that America's theatre critics would have toward his *avant-garde* work. Many of these critics considered it their obligation to lead Broadway out of its cultural quagmire and settled upon a cocktail of academic erudition and character assassination in their reviews to do so, a bitter hemlock that Williams was forced to ingest. They looked for ways to lure the nation back from the glitz and gild of Tinsel Town to the stolid values of America's Great White Way. And since Williams was as much Mr Hollywood as he was Mr Broadway by the late 1950s (Palmer and Bray 2009: 2–3), perhaps more so, the rejection of one implied the damning of the other. Williams, who for them represented the fulcrum upon which the balance of America's artistic mores tilted toward the fast and easy sensationalism of pop culture, had to be made an example of. And that he was.

One theatre critic in particular, Robert Brustein, singled Williams out as the rotten apple that spoiled the bushel of emerging playwrights on Broadway. His ruthless attacks—as much against Williams's person as against the plays he wrote—ushered in with alacrity the era of ill-feeling, the likes of which Williams had never seen before among New York's elite theatre critics, save the august George Jean Nathan, his avowed nemesis. Williams, who almost always responded to his theatre critics in private or public letters to the editor—whether to defend his play or to thank them for their astute analysis—was largely unprepared to confront let alone combat the likes of Brustein, and the plethora of incomplete and unmailed letters to the *Times* theatre critic that Williams wrote over several years attests to the uncertainties he faced about his work and his legacy in the American literary pantheon.

If Williams's theatre shifted drastically in the 60s, then, it was hardly his fault; it had nowhere else to go. He did not so much force change but was forced to change by the various circumstances connected with mid-century American theatre culture. Williams simply morphed along with his plays, a necessary chrysalis. But if death, drugs, and alcohol fueled his physical decline, his artistic decline was largely engineered for him. Therefore, while the various Williams scholars are correct in their reasoning behind *why* Williams's star fell in the 60s, they are perhaps less precise in discerning *how* that decline manifested itself. This essay explores how Williams's attempt to keep pace with the nation's evolving cultural aesthetics led him down a literary path that critics refused to follow, and while American theatre culture was itself arriving at a fork in the road, the direction it chose to take was incompatible with Williams's vision of the postwar American stage.

## "Stupidity is no longer profitable": Williams and his Critics, 1937–1948

In her book *The Politics of Reputation*, Annette Saddik argues that Williams's tarnished image as America's preeminent playwright from

1963 onward was largely orchestrated by the New York theatre critics. In establishing her thesis, Saddik draws on the distinction theatre critic John Gassner makes in his 1954 collection of essays *The Theatre in Our Times* between the theatre *reviewer* and the theatre *critic* (23). While the former generally reports on a play's audience appeal, the latter analyzes that play's intellectual merits in an attempt to buttress the theatrical dimension of America's world-class letters. Though Gassner maintains that theatre critics had no interest in determining the success or failure of the play, they did precisely that. To support her thesis, Saddik reproduces excerpts from the many reviewers' and critics' columns written about Williams's theatre over the years, but because her study was completed before the publication of Williams's letters, she did not include the responses Williams wrote to these critics, which are revealing in the sense that they demonstrate how Williams was not going to sit idly by and watch his reputation getting destroyed.

Whether a play of his received glowing or glaring reviews, Williams often took the time to reply to his supporters or detractors. One supporter, *New York Times* theatre critic J. Brooks Atkinson, received the majority of these letters, not just because his criticism was generally laudable but also because Williams found in Atkinson a soul-mate for America's experiment in the plastic theatre: "Why are you so good to me? I certainly don't deserve it, although I do try" (L2: 533). At the end of one of his letters to the editors of the *Chicago Herald-American*, Williams praised Atkinson for believing that theatre has "another purpose than entertainment and profit": "If theater itself is important, the criticism of it is equally so. For it is the attitude of the critics that determines the direction of change in theater. And change is imminent" (L1: 547; cf. L2: 18). Whereas many critics failed to see the plastic nature of *A Streetcar Named Desire* and *Summer and Smoke*, Atkinson did not:

> At last a criticism which connects directly with the essence of what I thought was the play– . . . . I wanted to show that people are not definable in such terms [i.e., alcoholic or nymphomaniac] but are things of multiple facets and all but endless complexity

that they do not fit "any convenient label" and are seldom more than partially visible even to those who live just on the other side of "the portieres". (L2: 137; cf. 207–8)

With his other critics, the exchanges were less cordial, but they always remained courteous. Williams was a Southerner after all, and even in St Louis he had learned that people may agree to disagree but did so with respect. In the 1930s, for example, when Williams began his theatre career with the Mummers in St Louis, his plays were reviewed by local theatre critics who, though curt at times with his plays, were not intentionally hostile to the playwright himself. Once Williams had demonstrated to his theatre reviewers and critics that he was a talent to contend with, their expectations grew more demanding. When he followed *Candles to the Sun* a little less than a year later with *Fugitive Kind*, Williams soon learned that theatre critics could be as intolerant as university professors. Colvin McPherson felt that Williams was "merely loafing around" with very little "to say" in this rather "weak" play, and Reed Hynds, who thought the play was a "step forward" for Williams, found it "confused" and "inconclusive" (17). As he would later do with Atkinson, Williams wrote McPherson about his review of *Fugitive Kind*, which was "temporarily painful" but which proved a "benefit" in "the long run": "I don't want you to think I only thank people for favorable reviews so I am writing to say I appreciate your sincere and direct comments upon my new play" (L1: 118). Williams added that he felt any criticism which would help the playwright achieve artistic truth was welcome, "if he recognizes his failures and has an ideal of perfection" (L1: 118). It was a stock response he would send to his critics well into the late 50s.

The 40s saw Williams putting that credo to the test, and the first challenge would be one of the hardest for Williams to digest. Again, though, while the play *Battle of Angels* was lathered in the press, Williams himself was not. One anonymous reviewer for the *Boston Post* even found the play to be the product of the "imaginative brain of a genius" ("Miriam Hopkins at Wilbur" 1940: 8). If another anonymous reviewer mentioned that the play was deemed "putrid", there were enough parties involved to share the blame, including the

Theatre Guild which produced it and the Wilbur Theatre owners who allowed it to be staged. As Claudia Wilsch Case argues:

> If the audience was horrified, the Boston reviewers were not pleased with *Battle of Angels* either. . . . The reviewer for the *Boston Transcript* called *Battle of Angels*, "a stumbling pointless affair" ("Miriam Hopkins Returns"), and the *Boston Globe*'s critic referred to it as an "embarrassment" for the actors who appeared in it ("Plays Here"). Although the play's "symbolic implications" were lost on most reviewers, a couple of critics recognized Williams's raw genius. "Given a few years in the theatre," Elinor Hughes noted in the *Boston Herald*, "and Tennessee Williams should add craftsmanship to imagination and produce important work." In a similar fashion, Elliot Norton commented in the *Boston Post*, "If he can learn to walk with the theatre's craftsmen, he may find himself riding the clouds with the theatre's dramatists. His talent is most interesting." (2006: 63)

From the *Clarksdale Register*, which bemoaned the "dirt" that Williams had written (8 January 1941), to the *Boston Globe*, which accused Williams of having given "the audience the sensation of having been dunked in mire" (31 December 1940), in the tally of things it was the play that had caused the stir. Williams wore such criticism proudly, being the bohemian activist that he was, for as direct as the reviews were, they were proof that he was shaking up America's bourgeois theatre culture. George Jean Nathan of course hated the play and chastised the Guild in his *Esquire* review (April 1943) for turning down Sean O'Casey to produce *Battle of Angels*, which solicited this response from Williams in his notebook: "Nathan's horrible comment in Esquire has been unreasonably depressing—the play which seemed the only way out is a fading promise and there is really no good omen" (N: 361). That good omen would arrive 4 years later in the form of *The Glass Menagerie*.

Claudia Cassidy and Ashton Stevens are credited with having kept *The Glass Menagerie* on stage long enough for the play to work its magic. Famous now is Cassidy's comment: "If it is your play, as it is mine, it reaches out tentacles, first tentative, then gripping, and you are caught in its spell" (1944: 11). Stevens also championed the play in his reviews for the *Chicago Herald-American*. In February 1945, Williams wrote the editors of the paper, thanking them for being part of the "little band of drama critics whose tenets of faith in a certain type of theater . . . have been largely responsible for holding that misshapen thing", but voicing his concerns over the Broadway bean-counters who, "when they swallowed the theatre they also swallowed these critics—this little band of a dozen or so—here and there in America, who did not regard the theater as a business or a slot-machine or a concession at a carnival or a race-horse" (L1: 546). Theatre producers, who declared themselves "custodians of an art which to me is religion", had no business "gobbling up the theater" (L1: 547).

Despite the critical and commercial success of *The Glass Menagerie*, Williams saw the playwriting clearly on the wall: Odets's *Night Music* (1940) and Saroyan's *Love's Own Sweet Song* (1940) were also plays for the plastic theatre, but they were never allowed to flourish. Williams had read Saroyan's plea to the *New York World-Telegram* to bring new and young playwrights "out of obscurity" and "to get them to appear as little damaged and compromised by the disorder in the theatrical world as possible" (L1: 235). It was his opposition to mixing money and the arts that prompted Saroyan to turn down the Pulitzer Prize for *The Time of Your Life* (1939). Williams wrote Saroyan in November 1941, praising him for his values. Williams admitted that he had had the luck (e.g. the benefit of various grants) to write what he wanted instead of what was desired by producers: "Well, I can't do the second—and my suitcase is getting terribly crowded" with material that is "[i]nteresting but not suitable" (no pun intended, alas):

> Undoubtedly our artistic climate is going to change through the world situation. People are going to realize to their amazement that stupidity is no longer profitable, even the little people are going to learn (bitterly) the necessity of thinking. . . . People

will want to read, see, feel the living truth and they will revolt against the sing-song Mother Goose book of lies that are being fed them. (L1: 359)

Despite echoing Saroyan repeatedly throughout his own life about the ills of Broadway's moneyed interests, Williams never found it necessary to turn down an award, or the money that came with it.

Williams was, of course, correct in his assessment, as the critical and commercial success of *The Glass Menagerie* and *A Streetcar Named Desire* after it—both plays for his plastic theatre—would bear out. While Broadway never let go of its art for profit's sake credo, its audience and critics *did* appreciate both plays' delicate handling of mature material. Where Williams first erred, however, was in his believing that audiences and critics would remain faithful to his "living truth" theatre throughout the 50s and into the 60s. As irony would have, American theatre culture evolved and critics began accusing him of having resorted to writing an anti-intellectual "Mother Goose book of lies."

When *The Glass Menagerie* did make it to the Playhouse Theatre on Broadway the following spring, Louis Kronenberger found it "interesting and sometimes absorbing theater" but regretted that the play had "a great deal wrong with it" (1945: 16). Joseph Wood Krutch announced later:

After the final curtain had descended, the unfamiliar cry of "Author – Author –" rang through the auditorium, and next morning the reviewers staged what is commonly called a dance in the streets. Undoubtedly some of this enthusiasm was for the acting and the production, especially for the performance of Laurette Taylor, who got everything that was to be had from the character of the pitiful and terrible old woman who is the central figure. But undoubtedly the enthusiasm was also and in almost equal measure for the playwright, a young man named Tennessee Williams previously known chiefly to prize committees and to the editors of avant-garde magazines. (1945: 424)

Among the New York critics, only George Jean Nathan openly had it out for Williams (N: 742–3). His review for the *New York Journal-American* claimed that the "wooden" role of Tom Wingfield was entirely "rewritten" by Dowling in order to add "some living plausibility" to the play. Whatever praise Nathan could muster, he attributed to the play's production, which he said camouflaged its faulty structure. Nathan concluded that *Menagerie* was "a freakish experiment and replete with such delicatessen as moving picture titles of silent drama days thrown intermittently on the scenery", that it was "metamorphosed under Dowling's guidance into the unaffected and warming simplicity that it should have had in the first place", and that it was "[d]eficient in any touches of humor" (C: 14–15). In an essay written on 9 April 1945, "A Reply to Mr. Nathan", Williams laid out most of his complaints against the embittered critic. The response, which Williams wisely chose not to publish so early in his career, defends, among other things, his acceptance of removing the use of the play's screen device, which greatly altered its "sculptural" design:

> Truth is something that I have set up as my single standard, both as a writer and as an individual—this may sound like a very pompous statement and you may think me a very pompous young man for saying it—but I do say it with all earnestness, and will repeat it as often as I am given occasion such as the present. (NSE: 193)

In spite of its defense, the tone of the essay nonetheless remains respectful.

Williams *did* send letters to other drama critics about their reviews, such as Burton Rascoe of the *New York World-Telegram*, who published a critical piece that was rather harsh on the printed editions of Williams's plays. As Williams wrote on 11 August 1945:

> I was very agreeably surprised when I returned to town this week to discover these articles, which I read for the first time, were not attacks at all but *really quite fair and reasonable*

and in some respects *more charitable* than I myself would be inclined to speak of them. You have a command of irony and a wit that could make the object squirm, as Mr. Nathan has frequently done, but there is a distinct difference in that your motives are obviously more humanitarian. You don't feel that an effective attack is necessarily a savage one. (L2: 16, emphasis added)

Williams then repeated his diatribe against "the commercial theatre": "When you are for something you have to make negative comments on whatever it is you would like to see revised or improved on" (L2: 17). Again, if Rascoe had criticized anything in his column, it was the faulty structure of *The Glass Menagerie* and not the playwright himself, and for that, Williams admired the critic.

Williams would later cross pens with Eric Bentley, drama critic for *Harper's Magazine*, and later, *The New Republic*, over questions concerning his artistic "truth" in *Streetcar*. In a July 1948 letter, Williams wrote to Bentley, "Yours is the kind of criticism that the theatre desperately needs and which is supplied by few others. However, that is all the more reason why certain questionable attitudes of yours should be questioned" (L2: 203). Williams did not write his critics in order to strike up friendships that he knew would influence their reviews of his plays (Kenneth Tynan was living proof of that later in the decade). He wrote them to clarify the reasons behind the ambiguity in his plays, and he always stood his ground. Later, when Bentley wrote in his book *The Dramatic Event* (1954) that Kazan had "virtually co-authored" *Streetcar* (L2: 560), Williams even threatened legal action. A critic like Bentley was for Williams an ass because "it doesn't seem that Mr. Bentley's aim is to get to the truth" (L2: 560). As Devlin and Tischler note, after his play *Truckline Café* (1946) received a "savage attack", Maxwell Anderson protested in the *New York Times* about the "enormous increase in the reviewers' power" and their virtual "censorship over the theatre" (L2: 209). Williams's earlier predictions about the rise of the omnipotent theatre critic were coming true.

## "A radical departure": Williams and his Critics, 1951–1958

Williams could not entirely dismiss the wave of negative criticism that his mid-century plays received because he himself often doubted them. He felt that he was repeating himself, as the critics had said, and indeed wanted to find new material that would display the expanse of his artistic talents and intelligence. As he wrote in an unmailed letter to Brooks Atkinson in June 1949: "The trouble is that you can't make any real philosophical progress in a couple of years. The scope of understanding enlarges quite slowly, if it enlarges at all, and the scope of interest seems to wait upon understanding. In the meantime there is only continued observation, and variations on what you've already observed" (L2: 258–9). Yet, a playwright without a play on Broadway is a forgotten playwright, and Williams knew that the best he could do was stay true to his plastic theatre and find new human issues to explore. He admitted to Atkinson in 1951 that he thought *The Rose Tattoo* was such "a radical departure" (L2: 369). Atkinson's thoughtful review in the *New York Times* on 5 February (again, not "positive" but intelligent in its criticism), along with those in "The News and The Trib," gave him the courage "to go on working for the theatre" (L2: 369).

Because Williams was no longer a newcomer in the 50s, the intensity of his relationship with the theatre critics grew proportionally with their expectations of his work. He had already won all the major theatre awards and had thus proven his mettle, but Williams's armor was still thin, and the more he found his work under attack, the more he turned to the bottle (prescription and otherwise) for comfort.[14] As expected, the general tenor of the reviews and critiques was that Williams was not reaching the heights he had achieved with *Menagerie* and *Streetcar*. But a new element had entered into theatre criticism, which had less to do with evaluating the plays themselves and more to do with preserving the critic's political image during an age rife with false accusations. Referring to the fervent antiliberal direction that America was then taking, which climaxed with the House Committee on Un-American Activities hearings, Williams admitted to

Atkinson in May 1952 that "[t]hese times must be difficult for a critic as they are for a writer" (L2: 425). Instead of returning to the safety of the closet as William Inge had done in his theatre, William thumbed his nose at the American right with the production of a left-leaning homophiliac play, *Camino Real*.

Atkinson remained upbeat about *Camino Real* in his review, although he was the rare nightingale among the cacophony of crows. And Williams typically thanked him for his "discerning and sympathetic notices" but needed to clarify one major point which would preoccupy him for the rest of the decade: "I can't believe that you really think I have painted the world in blacker colors than it now wears, or that it is melancholia, psychopathic of me, to see it in those shades" (L2: 462). Williams was hurt, and he thought his "pride" should have kept a "stoic silence about my hurt", but "I don't think pride should prevail in my relations with you, the one who has most bravely, consistently stood by me in the past and for whom I have such grateful affection, in whom I feel such trust, and from whom I have no secrets as imperfect artist and person" (L2: 462).

*Camino Real* provided one of the tectonic plate shifts in American theatre culture, for unlike *The Crucible* by Arthur Miller, which also denounced McCarthyism, the play educed an anti-intellectualism in Williams, a political naiveté, that was not apparent in his previous plays. He wrote Walter Kerr about his "cynical" review of the play (*New York Herald Tribune*, 29 March 1953) to "get a few things off my chest in reply", which included convincing Kerr of the play's honest representation of the American "night-mare" at the time:

> Mr. Kerr, I believe in your honesty! I believe you said what you honestly think and feel about this play, but I don't think you fulfilled your entire obligation as a critic. . . .
>
> If I had not been deluged, literally, with letters and wires expressing outrage over the play's critical reception, far more than for all my other plays put together . . . I wouldn't have the nerve to question your verdict. But silence is only golden when there is nothing to say and I still think I have a great deal to say no matter how badly I say it. (L2: 463, 464)

Williams insisted that, loyal to his earlier precepts, this play was not written to make money but to send a message and to be true to its artistic mission. Famous now is Kerr's reply: "What terrifies me about 'Camino Real' is not what you want to say but the direction in which you, as an artist, are moving. You're heading toward the cerebral; don't do it. What makes you an artist of the first rank is your intuitive gift for penetrating reality, without junking reality in the process" (N: 565).

A few days later, Williams commiserated with Brooks Atkinson "over the play's treatment by critics", claiming that there was a lot of "grotesque comedy in this work," of the type he would exploit more fully in the 60s, and that its dominant trait was

> traceable to the spirit of the American comic-strip and the animated cartoons, where the most outrageous absurdities give the greatest delight. . . . I thought that this art-form softened up my American audiences for the manifest illogicalities of Camino! (More's the pity!) The Messrs. Chapman and Kerr—(I stopped reading the notices after those came out—except for Hawkins which a true friend read over the phone at 3 A.M. when a combination of nembutal and seconal still hadn't worked)—were obviously not willing to be budged one centimeter from the strictest of literal approaches . . . toward something that literally got down on its knees and begged for imaginative participation. (L2: 469)

All of his writing is to express "a feeling of outrage against hypocrisy and brutishness" and "when it stops being about those things it will be finished. (Me, too)" (L2: 470).

A few months later, after the initial shock of the reviews for *Camino Real* had worn off, Williams once again confided in Atkinson: "Book-burning and banning and so forth is having a fearful ascendancy these days, and that's why I think a single honest and courageously outspoken critic is more important to us right now than writers are, since the latter cannot function at all without the support of the first" (L2: 486–7). He concluded his letter with a quip that pretty much summed up the widening gap between Broadway's playwrights and their critics: "Well, that's about all, right now—except for a funny remark that George Kaufmann made on the ship coming over about Eric Bentley's new book. He said the full title is 'In Search Of A Theatre, and God Help It If I find One –'" (L2: 488).

It was only logical that Williams would turn next to the world of mendacity in *Cat on a Hot Tin Roof*, for he found Broadway seething with it. George Jean Nathan, expectantly, attacked Williams directly in his review of the play, saying that its characters "are presided over by an interlocutor in the person of Williams whose too many pre-performance drinks have gone to his head" (*New York Journal American*, 5 April 1953). Walter Kerr also turned on the playwright himself by hinting that Brick's homosexual "mystery" was really Williams's. Williams obviously thought it useless to respond to Nathan, but he did write to Kerr about his complaint of the play's "evasion" of the truth surrounding Brick's alcoholism and thanked even him for his "keen intelligence" (L2: 570). Williams later published a more thorough rejoinder to Kerr's review, insisting upon Brick's epistemic dilemma in understanding for himself what his alcoholism entailed. Again, though more heated than their previous exchanges, the debate nonetheless centered on character, plot, and theme and not directly on the writer's own homosexuality.

Equally predictable was Atkinson's support, with Williams writing to him immediately after opening night on 24 March 1955 to thank him for his "lovely notice":

> I can't explain to you or myself or anybody why the reception of this play meant so damnably much to me, why I was so disgustingly craven about it, why the wait for the morning notices to come out was the most unendurable interval of my life. Of course it's always been like that, every time since it started with that little theatre in Saint Louis in 1938, but it gets worse instead of better, and before I go through it again, I've got to sit down with myself long and privately and try to figure out what makes it and what I can do about it besides not writing more plays. (L2: 569)

As the years passed, Atkinson, like Kerr before him, found it more and more difficult to maintain the same level of exuberance he had expressed in earlier reviews. When *Orpheus Descending* was next in line to the slaughter, Atkinson still managed to support Williams in spite of the hostilities leveled against the playwright: "I believe I've always written you a letter of thanks for an appreciative review after openings of my plays," Williams wrote him on 24 March 1957, "and I see no reason to discontinue the practice on this occasion even though the appreciation, on this occasion, was more qualified than usual. It seems to me that several of the critics failed to regard the play in its true light, as a dramatic poem" (L2: 644). "Naturally," he added, "I don't know for sure if I am right or the critics are right" about the play being a poem instead of a melodrama, as it was deemed. "I've always felt a silly embarrassment about having social contact with theatre critics because I feared it might seem like an attempt to disarm them in their attitude about my work" (L2: 644). He wanted to meet with Atkinson to talk privately about his work, to "take the kid gloves off and put the verbal boxing gloves on with me" and "I think I can take it" (L2: 644).

Nearly two decades of theatre criticism culminated with the reviews of *Orpheus Descending*, and despite the blows he had withstood over the years, Williams emerged near the end of the 50s still very much in command of Broadway and its theatre critics. He would confirm that place with *Suddenly Last Summer*, which to his surprise was admired by the majority of the critics. Even Kerr chimed in with Atkinson this time, praising it as "a serious and accomplished work" (1958: 16). It would be his last triumph of the decade, however, and the penultimate one of his career. As he prepared *Sweet Bird of Youth* for the following season, the mid-century sea change was already in motion.

What all of these early letters that Williams wrote to his reviewers/critics evince, then, is an overwhelmingly respectful rapport between playwright and critic in the manner in which they both defended their interpretations of a given play. If Williams himself were ever criticized, it was generally for his artistic limits in delivering to the audience the message intended in the play. As the decade progressed and the nation grew frightfully more conservative compared to the likes of Williams, his plays rang less true with the critics. Eventually, the audiences, too, would find them false, but for the exact opposite reason as his critics: once at the vanguard of American culture, the plays now seemed stale, passé. As Saddik points out in discussing Clurman's collection of his theatre reviews, *Lies Like Truth*, "the reviewers" rejection of disturbing aspects of Williams' early work which Clurman brings out . . . was rooted in the fundamental expectations of an established theatre criticism which reflected American political values and assumptions of the 1950s and early 1960s" (142). With audiences tugging him in one direction and theatre critics in another, Williams did not know in which direction to turn. So he went off by himself instead.

## "A butterfly to a cannon": Williams and his Critics, 1959 and Beyond

Williams's early experiences with theatre reviewers and critics demonstrate how ill-prepared he was for the likes of the critics of the 60s and 70s. Annette Saddik argues that American theatre reviewers and audiences, at first baffled by the likes of a Samuel Beckett or Harold Pinter, gradually came to accept the European imports, but the "same courtesy was never given to Williams" (147). As she concludes, "His later reputation, therefore, tells us more about the critical biases in the popular and academic press in this country than about Williams' work per se" (150). If Williams's habit of responding to his reviewers and critics in the previous decade had helped him overcome his personal doubts about being the nation's most important playwright, now, in the spring of 1959, the year that would announce his future rupture with Broadway, that resolve was dissipating. The "Prayer in Rehearsal" that he wrote for himself during *Sweet Bird of Youth*'s tryouts in Philadelphia attests to the playwright's fragility, and, despite the play's modest commercial success, the chorus of critical attacks published in the various papers and magazines presaged the beginning of the end. One of *Sweet Bird*'s harshest critics was Robert Brustein, a relative newcomer to the New York theatre scene. Brustein, whose scathing review of the play as "corn-ball" and its preopening piece in the *New York Times* as "embarrassingly explicit," haunted Williams for several years and set the playwright on a course incompatible with New York's theatre critics.

In his June 1959 review for *Encounter* titled "Sweet Bird of Success," Brustein charged Williams with writing dishonestly by hiding his interest in incest:

> the play is interesting primarily if you are interested in its author. As dramatic art, it is disturbingly bad—aimless, dishonest, and crudely melodramatic—in a way that Williams's writing has not been bad since his early play, *Battle of Angels*. But if the latter failed because its author did not sufficiently understand his characters, *Sweet Bird of Youth* suffers both from his ignorance of, and obsession with, himself. (59)

Pretty harsh words for a junior theatre reviewer fresh out of graduate school. Brustein's comments here, and in another review a few weeks later, had cut Williams so deeply that it forced him into a mode of self-reflection more profound than even Dr Lawrence Kubie had managed during their psychoanalytical sessions together 2 years earlier.

If you were looking to pick a fight with Williams, all you had to do was call him a liar. George Jean Nathan did it back in 1945. In the case of Brustein over a decade later, the charge of dishonest writing sparked a flurry of attempted responses that Williams had this time planned to publish in the *New York Times*. Some are short and poignant addresses to Brustein, appropriately called ["Reply to Professor Brustein"]; others are longer musings on American theatre culture in general, and Williams's in particular. They carried many titles, from "Some Philosophical Shop Talk" to "These Scattered Idioms," two titles that he would alternately use for the memoirs he was currently drafting.

The unpublished fragment pages directed specifically at Brustein number in the dozens. None is polished; most are rambling; some even incoherent. "As I write this," Williams notes in one, "I know the immodesty of it, but I have just completed a hard and excited day's work on my next public address to you, and my nerves are not in a state in which I can talk to you with that control out of which an air of modesty comes. If I ~~mailed~~ dispatched this piece right now, I would die of shame tomorrow" [3].[15] Yet in those passages of lucidity, Williams offers some of his best criticism of contemporary Broadway and its critics.

In one fragment, Williams writes, "Dear Professor Burstein [*sic*]: I read your piece in 'Encounter' with understanding and appreciation of some valid points made, but I would like to discuss with you the charge of 'dishonesty' that you make against me" [19]. Williams goes on to describe how explicit theatre is his contribution to the dramatic arts in America, which needed to be confronted with the unpleasant truths that fill the silence between people. His theatre, he maintains, opened up the nation's dialogue on topics heretofore taboo: mental illness, rape, and hypersexuality.

In another draft entitled "Embarrassingly Explicit", Williams adds that his theatre even functioned as the nation's psychotherapist, where "personal therapy", which is all creative art for Williams, "is only successful if it is therapeutic to <u>others</u>, and in the Broadway theatre the others must be many" [2]. All creative writing is a form of psychotherapy that should produce a catharsis, both in the playwright and in his audience: "I cannot be cured of explicitness in my plays or my efforts at prose. You see, I feel with all my heart that writing must not be separated from the total truth of the writer's self, and I am by nature explicit" [1]. Williams's plays grew overly self-conscious in the 60s, and just as Williams had left Kubie's couch when he grew tired of the therapy, American audiences began leaving Williams's theatre when they felt that they had seen it all before.

In another essay fragment that begins ["The last time I wrote . . ."], Williams writes:

My theory about creative art is that it must, or should be, as close to your intensely personal experience as possible and even if you should betray that dreadful and something disgusting thing, an excessive concern with yourself, you must go for broke with the hope that there are people enough, with the same inclination or disease, for your work to be understood and partly excused by a majority of them. [1]

He continues in this draft to explain how art in general cannot be anything but personal and about how a writer's confrontation with life's frightening experiences is an expression of that art.

Another aspect of Brustein's attack was that Williams's theatre was closing doors, rather than opening them, to advances in American drama. There were "[V]iable stage works" being suppressed, he claimed, in order to leave room for Williams on Broadway. He and other "cornball" playwrights like William Inge were, in effect, holding court on the American stage and blocking the way for first-class novelists to arrive on stage. As Williams replied, "Our early works opened some doors but our later work hasn't turned those doors into walls against those pointed to come after us" [8].

In each of these draft fragments, Williams attempts to justify his vision of the dramatic arts in America at mid-century They also provided Williams with the opportunity to reflect personally on his own art after 20 years in the theatre, and what he discovered about himself, and about his critics and audiences, confirmed that he and the American public had entered a formal period of separation, or "adjustment"—the title of the play he was writing at that time—that climaxed a few years later in a full divorce. There was, of course, a moment of reconciliation—*The Night of the Iguana* in 1961—but even there Brustein led the charge against Williams in *The New Republic*, calling it "a little nocturnal mood music for muted strings" which is "very short on plot, pattern or theme" and "tired, unadventurous and self-derivative" (1962: 20). Williams responded in an open letter intended for the *Times's* readers about the nature of contemporary American theatre and the relationship between its "intellectual" playwrights and its "pedantic" critics.

It was not just the content of Brustein's review which bothered Williams, however. It was also the tone. If Williams's critics up till now did not always like his plays, there was at least a sense of decorum among them (save Nathan) in how they framed their objections. As Williams said elsewhere to Brustein and the other "intellectuals" of these "New Critics", "Sound criticism stops where malice begins . . ." [4]. For critics like Brustein, Williams's plays were not intellectual enough to provide nourishing food for thought, and the malice toward Williams would not only continue throughout the 60s, but would also reach fever pitch. Richard Gilman's *Commonweal* article, "Mistuh Williams, He Dead," Stefan Kanfer's reference to Williams as an "infantile" "White Dwarf," or *Time* magazine's comment that *In the Bar of a Tokyo Hotel* "seems more deserving of a coroner's report than a review" (75) were more the standard than the exception of criticism leveled against Williams by the decade's close.

There was something new about academic critics like Brustein that Williams was not prepared for. Brustein was not "old school," that gentleman-critic to whom Williams had been accustomed for the last twenty-some years. He did not like Nathan, but he at least respected the venerable theatre critic. He had to after all. Nathan was not going anywhere, and he did wield influence over those who attended Williams's plays. For Williams, Brustein was the "new hatchet-man for the soi-disant 'New Critics,' the ones that assail us cornball playwrights in the literary and academic quarterlies with a ferocity that matches the 'rumbles' between the 'The Assassins' and the 'The Sinners' over the contested turfs of upper West-side Manhattan" [4].

This new theatre criticism emerged from what Williams denigrated as the "Groves of Academe," theatre reviewer as scholar-critic whose knowledge of American drama came out of learned books and not out of years of exposure to Broadway. Williams experienced firsthand postwar theatre criticism in America's migration from newspapers like the *New York Times* to magazines like *Time, Harper's,* or *The New Yorker,* to finally academic journals like the *Tulane Drama Review* (Saddik 1999: 23–4). Commercial publishers were also publishing nonfiction books of theatre criticism like Bentley's *The Dramatic Event* (1954) or Brustein's *The Theatre of Revolt: An Approach to Modern Drama* (1964).

On the other side of the Broadway aisle, across from the "soi-disant 'New Critics'" sat the more traditional reviewers, those who clung to the schmaltz of TV's *I Love Lucy.* Their criticism against Williams also began mounting in the late 50s, but it was fuelled by what the reviewers considered as affronts to the nation's mores more than bouts of its anti-intellectualism. If they felt that Williams was out of touch with American audiences, it was not because his plays lacked intellectual punch but because those punches were always landing below the belt. These reviewers no longer had the stomach for the kind of theatre violence with which Williams had established his name. The public that these critics spoke for desired light comedies or moral American melodramas about family issues, such as those programs that filled the time slots on prime-time television. Williams had appeased them with *Cat on a Hot Tin Roof* to a certain extent, but since 1955 he had veered sharply off course: *Baby Doll*, *Suddenly Last Summer*, and *Sweet Bird of Youth*. Marya Mannes wrote in her 1960 essay "Plea for Fairer Ladies" that recent Broadway plays like his were "snake pits" worthy only of a "psychiatrist or a nurse in a mental institution [who] would have spent several hours of so many nights in the company of addicts, perverts, sadists, hysterics, bums, delinquents and others afflicted in mind and body" (16).[16] Williams again felt the need to defend himself and the American theatre in general, which he did in his *New York Times* essay "Tennessee Williams Presents His POV" (1960). In the various drafts to this essay, one essay fragment was titled "The Good Men and the Bad Men" (c. 1960), which bore the crossed-out subtitle, "Get The Corpse out of the 'Copter." In it, Williams opines on the fact that while violence is allowed to dominate American cinemas and pervade the nation's television screens, it is reviled on the Broadway stage.

Williams's view was that popular culture, fuelled by postwar jingoism, was responsible for generating a binary violent impulse in American mores in the 50s that pit the good "white hat" guys against the bad "black hat" guys, and that this epistemological banality was keeping audiences from recognizing that violence in his plays was not diametrically opposed. In short, TV Nation was killing Theatre Nation by proscribing certain modes of acceptable social interaction and by anesthetizing the public to real forms of human tragedy. As the nation thickened its skin to violent projections, Williams felt forced to up the stakes in his plays. But where could Williams logically go, having already dramatized rape, castration, and murder? Williams had only two viable directions: the absurd, such as the *Guignol* violence of *The Gnädiges Fräulein*, or the surreal, such as the tragedy-within-the-tragedy of *Out Cry*.

A few years earlier in the essay "The World I Live In" (1957), Williams wrote that he did not "believe in villains or heroes—only right and wrong ways that individuals have taken, not by choice but by necessity" (NSE: 85). His plays in the 60s were in fact pastiches of his earlier works, and instead of Blanche getting raped, the Fräulein gets her eyes pecked out by a giant grotesque bird. Instead of Chance getting castrated, Felice gets lost in a never-ending play about suicide. With a country polarizing its Cold War beliefs between right and wrong in ways it had not done before World War II, Williams now firmly believed

> that evil is not identifiable with places or beings in them, but a thing, a disease, afflicting these beings and places, with nothing to show that xxxxxxxx it was ever deliberately and consciously chosen. And finally, this: I don't buy the cynical comment, made by someone somewhere, that God, in whom I believe, is on the side of the heaviest artillery. I believe as much as I am able that He prefers a butterfly to a cannon. ("Good Men" [5])

Williams understood that it was "risky" for him to show the nation that its pop culture was persuading it "to believe that the human race is really and truly divided between cops and robbers, ranchers and cattle-rustlers: the good and the bad":

> My message is that I don't believe there is any such sharp definition, certainly none shape enough to excuse the bang-bang and the rat-a-tat-tat, and the upliftingly, musical, and luminous finale of a movie or TV drama in which there has been great carnage with the good men walking off, smiling, or kissing to kiss their sweethearts. ("Good Men" [1])

As for the good men of the war films so pervasive in American cinemas or the cowboy on Saturday afternoon TV, Williams knew that they were "good men" because "they were our men": "I say that I may be making this admission at some risk of popular reputation because our popular culture has been ~~given~~ giving us the "hard sell" on something which is basically erroneous: namely, the idea of original sin as applicable to some and not to others" ("Good Men" [2]). Williams voiced a similar opinion to Edward R. Murrow in May 1960 on his *Small World* telecast for the Columbia Broadcasting System, arguing his case for "the light and the shadow" (C:77) sides to human nature and how emotional violence is the necessary obstacle to love.

Williams's discussion of violence in American culture and how he saw all couples, gay and straight alike, working through their relational problems was no doubt inspired by his own troubled life with Frank Merlo. But he also tried to deconstruct America's polarized vision of its war heroes by moving them from the battlefield and into the bedroom. *Period of Adjustment* attempted to recast Hollywood's matinee culture within a framework of serious comedy. Two Korean War veterans demonstrate that goodness is relative and that heroism is achieved more in the mundane domestic struggles to keep a marriage alive. In a fragment to the play's preopening piece "Prelude to a Comedy" (1960) that begins "and in this way we fight the bang-bang" (c. 1960), Williams writes:

> In my new play about human adjustments, and the enormous difficulties of them, the misunderstandings xxxxxxxx, the pride and the wounds of pride, the aggressions and counter aggressions, it may be that I was all the time trying, without knowing I was, to state my total disbelief in and rejection of the black-and-white differences among individuals, nations, and hemispheres on this planet, my conviction that the world is passing through a period of adjustment like the two young married couples in my play, and that the only hope lies in our finding patience, insight and tolerance, (those things that are the trinity of wisdom,) to stop thinking in terms of "My daddy can beat your daddy," the yells of little boys, the bang-bang and the rat-a-tat-tat or last big boom of the "good men" destroying the "bad men," but in the infinitely difficult but infinitely necessary [texts breaks off here]. [3]

In "Some Philosophical Shop Talk, or An Inventory of a Remarkable Market," another draft to the essay "Prelude to a Comedy," Williams explains how he believed, perhaps naively so, that "Broadway society" were not "cultural cannibals" but "terrifically knowing," knowing when a scene is being overacted to counter its lack of poetry or a set is "lovely to look at but awful to play on," discerning "a gag line from one that is honestly amusing," and remaining "color-blind to purple patches in a sometimes pretentious script" [5]. He thought they would see that his characters were not derivative of pop culture icons but rather their pastiches. He at least thought that his critics, "New" and old alike, would have recognized this fact about his 60s' plays. Neither the audience nor the critics, however, could see that Williams's drama had evolved.

Once television broke the taboos against portraying gratuitous violence and the breakdown of social values, there was no need to see it anymore on stage, at least not realistically. His 60s' plays instead offer his unrealistic vision of violence in America, which was surely more metaphysical than cinematic or even naturalistic. Williams's theatre had thus fallen between the cracks of the "intellectual" and "moralizing" theatre critics in America who greatly influenced the success or failure of any play. And as the 60s wore on, and Williams's dependency and depression pushed his theatre into more personal and absurdly violent directions, the reviewers lost interest and the critics lost patience.

## "Assassins, before, now, and after": Conclusion

Williams's relation with American audiences and theatre critics throughout his life was tenuous at best. If he had helped see the nation through its prewar sexual adolescence, he could no longer speak to it as a fully sexed adult, and audiences and critics no longer found his work of interest or of national value. While his tantalizing stories rang true to modernist Americans in the 40s and 50s, anything he seemed to offer their postmodern sons and daughters in the 60s and 70s seemed, on the one hand, a hackneyed repetition of his earlier plays or, on the other, an overly and overtly personal exegesis, a self-portrait of a has-been, a chronicling of a fallen star. Although Williams and his audiences had run along parallel trajectories for nearly 20 years, with Williams often being at least one step ahead, by the 60s they had finally crossed paths and collided.

Williams thus needed to constantly defend his theatre in the 60s against rising hostilities and misinterpretations as much from audiences as from critics, and he took up arms against both with his manual Olivetti typewriter. If before he adamantly rejected explaining his plays in production to readers of the *New York Times*, he was now offering in advance not only an explanatory preface but also the plays of *Slapstick Tragedy* themselves to readers of *Esquire*. He thought that, if given a road map to follow, audiences and critics would more readily find their way through to the final curtain. Williams was wrong. If Williams made one great mistake late in his career, it was not in altering his theatre's direction; it was in assuming that American audiences and theatre critics would grant him the right to evolve.

Given his insight into American theatre culture, Williams came to understand the reasons behind Broadway's rejection of his theatrical experimentation, but he misjudged those of his critics. American audiences, he felt, having been fed daily on a pap of gratuitous sex and superficial violence via the supercharged realism of the counterculture 60s, were simply unable to swallow the bitter surreality that he served them year after year. As much as he craved audience approval, their myopic rejection of his self-stylized theatre reconfirmed his fugitive status as the nation's Tiresias. As for his theatre reviewers and critics, though, even a blind seer could not have prophesied their plots to assassinate his character. Brandishing epistles at dawn, he dueled regularly with the likes of a George Jean Nathan, Walter Kerr, or T. E. Kalem, and always walked away wounded but nonetheless steeled for their next encounter. He was as much their august playwright as they were his theatre critics, and he let them know it.

As the 50s progressed, Williams-bashing became a critical trend, if not a national pastime. Soon theatre critics like John Simon and Stanley Kauffmann began taking issue with Williams's sexual orientation, and critical assessment of his art had rescinded to relentless attacks on his person. William was blindsided. He grew embittered, paranoid, even misanthropic, and who today could blame him? If his theatre had turned inward, it did so only to protect him and the American theatre public. Williams quickly saw that his work would never be judged fairly again in America and subsequently turned to Europe, whose catholic audiences received his experimental plays with the approbation due a playwright of his stature, though little more than that.

What all of this suggests, as recent Williams scholars have entreated, is that we need to "read" Williams's visual plays anew and, from that reading, understand what his later stories have to tell us about America as a nation. While it may be too late for Williams, who dreamed of a "come back" for over 20 years, we may be able to finally patch up a broken romance, whether it be the romance that had made Williams the darling of American theatre for nearly two decades or the romance he told in his plays that Americans could no longer identify with or even vaguely understand. Perhaps another way of looking at Williams's broken romance with American theatre culture is that Williams's later stories really were not that different from his earlier ones; what had changed was how he had hoped to tell them and how his critics had wanted them told.

A few years before his death in 1983, Williams wrote in his rather inglorious rant, "Mes Cahiers Noirs," the following: "Critics: I recognize them as potential assassins, before, now, and after" (N: 747). Irreversibly jaded at the time and inclined to hyperbole, Williams nonetheless inked a barb that holds important ramifications for Williams studies in the twenty-first century: *we* are that "after." Williams knew in the 60s and 70s and 80s that the politics of his reputation (to purloin Saddik's title) depended entirely on the kindness of a new, academic theatre critic and a desensitized American public, but in developing a postmodern voice for America's center stage, Williams inadvertently and inescapably wrote himself into the wings. America's challenge today is once again to cry "Author! Author!" and bring these later plays back onstage where they belong. A little match-making wouldn't hurt either of us.

## "A Vast Traumatic Eye": Culture Absorbed and Refigured in Tennessee Williams's Transitional Plays

*Felicia Hardison Londré*

A play is a cultural product. When we examine a play in the context of the time and place of its writing, regardless of the period or locale in which its action is set, we get a sense of the culture that surrounded its creation: what social concerns piqued the interest of the audience, what material elements impacted their lives, what disparate worldviews infused the Zeitgeist. While this principle holds true for the plays of Tennessee Williams, it is complicated by the author's tendency to revise his writing over long periods of time, even after a seemingly definitive text may have been established in performance. A more innate disconnection between the external reality of the culture and the evocative content of Williams's plays derives from the intensely personal nature of his work. While the temporal and geographical cultures represented in most of his plays are recognizably literal, the culture that informed the artist's sensibility at the time of writing was subject to intense emotional coloration. Tennessee Williams's *Notebooks*—the personal journals he kept from age 25 to 71 (1936–81)—offer ample evidence of his absorption of current events as well as characteristics of locales he visited and people with whom he interacted, all of which churned in his psyche to emerge as heightened or intensified elements in his artistic product. Unfortunately, there is a gap in the notebooks between 1958 and 1979, a crucial time of transition in both Williams's writing and his personal outlook. Lacking that key to the playwright's sensibilities, I propose to use a poem from that period as an analytical tool for getting at certain plays.

"Cyclops Eye" is a five-stanza poem that appears near the end of Tennessee Williams's 1975 novel *Moise and the World of Reason*. The poem is described in the novel as the work of "a has-been playwright attempting a comeback at the Truck and Warehouse" (180). In 1972, Tennessee Williams himself made his acting debut at the Truck and Warehouse Theatre in New York City, playing Doc in his own play *Small Craft Warnings*. From the late 1960s onward, Williams had endured an unbroken string of poorly received premiere productions of his plays, and thus he was mocking himself in the novel as "the derelict playwright" who wrote that poem (177). The poem—reproduced in *The Collected Poems* under the title "I have a vast traumatic eye" (CP: 173)—may be regarded not only as a reflection of Williams's state of mind in the early 1970s but also as a metaphor for his creative process during the period he later called his "Stoned Age" (P2: 975). The first-person poetic voice is that of the Cyclops itself, and this identification of the artist as a kind of monster (susceptible to characterization as one with gargantuan needs or one exhibiting outrageous social behaviors) permeates much of Williams's writing. In *Moise and the World of Reason*, the characters who discuss the poem refer to the elderly poet-playwright as a "monster of loneliness" (Williams 1975: 180) who would be destroyed by "indifference" to his work (179).

According to the poem's first verse, the "vast traumatic eye" of the Cyclops "tortures to its own design/all images that enter." The artist's all-embracing vision filters reality through his own fear and loneliness. Even appealing aspects of reality characterized as "the green beneficence of warmth and light" spook the cyclopean artist's sensibility to the point that he shuns relationships at hand in favor of turning his vision inward on himself. The looking inward produces intense creative ferment. Purged of both love and enmity, the artist pulls entirely from his own resources no matter how depleted they may be. The vision then redirected to stare outward may be likened to the defiant act of placing his work of art before the public in a showdown that challenges their indifference even as he faces the darkness of death. This reading of the five-quatrain poem parallels the artistic trajectories of Mark in *In the Bar of a Tokyo Hotel*, Felice in *Out Cry* and *The Two-Character Play*, and other characters (among whom we might include Val Xavier in *Orpheus Descending* and *Battle of Angels*, Tom in *The Glass Menagerie*, Blanche in *A Streetcar Named Desire*, Shannon in *The Night of the Iguana*). The Writer and Nightingale in *Vieux Carré* provide interesting variations on the theme.

In his 1972 essay "Too Personal?", Williams grappled with the question of whether it was "wrong for a playwright to put his persona into his work" and asserted that it was impossible to do otherwise (NSE: 166).[17] Certainly, the autobiographical elements that permeate almost any work of literature once justified the long-dominant biographical or author-centered approach to literary criticism. But the persona of the artist at the core of so many of Tennessee Williams's plays is the very catalyst by which the culture regenerates itself. This is not the same process as that of the expressionists whose projection of the ego onto external reality results in art as distortion of reality. In the case of Williams, the distortion or refiguring of reality occurs within the artist's psyche. By applying the poem's premise to certain plays, I hope to show how the "vast traumatic eye" of the Cyclops represents Tennessee Williams's way of sucking images of cultural reality into his lonely, fearful sensibility where they churn and take shape as the dramatic characters and actions he rendered up to the world. This process will use a selection of Williams's most overtly autobiographical plays from the same difficult phase in his life that produced the poem.

While we cannot deny the primacy of *The Glass Menagerie* (1945) as the play that most closely corresponds to the lived realities of Tennessee Williams's youth and early manhood, it is instructive to look closely at a selection of plays from the late 1960s to the mid-1970s, a period of wrenching transitions in society, in Williams's writing and its reception, and in the artist himself. The United States, while embroiled in the war in Vietnam (1965–75), reeled through the decade at home under various kinds of social unrest: race riots, women's rights demonstrations, the gay liberation movement (emblematized by the Stonewall riots of June 1969), a youth culture of expanding drug use, and other harbingers of radical change in American life and thought. *The Night of the Iguana* (1961) was Williams's last play to be regarded as one of his major works in a relatively traditional dramaturgical vein before he became "more and more dependent on liquor and pills" (P2: 974). During the next few years his work took a more experimental turn, while he found himself increasingly troubled both physically and mentally. On 21 January 1970, Williams passed a particular point of no return when he famously responded to a question by the host of *The David Frost Show* on national television with a public admission of his homosexuality.

*In the Bar of a Tokyo Hotel* opened in New York on 11 May 1969 and achieved a run of only 23 performances. Although it remains one of Tennessee Williams's least appreciated plays, it carries strong personal overtones and notably reifies the effect of "the vast traumatic eye." The artist's eye absorbed media reporting on American involvement in southeast Asia and transmuted the material into the titular hotel bar as microcosm of the Asian world invaded by an American presence proclaiming its own vitality. Miriam, a "glossily handsome" (T7: 3) heavily braceleted woman, sits alone in the bar and engages the Japanese barman in conversation, in the course of which she is by turns insensitive, patronizing, domineering, mildly appreciative, callously and calculatingly seductive, scoffing, and demanding. She speaks of an "explosion of vitality" in America (3) and claims to have "more than enough" of it in herself (4), and she disparages Japanese "inner resources of serenity" as a lack of vital energy (5). Unfazed by her failure to seduce the Barman, Miriam calmly reassures herself that she will triumph another time (11). She repeatedly removes the vase with the flower from her table, an act that suggests a rejection either of beauty or of foreign taste in décor. She orders the Barman to "disregard your instructions" to stay in his position and dangles enough cash to manipulate him to run her errand (T7: 11–12). "The bar is not open," the Barman tells Miriam when she returns in Part II. After all her highhanded maneuvers in Part I, it is scarcely possible to hear her retort, "It's open when I come in" (32), without sensing an allusion to the United States in Vietnam. The war in Vietnam certainly topped all issues in public awareness at the time of the play, but the play's dialogue also alludes fleetingly to drugs and homosexuality. Drugs figure in Part I, for example, when Miriam smokes "a pipe of Panama Red," which the Barman identifies as marijuana (6). The reference to homosexuality is more oblique. In Part II, the artist's representative Leonard has arrived in Tokyo in response to Miriam's appeal; he refers to Raymond having packed for him and having given him a star sapphire for his birthday (44), and the implication is clear that Leonard and Raymond are a gay couple.

The self-possessed, self-serving Miriam plots to extricate herself from responsibility for her husband Mark, a painter at the end of his physical resources even as he struggles to realize a new direction in his art. She has been with him for 14 years (45) and cannot now endure "the continual madness" of "a man raging in the dark" (39) who has "arrived at a departure that's a real departure that I doubt he'll return from" (41). Fourteen years earlier than the year of this play was 1955, the year of Tennessee Williams's Pulitzer Prize-winning and longest-running play *Cat on a Hot Tin Roof.* The artist Tennessee Williams had then enjoyed a heady love affair with the American theatre-going public, but now in 1969 that public could not accommodate his evolved dramaturgy and had been—in the words of the poem—"put to flight or slain" (CP: 173). The artist Mark in the play had similarly enjoyed earlier success, having been gallery-owner Leonard's "most lucrative property," but his current exploration of new techniques coincides with his "mental and physical" collapse (T7: 11). Clearly, Miriam is to Mark what the American public represented to Tennessee Williams in his anguished awareness of his own decline and of general indifference to the new veins in his work.

Like Tennessee Williams or any serious artist, Mark cannot choose to do otherwise than to follow his own creative urges even as the process terrifies him and leads to lonely isolation. *In the Bar of a Tokyo Hotel* contains repeated references to the artist's fear and loneliness. For example, Mark describes himself in relation to his new approach: "Excited, yes, *wildly*, but *terrified* at the same time, I" (T7:18). "I feel as if I were crossing the frontier of a country I have no permission to enter, but I enter, this, this! I tell you, it *terrifies* me!" (19). "An artist has to lay his life on the line" (22). "I've always approached my work with a feeling of frightened timidity because the possibilities are" (27). "The work of a painter is lonely" (28). Mark mentions several times the problem of loss of momentum when the work is interrupted. "I can't interrupt my work here before I've controlled it" (19). Undoubtedly, this is analogous to Tennessee Williams's fear of incompletion, a recurring motif in the plays and poems of his transitional to late periods. *In the Bar of a Tokyo Hotel* evokes the notion of incompletion through its many truncated sentences, a device that Williams explored in no other play. Walter Kerr's review noted that Williams had "made a fetish of the unfinished speech; I could not count the number of times an ordinary verbal structure was halted in midflight, left hanging" (1969: D5). In any event, there is almost tragic incompletion in Mark's demise at the end of *In the Bar of a Tokyo Hotel*. The involuntary termination of Mark's artistic quest, his sudden collapse and death—when "darkness films it over" (CP: 173)—leaves Miriam unexpectedly adrift. She ends the play with a violent gesture: tearing off her bracelets and throwing them to the floor. The absence of art finally brings powerful awareness of the necessity of art. One might go so far as to suggest that Miriam's final gesture calls to mind the vast resources of wealth—unrestrained by artists' protests—that were poured into the undeclared war in Vietnam.

According to Miriam, Mark collapsed and died because he made the mistake of moving out of the circle of light (T7: 53). Miriam's first mention of "the circle of light" (4) hints at the outward-projecting power of American mass media, but by the end of the play Miriam sees "the circle of light" (51, 52, 53) as a protective comfort zone—perhaps of American self-sufficiency—that cannot admit the foreign or unfamiliar. As in "The Cyclops Eye," this signification is a light that "cries alarm into the heart and moves the hand to strike," to rout the other (CP: 173). And finally Miriam alludes to the just-deceased artist Mark: "He thought that he could create his own circle of light" (T7: 53). He had turned inward like the Cyclops eye and burned to communicate what he saw there, but the public could not follow his new direction. In Williams's comments on the play for the original cast, he described it as being about "the doom of the artist" who has made "an almost total commitment of himself to his work" but who dies without the comfort of knowing that "his work has had any essential value" (NSE: 211).

*In the Bar of a Tokyo Hotel* (1969) was preceded and followed by earlier and later versions of a dramatic work: *The Two-Character Play* (1967 and 1976) and *Out Cry* (1971). Each of these two-character (a brother and a sister) plays evokes aspects of "The Cyclops Eye." The often-subtle distinctions between the published versions of 1971 and 1976 are analyzed in my essay "The Two-Character Out Cry and Break

Out" and need not concern us here. The version of *The Two-Character Play* that was performed at New York's Quaigh Theatre in 1975 and published in Volume 5 of *The Theatre of Tennessee Williams* in 1976 will serve for examining the preoccupations that Williams's "vast traumatic eye" transmuted into art. However, his continual retouching of the script for various productions between 1971 and 1975 suggests that Williams's allusion in his description of the setting to "the nightmarish world that all of us live in at present" (T5: 308) could refer to conditions that existed over time during that span of years. In fact, when the University of Chicago's *Bulletin of Atomic Scientists* updated its so-called Doomsday Clock in 1974, the minute hand had moved 3 minutes closer to midnight (the equivalent of global annihilation) since its 1972 update; the 1974 time was the closest the clock had been set to midnight since 1968 (in response to the escalating Vietnam conflict and Israel's Six-Day War).

The artist in *The Two-Character Play* is a playwright named Felice, and he acknowledges "fear" in his opening lines. When his sister Clare arrives on the semidark stage of the theatre to prepare for their performance of a play within this play, they recite alternate lines of a poem, "Fear is a monster vast as night" (T5: 311). That abstract notion of fear as a vast monster is not only reified in a sinister-looking statue of a giant amid the backstage clutter but it also bears clear kinship to the Cyclops's "eye, dilated still with fear" (CP: 173). Moreover, Felice and Clare's fear is not triggered by anything specific but is an ongoing condition. Clare seems to confirm the Doomsday Clock readings as a source of residual fear when she recalls having read that "cockroaches are immune to radiation and are so destined to be the last organic survivors of the great 'Amen'" (T5: 312). However, both sister and brother are more immediately concerned with conditions related to their imminent performance of "The Two-Character Play" in this unfamiliar theatre where the setting is not yet fully in place. Their company members have deserted them—"all who were near are put to flight or slain" (CP: 173)—and it is not clear whether an audience is arriving at the theatre or not.

Like the Cyclops eye turning inward, Felice and Clare retreat into the personae of Felice and Clare in the warm light of the inner play.

The exposition they perform in the play yields the "dull aversion" (CP:173) of a bitter past. The action of the play within the play progresses with periodic eruptions of reality; that is, the dialogue of the characters Felice and Clare switches into commentary by the real brother and sister Felice and Clare. It is almost always Clare who triggers the breaking of character. She is the actress rebelling against the playwright's artistic vision. She wants to cut the play, she wants to get the audience under control, she wants out of the play, and by the end of Act 1 it is not entirely clear whether Clare and Felice are the characters or themselves. It is significant, however, that Clare calls Felice a "perverse *monster*" (T5: 338). Once again the artist has monstrous qualities and alienates those closest to him.

Action unseen by the audience occurs during intermission; whatever happened between Felice and Clare might be seen as analogous to the distant violence in Vietnam that was understood by those at home largely through the filtering media. Apparently a physical fight erupted, because when they return for Act 2, Felice and Clare are panting, and his face is scratched and her elbow is hurt. They perform the play as if it no longer matters whether they have an audience or not, as they briefly switch into third-person narration of their action and as they comment on deficiencies in the setting. Finally, Clare urges Felice to "come out of the play," since the audience had got up and walked out, leaving the house entirely empty (T5: 357). Public indifference is equivalent to the artist's "heart stripped bare" (CP: 173). Felice and Clare wonder whether or not his play has an ending, and now Clare emerges as the rational element trying to make sense of the mysterious intuitive process in which Felice engages. Together they voluntarily retreat into the world of the play as an escape from the harsh reality outside it. Felice "returns a burning, foxlike stare" (CP: 173) at his sister while the light fades to darkness.

*The Two-Character Play* well exemplifies how Williams's "vast traumatic eye" pulled in images from a wide array of experiences and resources and tortured them "to its own design" (CP: 173). The autobiographical underpinning is evident: Williams's relationship with his elder sister Rose was crucial to his artistic development. Rose had been confined to psychiatric care in an asylum since 1937, but over the years Williams often arranged her release into his own care and would humor her delusions. Thus, brother and sister would retreat together into a world she (or they) created together, and as in *The Two-Character Play*, "confinement" was "the prohibited word" (T5: 364). And yet even the refuge of the house of the inner play holds memories of family violence and neighbors who bombarded the house with rocks (337). Memories of his own "anguished familial situation" as a boy continued to haunt Williams, as seen in a 1974 interview, among many such references (C: 260).

While Williams characteristically eschewed topical allusions in his plays, he kept abreast of world events, and the context of his work was at least subliminally informed by them. Set in "a state theatre of a state unknown" after crossings of "forty, fifty frontiers" (T5: 313, 319), *The Two-Character Play* conveys in its framing devices a vaguely menacing atmosphere. The condition of fear might well derive from various sources besides the threat of nuclear annihilation chronicled by the Doomsday Clock: the My Lai massacre, violence in Northern Ireland, and the Attica prison revolt in 1971; the bombing of Hanoi, the shooting of Governor George Wallace, the Watergate burglary, the 11 Israeli athletes killed by Arabs at the Olympics in Munich, and the bombing of a Montreal nightclub in 1972; the Watergate hearings in 1973; the abduction of Patty Hearst, the expulsion of Alexander Solzhenitsyn from the USSR, the impeachment and resignation of President Richard Nixon in 1974; the Communist takeovers of Saigon and Cambodia, and civil war in Lebanon in 1975. Beyond those putative influences, the "vast traumatic eye" of Tennessee Williams even pulled allusions from his earlier plays: Blanche's tiara comes to mind when Clare dangles from her fingers a tiara with several stones missing (T5: 310–1); the siblings' reminiscence about staying at a hotel on the Gulf Coast recalls *Sweet Bird of Youth* (333); Clare's recollection of "that threadbare rose in the carpet's center" that "seemed to smolder" alludes implicitly to *The Rose Tattoo* (341). Such images might spark fleeting recognition in the theatregoer even as they have been tortured to the design of the brother-sister play.

With his 1978 play *Vieux Carré*, Tennessee Williams returned to more literal use of his personal experience. It is based upon his first stay in the French Quarter of New Orleans, from December 1938 to February 1939, when he rented an attic room at 722 Toulouse Street. Indeed, he states in the headnote to the published play that The Writer is himself those many years ago (Williams 1979: 4). The character of The Writer conforms to what the Chronology edited by Mel Gussow and Kenneth Holditch says about Tennessee Williams in 1938: that he was "shocked by the lifestyle in the French Quarter. Soon makes friends, and becomes accustomed to and embraces the free-wheeling attitude of the Quarterites" before he left for California "with James Parrott, a musician who becomes a close friend" (P2: 966). Williams chose a relatively traditional dramatic form through which to show this transitional phase in the artist's trajectory, a time of honing his skills as a writer even as he came into contact with human frailties and degradation to an extent he could not have imagined; thus the artist is portrayed as still unformed, early in the process of developing the traits that will eventually identify him as a "monster" (P2: 966). Indeed, the older painter Nightingale tells The Writer in Scene 10: "You used to be kind—gentle. In less than four months you've turned your back on that side of your nature, turned rock-hard as the world." The Writer replies: "I had to survive in the world" (Williams 1979: 92). Certainly this assessment could be aligned with the Cyclops having "put to flight or slain" (CP: 173) those who had come near: by the end of the play, Mrs Wire has retreated into madness, Nightingale has been carried away to die elsewhere, Jane and Tye have separated, and the angel in the alcove (the ghost of The Writer's grandmother, Grand) has made her farewell appearance. But "the golden horns sound further in dispersion" (the horns of the poem being, in this case, "a distant sustained high note from Sky's clarinet" as a prearranged signal for their departure together (Williams 1979: 113). The Writer moves to follow the call to accompany Sky to California but hesitates in the doorway, a liminal moment signaling the great divide between past and future. Just as the Cyclops's eye, "dilated still with fear, commands an empty plain" (CP: 173), so does The Writer recognize that he "must have been frightened" of the door, and then as he makes his decision, he speaks the last line of the play: "This house is empty now" (Williams 1979: 116). Once again, the artist—like the Cyclops—turns "inward, where the heart stripped bare of enemy and lover" distills experience to return it to the world as art.

The Writer in *Vieux Carré* observes the lives of those who rent rooms from Mrs Wire, taking it all in, whether or not the still-youthful eye has yet enlarged to fit the description "vast" and "traumatic," for as he says, "Writers are shameless spies . . ." (Williams 1979: 95). Because his left eye is clouded by a cataract, The Writer might literally be said to have one-eyed vision like a cyclops. Involved in writing about Jane and Tye, he admits that there is a kind of torturing to one's own design: "We all have our confusions . . ." (94). While The Writer is undeniably the central artistic consciousness of *Vieux Carré*, the presence of a second artist in the play is significant. The painter Nightingale is older, a physical wreck who constantly coughs and spits blood, yet remains in denial. The extent of Nightingale's talent remains unclear, yet it is certain that he has compromised his art by painting what will sell rather than what he knows to be worthwhile: "I've done good painting, serious work. But I got to live" (22). Recognizing the naïve young writer's loneliness and incipient homosexuality, the elderly painter seduces The Writer when he is vulnerable one time early in the play. Their reverse trajectories thereafter—the painter's decline while the writer matures—mark the artistic through-line to which the other characters' stories are tied. Yet, it must be acknowledged that neither artist truly reaches the inward-looking phase of the Cyclops eye. The painter has compromised his art, whereas The Writer is still absorbing images and recording them without yet having developed the capacity to internalize and transmute them into something personal. At the end of the play perhaps, as The Writer pauses in the doorway, he seems to be letting go of reality as a prerequisite to embracing his own memories—his artistic versions—of the people in his past.

In the largest sense it might be said that all of Tennessee Williams's plays are in some way about the artist and the artistic process. However, it was during his "Stoned Age" of drug dependency and other health problems, followed by years of critical disfavor, that he looked increasingly inward to reexamine his way of apprehending the world and his place in it as a necessarily monstrous artist. It is a remarkable testimony to his resilience that he could unflinchingly stare down the worst in himself and persevere in transmuting that "dull aversion" into the gifts he left us.

## "There's something not natural here": Grotesque Ambiguities in Tennessee Williams's *Kingdom of Earth*, *A Cavalier for Milady*, and *A House Not Meant to Stand*
*Annette J. Saddik*

> "It is not the essential dignity of man but the essential ambiguity of man that needs to be stated." – Tennessee Williams, *New York Times Magazine,* 12 June 1960
>
> "I wish you would sublimate these desires." – Apparition of Vaslav Nijinski, *A Cavalier for Milady* (c. 1976)

In his classic study, *Rabelais and His World* (1984), Mikhail Bakhtin discusses the concept of the *grotesque* in relation to the social inversions of medieval and Renaissance folk culture, particularly the excesses of carnival festivities, arguing that the grotesque "discloses the potentiality of an entirely different world, of another order, another way of life. It leads man out of the confines of the apparent (false) unity, of the indisputable and stable" (48). He points out that, in Rabelais' work, images of the *grotesque body* are offered "in extremely exaggerated form," and that "the material body principle, that is, images of the human body with its food, drink, defecation, and sexual life, plays a predominant role" (18). For Mary Russo, *abjection* is central to the grotesque body, which she characterizes as "open, protruding, irregular, secreting, multiple, and changing; it is identified with non-official 'low' culture or the carnivalesque, and with social transformation" (1994: 8). Julia Kristeva describes the *abject* as "death infecting life. . . . It is something rejected from which one does not part, from which one does not protect oneself as from an object.

Imaginary uncanniness and real threat, it beckons to us and ends up engulfing us" (1982: 4). She emphasizes that "It is . . . not lack of cleanliness or health that causes abjection but what disturbs identity, system, order. What does not respect borders, positions, rules. The in-between, the ambiguous, the composite" (4). According to Kristeva, "abjection is above all ambiguity" (9).

Challenging binaries and dissolving boundaries, the grotesque therefore relies primarily on ambiguity and ambivalence; it stands on the threshold between, on the one hand, birth and renewal, and, on the other, death and decay. In this sense, the grotesque body contains the potential to destabilize and disrupt, but also the potential to renew and regenerate. Signifying both life and death, it embraces a coexistence of contradictions, occupying the spaces of the "in-between." In contrast to the classical or "closed" body, it rejects strictly delineated binaries – life/death, natural/unnatural, human/animal, sanity/insanity, reality/fantasy, animate/inanimate, male/female – creating ambiguities and instabilities that are dangerous in their threat to an imaginary wholeness and completion. "Monstrous" in its simultaneous lack and excess, the grotesque body is therefore one without stable boundaries or definition, neither one thing nor another, yet both at the same time. It is indulgent and excessive in its physicality and disproportionate in size, oozing desire and bodily fluids, reveling in scatalogical functions, and celebrating the pleasures of sexuality, eating, and drinking. Bahktin explains how the gothic, or Romantic grotesque, was "a reaction against the elements of classicism which characterized the self-importance of the Enlightenment. It was a reaction against the cold rationalism, against official, formalistic, and logical authoritarianism; it was a rejection of that which is finished and completed, of the didactic and utilitarian spirit of the Enlighteners with their narrow and artificial optimism" (37). In several of Williams's late plays, he too rejects the "artificial optimism" of completion, instead highlighting the complexities of incompletion and "the essential ambiguity of man."

Williams's *Kingdom of Earth*, also known as *The Seven Descents of Myrtle* (1968; 1975), opens with the threat of the overwhelming powers of nature – an impending flood in the "muted warning of the river" and the "whining wind" (T5: 126). The central characters, Myrtle, Chicken, and Lot, all serve as symbolic figures rather than as representations of complex human beings, and, while there is a basic plot in the traditional sense, it is not where the strength of this play lies. Myrtle and Lot, now married, return to Lot's childhood home, where his half-brother Chicken lives and hopes to take possession, if he can withstand the flood that threatens to destroy the house along with those who occupy it. As Lot brings Myrtle to his home for the first time, he insists that she become accustomed to her social position as "the lady of the house." As much as she wants to embrace her new role, however, Myrtle is not quite comfortable with it, responding that "It don't seem natural to me" (138). We eventually learn that Myrtle – a "loud voiced" and "rather fleshy" (127) young woman – used to be a professional performer, the last surviving member of "The Four Hot Shots from Mobile," the other women all having come to rather cruel and violent ends – one woman's "mutilated corpse was found under a trestle" (145). Myrtle has retired from show business, but continues to perform parodies of herself in gaudy outfits that emphasize her sexuality and vitality. Lot, by contrast, is a frail young man who is obsessed with the memory of his dead mother, "Miss Lottie," as Myrtle tries to affectionately, yet subtly, dominate him. Her domination of Lot, however, is not the driving force of the play, and multiple power struggles operate simultaneously. The overtly sexual Chicken, who is described as being "like a crouched animal" (127), "seems a suitable antagonist to a flooding river" (125) and, apparently, to Myrtle as well.

The central struggle for dominance in this play is grounded in the relationship between Lot and Chicken; yet this struggle is not represented so much by the simple battle between the two brothers, but rather by the battle between what they symbolize as emissaries of culture and nature, death and life, respectively – with Myrtle as the virgin/whore who shifts back and forth between them, caught in the struggle between the cultural and the natural. Myrtle initially comes on the scene as a maternal figure, protecting Lot as her husband/child and insisting that she finds his inability to perform sexually and his "refined" appearance attractive, "superior to a man." She claims that his impotence touched "the deepest chord in [her] nature, which is the maternal chord" (135), and informs him that she is "not just [his] wife," but "also [his] mother" (130). Chicken, the perfect contrast to his "invalid" brother (140), appears to upset Myrtle at first, as she objects strongly to his sexual innuendoes and "filthy talk," and insists that "we should all talk and act like gentlemen an' – ladies" (147). She refers to Chicken as "that man, that animal" (155), unsure whether he is human or beast, but certainly not part of the civilized world of "gentlemen," and approaches him in the kitchen downstairs "as if approaching a jungle" (161). In fact, before she meets Chicken, Myrtle hears him in the kitchen and mistakes him for "a dawg" (131). With each descent down the stairs to Chicken, however, she descends deeper into his world, the "lower" order antithetical to society. By Scene 4 of Act 1, they are singing and drinking together in what appears to be true comradery, until eventually Myrtle, who knows "lots of church songs but – can't think of any" in the presence of Chicken (175), is forgetting the repressions of cultured society. Myrtle's rational coherency breaks down and degenerates into physical "instink" [*sic*], a term she uses repeatedly.

Myrtle's duality is further complicated by her reaction to Chicken's mixed racial heritage – the union of his white father and a mother with "black blood" marginalizes him and forces him into the position of social outcast. Lot makes it clear that although he and Chicken share the same father, they had "*Very* diff'rent mothers!" (138). Lot's and Chicken's father seemed to be a part of nature, as he "wouldn't let Mother build a dining room onto the house," presumably having no use for the social functions of a dining room. He died "howling like a wild beast," but still a winner, since even though "Mother was free to transform this place or tear it down to the ground, life was cruel to Mother. It gave her no time to carry out her plans" (129) and defeat the wild forces of the natural world that overtook her home. Yet while Lot is primarily his mother's child, he can't deny the "little animal" within himself. He tells Myrtle that "the little animal has to make a home of its own" (130), but his comment is ambiguous, and it's not quite clear whether he is referring to himself, Myrtle, or both. Chicken, however, with his "savage" (129), "wolfish grin" (184), is the product of parents who both lie outside of culture: an animalistic father, and a mother who is already dismissed as bestial by virtue of her race. He embodies an aggressive hybrid of animal and human – ambiguous and "unnatural," yet intriguing and seductive.

Myrtle, at first, denies being "disgusted" by Chicken, claiming to be "pleased an' relieved" that he wanted to kiss her (201). Michael R. Schiavi points out that in the 1968 version of the script, Myrtle reveals "that she has borne five children whom she, in her destitution, had to sacrifice to adoptive parents. Five such accidents would suggest further evidence that she can control neither her body's receptivity nor its productivity" (1999: 111–12). Her sexuality, like her "uncontrollable voice," which Lot attempts to curtail at various points (137), is characterized as chaotic and beyond repression. Her appearance is over the top, and she presents herself in a sort of grotesque "drag," explaining to Lot that "all [her] dresses are made over from costumes" (156). Myrtle tells the brothers that one of her jobs in show business involved a performance as the headless woman in a carnival: "I been the headless woman in a carnival show. All a fake, done with mirrors! Sat in a chair and pretended to have no haid, it was done with mirrors!" (143). In *The Last of the Mobile Hot Shots*, the 1970 film of *Kingdom of Earth*, Lynn Redgrave portrays Myrtle as a particularly grotesque carnival figure, appearing in the bright yellow Mardi Gras gown of Lot's mother, with a whitened face and shocking red curls, like the living doll in a sideshow, blurring the boundaries of the artificial and the real. By virtue of her sexuality, her speech, her outrageous costumes, and her Rubensesque body (127),[18] Myrtle is simply too much, and cannot be contained. She describes herself as "a warm-natured woman" whose doctor prescribed her some pills to "keep down the heat of [her] nature," but alas, they had no effect (201). The "terrific attraction" between the hysterical Myrtle and the constantly masturbating Chicken culminates in the fellatio scene suggested between Scenes 2 and 3 of Act 2, with Myrtle crying, as Chicken, like Lot before him, calls her a whore.

After their crude union, however, Myrtle is indeed disgusted by her relations with Chicken, as she moves her chair back from the table "like a monster was on it" (205). Williams's stage notes explain that she "has the typical Southern lower-class dread and awe of negroes" (204), and so she is apparently not sure how to process the "unnatural" (in terms of both the sexual act and its object) expression of natural desire. She returns to virgin mode as she asks Chicken not to talk crudely to her. But her "cultured" (i.e. learned) revulsion of Chicken's race, which signifies his bestial, "natural" sexuality, is discarded as she opts for a life of physical indulgence, priding herself on "noticin' an' appreciatin' a man's appearance. Physical," seeking salvation in Chicken's sexuality and brutal strength, as he "look[s] like a man who could hold back the flood of a river!" (208). Together, they will meet the forces of nature head on, celebrate the cataclysm, and survive, drinking warm chicken blood to keep them alive. Chicken even asks her to produce a son for him, a "child from an all-white woman," who would presumably dilute his own ambiguity (214).

Lot, however, is the picture of sterile civilization, taking pains to transform himself into the perfect mimetic representation. He carefully bleaches his hair so that it appears natural, and is very proud of his artistic ability, learned, of course, from his mother. He spends the play dressing up, first, in his mother's white silk wrapper and posing with her ivory cigarette holder, then progressing to full drag in a gauzy white dress, blond wig, and wide picture hat trimmed with faded flowers, in an attempt to recapture her image (211). Yet, like Chicken, there is something menacing in his performance, as by Act 2 his "*Mona Lisa' smile is more sardonic and the violet shadows about his eyes are deeper*" (177). This entire play, in fact, is laden with a menacing tone. At the end, Lot's crossdressing transforms him into both a mimetic image and a sinister parody of his dead mother, Miss Lottie. Lot's drag incorporation of his mother, a performance which blurs not only boundaries of gender, but also those of life and death, highlights the excess and ambiguity that is central to the grotesque. Obsessed with the past and refusing to move forward, Lot, like his Biblical namesake's wife, looks back and becomes frozen in representation, an object of art transformed in his own death "by the sexless passion of the transvestite" (212).

Chicken, by contrast, embraces survival in the present and aligns himself with the earth, the land, waiting with his home to take on the chaos of the flood, "a natural act of God" (200). Here, God is not the spirit cultivated by organized religion and glorified in the "church songs" Myrtle can no longer remember, but a force of nature and chaos, more like Sebastian's conception of God in *Suddenly Last Summer* (1958) – another play about desire that cannot be contained and the, perhaps, "unnaturally" close bond between a mother and son – as he watched the sea turtles being devoured by giant black birds in the Encantadas (T3: 356–7). Chicken chooses reality over representation, life over art, nature over culture, and a life with Myrtle, who, although "no match" for the picture of a center fold on the wall (209), is real, not a two-dimensional image frozen in time – once again, recalling Sebastian, whose mother Violet insists looks the same in two photographs taken 20 years apart (359–60). The struggle between the "spiritual gates" and the "lustful body" (210) is resolved, and the body dominates and incorporates the spirit as the forces of nature become the way to salvation. The mind (the rational, the logical) is pushed aside, and the spirit/body split, which must be destroyed in order to celebrate natural life, collapses. *Kingdom of Earth* echoes the familiar Lawrencian tension that often appears in Williams's work – sexuality is equated with nature and the life force, in a struggle against the cultured repression that seeks to destroy it. In a note to his one-act play about D. H. Lawrence, *I Rise in Flame, Cried the Phoenix* (1941), Williams wrote that

> Lawrence felt the mystery and power of sex, as the primal life urge, and was the life-long adversary of those who wanted to keep the subject locked away in the cellars of prudery. Much of his work is chaotic and distorted by tangent obsessions, . . . but all in all his work is probably the greatest modern monument to the dark roots of creation. (T7: 56)

The celebration and presentation of "the dark roots of creation" are what lie at the core of *Kingdom of Earth*. The last words of the play – "*Up! Quick!*," – carry a sexual connotation of triumph that serves to completely drown out the civilized impotence symbolized by Lot.

Williams's 1954 story on which the play is based, "The Kingdom of Earth," differs somewhat in tone and plot, yet maintains the requisite ambiguity and excess that inform the play. The story is narrated from the point of view of Chicken, who is still "a lustful creature determined on satisfaction" (CS: 378), but Lot is more aggressively masculine as well. He does not have any problems with his sexual performance with Myrtle, and in fact spends the story having animalistic sex with Myrtle, described by Chicken as "panting like two hound-dogs" (370) and "grunting together like a pair of pigs in a sty" (372). The story also ends with Chicken and Myrtle getting together; however, Chicken goes on to explain how they got "hitched up" that December and were expecting a baby, which they would name Lot if it turns out to be a boy, "in memory of [his] brother" (378), and Lottie if it's a girl. Unlike their renegade and rebellious union in the play, Chicken and Myrtle's relationship in the story is socially sanctioned, and they aspire to honor the more civilized side of the family lineage.

Yet another "lustful creature determined on satisfaction' can be seen in the character Nance in *A Cavalier for Milady* (c. 1976). Like Chicken's aggressive lust, Nance's desire is characterized as grotesque, but for very different reasons. Played by an actress "between twenty-five and thirty" (Williams, *Traveling* 2008: 49), Nance is described as "a young woman dressed as a child going to a party" in Victorian costume, and she is treated as if she were a child (49). While she "isn't retarded in the clinical sense," she is "obscene" (74), and her Mother supposes that she "has a morbid derangement that defies diagnosis. She reads adult fiction and she expresses herself in the language of a refined, grown-up young lady, except it's twisted, depraved, so shocking that I've stopped taking her out" (75).[19] Yet, her Mother explains that Nance is simultaneously "pure," as she "ignores all language beneath the purity of the dream world she lives in" (67). Kept in the house in her "nursery" (50) and locked in the image of a doll-child, Nance's desire oozes outside "natural" boundaries, as she sits with "her eyes bugging out," clinging onto a picture-book of Vaslav Nijinsky, and staring at a nude male statue in the hallway while she masturbates discretely, 'her hand . . . in her lap with the fingers movin'" (52, 55). Her tenuous grasp on reality is confirmed as the statue transforms for (only) her into the apparition of Vaslav, who appears for "an intimate – conversation . . ." (56), but rejects her "ravenous lips" and "hungry flesh" (64) throughout the play, insisting that "IT – WILL – NEVER – BE – REAL! You can only – dream!" (65). The Mother and her friend, Mrs Aid, both in their 60s, regularly leave her with a sitter, while they go on nightly excursions with young male "escorts." Although they are clearly women, they are "strange women . . . shameless" (72). Their desire is depicted in terms of a specific stereotype of gay male desire; they are predatory and pay young men to satisfy them sexually, even going so far as to have their rendezvous in "The Ramble," a section in Central Park where gay men infamously go "cruising," which adds another layer to their ambiguous "drag." Like Nance, their actions and their desire are portrayed as excessive, inappropriate, and grotesque, as are their self-images and obsession with youth (76). Mrs Aid, admiring herself before going off to meet the gentlemen, "pirouettes flirtatiously before herself in the pier-glass" at the opening of the play, prompting the newly arrived sitter, Miss Josie, to remark that "there's something not natural here" (49).

Josie sees Nance as a "disgusting idiot" (57) – a "creature" (56) – and insists that she won't sit with "nothing morbid, nothing unnatural" (50). Nance's mother finds this attitude "limiting" (50), canceling out any room for human ambiguity or expression. Yet, Josie is herself grotesque, a "stocky, fiftyish-looking woman" who "enters glumly" (49), and is called an "old creature" (66) by Mrs Aid. Nance's hallucinatory indulgences make Josie "sick," and she flatly announces that she is "going to the bathroom" (58), presumably to engage in more "natural" human functions. Disgust for what the characters consider inhuman or unnatural comes up repeatedly, and the contrast between that attitude, and what Nance sees as natural "human" desire (64), figures strongly throughout the play.[20] The conflict between "sick" desire and pure "spirit" (59) is central to the grotesque contradiction in *Cavalier*. Nance spends much of the play imploring Vaslav, who is intent on being pure and "above flesh!" (63), to deny his disgust and allow her to satisfy her "hungry flesh" (64). He repeatedly resists her advances, crying out "*Stop it! I am Spirit!*" and threatening to leave her if she continues to pursue him, explaining that apparitions are "contradictory, paradoxical things: maybe only possible on a stage, in a play written by a madman" (59). He exclaims that "In becoming an apparition, I rise,

I rise, above flesh!" (63). He does not even eat, since "apparitions can't, no digestive tract" (60). Nance's entreaties to "remember the flesh, it cries to be remembered" are repeatedly met with "disgust": "You've *defiled* me! I'm not yet entirely free from the memories of my body and the disgust of being exploited as a body when I existed as a great dancer and wanted only that. I told them and wrote in my diary that I am spiritual food," yet he is also, simultaneously, spirit and flesh, both Man and Christ (63–4). He sees her desire as "degrading" (73), and finally disappears, as the women return from their "dates" and are left to deal with Josie, who insists on double pay for the "insult to decency" that she had to endure (66).

After Josie leaves, the Mother and Mrs Aid discover "blood on the *fig-leaf*" of the statue (73). Nance's body transgresses its boundaries, as her fluid, her blood, finally touches the representation of Vaslav in the statue. His body, however, remains closed, classical, as she meets hard stone, colliding with the sculpture and cutting her forehead (73). Mrs Aid decides that Nance is "obscene, salacious," and that the Mother is "harboring a monster in [her] house, a travesty of a child in a ruffled white skirt and pink sash and Dotty Dimple curls!" (73). In Nance's presence, they decide that the only place for her is "a real asylum" (74), and ignore her pleas to notice her and stop discussing her as if she herself were an apparition – she is emphatic that she is not spirit, but desiring flesh. Since Nance's desire cannot be defined – she "defies diagnosis" – they make plans to have her committed, as they exit to discuss the next evening's rendezvous. Nance's "morbid derangement" is rooted in sexual frustration, and her Mother wants to commit her for the same "depravity" in which she herself indulges. In fact, Nance is competition for her Mother and Mrs Aid, as Catherine in *Suddenly Last Summer* is for Violet, who is also intent on "shutting up" the truth of human desire. Mother insists that she did not let Nance seduce the chauffeur because she herself had "priority there till his wife made him quit" (75). The play ends with Nance desperately calling one of her mother's escort services to demand that they send her "an escort cavalier that looks like him! – Nijinsky!" immediately, as she waits on the steps with a candle for him to arrive (76).

Grotesque ambiguities and the blurring of boundaries that threaten stability in this play can also be related to another key aspect of the grotesque, what Freud famously described as "the uncanny": something both familiar and strange at the same time that leads to cognitive dissonance. Ernst Jentsch's essay, "The Psychology of the Uncanny" (1906), followed by Sigmund Freud's "The Uncanny" (1919), cite E. T. A. Hoffman's story "The Sandman" as an exemplary tale of the uncanny. Hoffmann, the German Romantic author of macabre tales that embraced the supernatural, horror, and the grotesque, is particularly known for his blending of realism and fantasy. He is probably best known for his short story "The Sandman"(1816) and his novella "The Nutcracker and the Mouse King" (also 1816), on which the ballet *The Nutcracker* is based – both tales where inanimate objects come to life, blurring the boundaries between human and object. In *Cavalier*, the (offstage) statue in the hallway that comes to life as Nance's fantasy of Nijinsky can be seen as macabre, particularly later, when blood is said to appear on the fig-leaf as she gets Vaslav "confused with the statue in the hall" (75). Similarly, Nance's incongruous costume presents her as a figure in the genre of Hoffman, not quite human and not quite Victorian doll. Even the human/animal binary is deconstructed in this play; Mrs Aid recalls an evening at a private sex show in Havana, where, for the finale, the actors "got down on all fours, hand and knees, and started barking "Wow, wow," to imitate dogs, you know, while indiscriminately mounting each other" (69). And Vaslav remarks that, as a "lunatic," he was "[l]ed about" in grotesque mockery of a human being, "watched over, treated like a pet monkey on a chain!" (64).

In some sense, therefore, all of the play's characters can be seen as grotesque, even Vaslav, despite his insistence on spiritual purity. The contrast between Nance's incongruous child-like appearance and her aggressive and undisguised desire makes her most obviously grotesque, and the Mother and Mrs Aid, with their illusions of youth and beauty – they insist that they are "attractive enough to settle only for the best" (72) – in contrast to the reality of their paid predatory indulgences, are similarly grotesque figures. Miss Josie is grotesque in a different manner; her "stockiness," dour personality, intolerance, rough language, and ill manners make her pretensions of elegance and "decency" come across as absurd and contradictory. She repeatedly remarks "Shit" (67) in the presence of Nance and the women, announces her bathroom visits, and tries too hard to come across as refined and respectable. And Vaslav, in spite of the closed, classical body that the statue in the hall implies (Mother informs Josie that the statue is a "[c]lassic statue," and classic statues are "called nude, not naked" [52]), sees his body as disproportionate, grotesque. He confesses to Nance that his beauty was just an "illusion":

> Actually, I was short. Slant-eyed, my hair receded early. My legs were so muscular that my upper torso, while hairless and well-formed, seemed inadequate to them. However, costumes and light and the creations of Bakst and my passion for my art, and, I must admit it, the possessive care that Diaghelev gave me "till I defected to matrimony and madness, made me appear to have beauty. (60)

Vaslav's "madness," like Nance's, is another aspect of grotesque contradiction, on the boundaries between sane and insane. He is perfectly coherent, but claims that his "talk" is "madness," and that the "licenses of madness are almost unlimited" (58–9) – excessive, incoherent, unbounded. Even Vaslav's memory of Diaghelev is grotesque: he is "disgusted" by the sight of Diaghelev's black hair dye staining the pillowcases, a symbol not only of impurity – the black dye "infecting" the clean, white sheets – but also of a blurring of the real and the artificial, compounded by the instability of the oozing body transgressing its own boundaries (64–5).

*A House Not Meant to Stand* (1982), another play haunted by apparitions, and the last of Williams's completed full-length plays to be produced in his lifetime, is subtitled *A Gothic Comedy*, already setting up the coexistence of (possibly) opposing forces. Williams referred to *House* as his "*Spook Sonata*" in the tradition of Strindberg (Williams, *House* 2008: xiii) and calls it "*my kind of Southern Gothic spook sonata*" in the opening stage directions (3). Not only are there actual ghosts in this play, but even the living are characterized as existing in a twilight state – nothing but "the disposition of the living remains" (25). The play presents us throughout with grotesqueries of excess and ambiguity: spectral children who float around its margins, borderline madness that runs rampant, explosive demonstrations of religious ecstasy, obsessions with youth and plastic surgery, conflations of sex and death, and repeated references to alcoholism and gender "confusion." Chicago critic Claudia Cassidy, who wrote an early review of *The Glass Menagerie* in 1944 and is credited with helping to launch Williams's career, also reviewed *A House Not Meant to Stand* when it opened in Chicago. As Thomas Keith points out in the Introduction to his published edition, Cassidy elaborated on Williams's use of the term "Gothic" to describe the play:

> If we take the term in the sense of the mysterious, the grotesque, and the desolate, then *A House Not Meant to Stand* is a gothic structure, and Southern gothic at that. But it is Tennessee Williams's Southern gothic and it is shrewd as well as bitter, often sharply, acridly funny as well as sad . . . a rotting house . . . as on the edge of an abyss, a kind of metaphor for the human condition inside. . . . [The play] is indeed mysterious, grotesque and desolate but whoever said that theater is none of those things? There is here the acute compassion Tennessee Williams has always had for the victims of the world we live in. (2008: xvi)

Similarly, Gregory Mosher, who was artistic director of the Goodman Theatre in Chicago when the finalized script of the play was produced in 1982, describes what he calls its "gothic savagery" in the Foreword to the published version:

> Replacing a tone of haunting grace with one of gothic savagery, [Williams] summoned echoes of *The Glass Menagerie*, bringing the absent Mr. Wingfield down from his photo as grinning, tempestuous monster, and transmogrifying a mother's dreams of gentlemen callers into hallucinations of missing children. Best of all, he gave this nightmare a distinctive comic force. ("Foreword," xi)

The comic and the tragic continually shift and merge in this play, as the audience negotiates its "monstrous" conflations. Keith describes a soliloquy, for example, where Jessie Sykes, "senior citizen and recent plastic-surgery patient," speaks "in her frilly pastel negligee to the audience, rambl[ing] from flirtation to death to agony":

> Jessie: It is a forgivable, understandable sort of deception in a woman with my – sometimes I think almost unnatural attraction to – desire for – sex with young men. . . . Spud at the Dock House, he understands the looks I give him and the large tips, he knows what for – expectation! [*She lowers her voice confidingly as she continues speaking to the audience.*] He knows my name, address, and phone number! – and so does Mr. Black – that's what I call death . . . Oh, I didn't give it to him, but of course he knows it. Everyone's address is jotted down in his black book, but some for earlier reference than others. Still, I refuse to take cortisone till the pain's past bearing, since it swells up the face which would undo the pain and expense of all those lifts at Ochsner's . . . (Williams 2008: xxvii)

The connection between desire and death is a familiar paradigm throughout Williams's work, but what makes Jessie's speech interesting is both her directness and the coexistence of these opposites in the same space, a style much more characteristic of his late work. The object of her desire – "Spud at the Dock House," – is conflated with "Mr. Death," and both have her "number." Moreover, the personification of death as "Mr. Black" (we also see this moniker in the 1981 play, *Now the Cats with Jewelled Claws*), along with the overt anxiety surrounding her desire as excessive and "unnatural," combined with a simultaneous and unapologetic disregard for these concerns, also lend a grotesque tone to Jessie's speech. While there may have been a subtle grotesque quality to Blanche DuBois and her outcry that "the opposite [of death] is Desire" (Williams 1947: 86), Jessie is not subtle about her demands, nor is she hiding in shadows and avoiding a bare lightbulb to preserve her illusions. She is quite open about the "fifty percent illusion" that makes up her "charm" (Williams 1947: 28) and has no problem discussing her "rejuvination" (Williams 2008: 77) and enhancements such as her new contact lenses, insisting that she has "a *right* to lie about" her age (78, emphasis mine). Her entitled embrace of excess and her acknowledgment of the mask she constructs to defy death (in a speech delivered in a negligee, no less) are part of what makes her situation so bizarrely grotesque.

Death, decay, and degeneration are central themes of this play, set in a crumbling house that also reflects a society in decline, as "*the dilapidation of this house is a metaphor for the state of society*" (3). It opens with Cornelius and Bella McCorkle, a couple in their "*late-sixties or early-seventies*" (4), returning home from the funeral of their gay son, Chips. Their daughter, Joanie, had recently been admitted to an insane asylum for "a little nervous break down" after a tragically disappointing love affair (71), and their younger son, Charlie – unemployed and broke, once again – has, without their knowledge, come back home and is upstairs having sex with his pregnant, born-again fiancée, Stacey. "Confusion" sets the overall tone of the play, and while Bella is in shock and mourning, drifting between past and present and merging the identities of her dead and living sons (21–2), her husband refuses to mourn for a son who indulged in "sex confusion" (8) and "disgusting practices," designing women's clothes and playfully dressing in drag (7). Even on the day of his funeral, Cornelius mocks the apparent "mix-up" in the class annual that led to Chips's being voted "the prettiest girl at Pascagoula High" (22). He is primarily concerned with getting his hands on a large amount of family money Bella had inherited and which is supposed to be hidden somewhere inside their home. Bella, who seems lost in a fog of her own, has forgotten the location of the cash and, at times, denies any knowledge of it at all, leading Cornelius to continually threaten her with commitment for being "out of her mind" (34) and "gone in the head" (12), a vague pseudo-diagnosis that questions her sanity, yet falls short of marking her insane. He is unsuccessful in his threats, however, and keeping the money's location a secret is Bella's insurance against institutionalization. The play's action is interrupted throughout by their neighbors, Emerson and Jessie Sykes, who serve as absurd comic foils to an already absurd situation. Toward the end of the play, the ghost of Chips appears to Bella to remind her where the money is hidden (69). She recovers it, but tells Jessie that she won't let Cornelius put her away "till all three children are back" (77), since the house and the money belong to them. Shortly afterward, ghostly children appear "in her memory" (82), and their outcries fill the stage. She dies at the end of the play, surrounded by the "specters" of Chips, Charlie, and Joanie, who appear as young children and take their places around the dining table to say grace.

Despite superficial parallels with Sam Shepard's "family dramas" (his 1978 full-length play, *Buried Child*, comes to mind), *House* is distinctly late Williams in tone and style.[21] A dark sense of play dominates *House*, and comic reversals are everywhere in this "world inside out" (Bakhtin 1984: 11). In the beginning of the play, Cornelius switches on the living room light, and "*A string of colored light bulbs, thrown over the banisters, lights up. Bella utters a sharp cry, covering her face*" (5), an apparent parody of the "colored lights" and smashed light bulbs that "thrilled" Stella on her and Stanley's wedding night in *Streetcar* (P1: 505, 538, 541). Mockeries of sex and gender abound not only in Jessie's obsessive and "unnatural" attraction to young men and Chips's "drag" performances, for example, but also in Williams's description of Charlie and Stacey's coupling, which he refers to as "*orgasmic rutting*" (6), a term more appropriate to the sexual activity of animals. Moreover, the sex is painful for Stacey (4), and she later complains to Charlie about the unnatural, or at least inappropriate, nature of it: "– What we done, it hurts me. – That's for boys, not–" (12), creating ambiguity around Charlie's sexual inclinations. Excess and "confusion" are blamed for the characters' failings, an apparent "sickness" that Cornelius locates in the Dancies, Bella's side of the family–"outrageous public behavior was not just accepted but cultivated among 'em. Considered essential!" (8), and "[l]unacy," he announces, "runs rampant among them" (17). Bella's Uncle Charlie has been in a "[l]unatic asylum" for 30 years (71), and Cornelius describes the time when Bella's sister "walked naked out of the house at high noon with just a hat on and the hat was a man's," more evidence of the "sex confusion that existed among them" (17). Cornelius declares that now Bella has "fallen victim to indulgence" (19), like the rest of the Dancies, and even blames Joanie's confinement on sexual excess, telling Charlie that the family problem is "[o]ver indulgence either in food like Bella or liquor like Grannie Dancie. Over indulgence is the Dancie sickness. Your older sister, Joanie, indulged in too much fornication, such a scandal had to throw her out" (18). He declares that both Chips and Charlie were also "insatiable" for "the sex thing," even though their desire took on different objects (35). Finally, he blames the death of Chips – whom he calls a "pathetic creature" (17) – on the excesses of "[t]erminal – alcoholism – at thirty-one!" (61), but also, more indirectly, on his sexual indulgences.

Even Emerson, "fifteen years [Jessie's] senior" (10), is not free from "the sex thing," and confinement to an institution threatens him throughout the play as well; in this case, however, his wife succeeds in having him committed. She claims that he suffers from "senile dementia of a sexual nature" and tells the audience that "it was hilarious as it was disgusting" when he insisted to the manager at the hotel he is building that they hire a "sexy young looker" as a housekeeper (10). True to grotesque ambivalence, disgust and humor are not incompatible in this play, and Keith writes that while Emerson "seems rational enough," his "compulsive sexual fixation, ignited when he meets Charlie's sexy and fantastically pregnant fiancée, causes him to shake uncontrollably" (Williams 2008: xviii) in a bizarrely comic, yet disturbing, scene: his "*voice . . . quiver[s] with the hunger that possesses some of the elderly for the young and lovely*" (44). The excesses of sexuality, madness, food, liquor, and general "outrageous behavior" all merge together under the mantle of "over indulgence," permeating the entire atmosphere of the play, both inside and outside the house. At the play's opening, Cornelius is denouncing the "consumerism" and "avarice – insatiable – avarice" that pervades society (5), and Jessie, more than once, expresses her concern that a "sex-fiend" is running around "at large on the Gulf Coast highway" (11; 70).

Keith calls the style of this play "hyper-realism" (xxvi),[22] and sees excess and extremes operating throughout: "Emerson and Stacey swing from unlikely extremes of the cartoonish . . . to the conventional. Cornelius and Emerson carry on dialogue that verges on the absurd" (xxvi), and Jessie and Emerson "play out two extremes of old age; Emerson the feeblest kind of simpleton, is incapable of survival while

Jessie is the most aggressive survivor in the play" (Keith 2002: 214). In the stage directions, Williams indicates that Bella's body is excessive, her *"way of moving suggests more weight than the actress needs to carry"* (4) as she *"shuffles ponderously"* (6), and Cornelius claims that that she "pants louder'n an ole yard dog" (16). Cornelius too is characterized as somewhat grotesque, *"slight in comparison to his distended abdomen"* (4), and crude in behavior as *"[h]e scratches his ass"* (8) and, later, *"lumbers to his easy chair and flops exhaustingly into it, massaging his belly"* (15). In Act 2, they stagger back inside from the storm, transformed into representations of chaos: Cornelius *"looks like an outraged and bedraggled old monster"* (47), while Bella, who ran out of the house in a *"state of delirious passion,"* (42), is now *"[w]ildly disheveled, suggesting an element of nature"* (46). In another version of the play, Williams was even more specific about Bella's status as a grotesque, contradictory figure, already implied in the incongruity between her appearance and the beauty that her name would suggest. Keith quotes from a draft fragment of *House*, titled *Our Lady of Pascagoola*, where Williams describes Bella as "a grotesque but heart-breaking Pieta," an "abstraction of human love and compassion – and tragedy." She should come across as, simultaneously, ethereal and Rubensesque – "an unearthly apparition" with "a quality of grace and loveliness," despite "the great accretion of flesh" (xxii). And, as Keith points out, "making [Bella's] character overweight allows an actress to more readily exploit the comic potential of her lines" (Keith 2002: 209).

Yet, perhaps the most bizarrely comical character in the play is Stacey, as she performs extremes in both appearance and behavior. While Bella is dying, Stacey is visibly pregnant with new life, her belly "distended" (60) and "protuberant with late pregnancy" (59). She emerges downstairs at the end of Act 1, covered in "a fantastic beach towel that shields her body from view from shoulders to knees. The faded towel is patterned with beautiful, stylized creatures of the sea: fan-tail fish of many colors, sea-horses, crustaceans, shells, etc.," and her face "has an ingenuous wide-eyed charm" (42). In Act 2, her religious fit is made even more bizarre by her fantastic appearance. And, like Bella, Stacey's name can be seen as a subtle pun, containing the "ecstasy" that possesses her. She is *"beside herself"* with hysteria, speaking in tongues and rolling on the floor (64–7), a scene worth quoting in part:

> Stacey: OH, IT IS COMIN' ON ME! WAIT, IT'S COMING, I FEEL IT, THE GIFT OF TONGUES! WHAHOOOOOOO! BE-BE, YAIS, BAH! OH, BLESSED! BE, BE, BE, BE, LIEVE! ALL, ALL, ALL COME FORTH! BAH! BOW! WALLAH, YAIS WALLAH! SALVAREDEMPTION IN ME, DEEP, DEEP SALVAREDEMPTION, GLORY IN ME, AH, GLORY, GO DEEP IN ME IN GLORY, AH, AH, GAH, WALLAH, WOMB! WOMB! WOMB . . . [*As if arrived at orgasm, she falls back onto the carpet*]. (65)

Her "bawn-again" (64) parody is, of course, overtly sexual and mockingly pornographic, as she uncontrollably cries out for "ALL, ALL, ALL" to "COME!" and implores the spirit to "GO DEEP" in her "WOMB!" Her "*post-orgasmic exhaustion*" (65) does not last long, however; she is "*repossessed by rapture*" shortly afterwards (66), as Cornelius dismisses her as a "pregnant lunatic" (67). This "pregnant" lunacy is at the core of *A House Not Meant to Stand* – a potential chaos, located in grotesque contradiction and ambiguity, that permeates the play and opens up the possibility of a new kind of rebirth.

All three plays discussed above revel in the ambiguity of the human condition that Williams engaged in his later plays, exploring the potentially regenerative power of the grotesque. By the late 1960s, Williams had overtly rejected realism's failed fantasies of stability and completion – the "straight" human heart that Blanche railed against in the film version of *Streetcar* – and instead asked us to consider the potential of new, unfamiliar possibilities that could be created through the coexistence of contradiction. Although these are certainly not "happy" or hopeful plays in any conventional sense, neither are they pessimistic or despairing. Going beyond such artificial binaries, they present, and even celebrate, life in all its complexity, exhibiting the spirit of "going on" that Williams was famous for championing. Chicken and Myrtle choose life over death in the union of their desire and their determination to survive the impending chaos of natural disaster, while Lot dies, frozen in representation, as he embodies a parody of civilized elegance. Nance, in fusing emotional fantasy and physical reality by acting to realize her desire in an escort who "looks like . . . Nijinsky," embraces life in Lawrencian fashion, if only for the short time she has before confinement limits her choices. She is not left staring at the statue in the hall in madness, nor is she pathetically waiting on the front porch for someone who will never come. She lucidly creates her own compromise and, in all likelihood, the escort she ordered will arrive to satisfy her longing. And even though *House* ends with Bella's death, Charlie and Stacey's new baby will ensure that "all the life" Bella was searching for will go on (35) – exactly under what circumstances is unclear, but the point is that there is no need to know for sure. We are far from the closure and conventional moral optimism, or pessimism, of domestic realism, heading toward the "undiscovered country" of creative, and perhaps unimagined, human possibility. At the end of the play, even Bella's own children return as ghostly figures to continue the cycle of renewal and rebirth, releasing their mother with a prayer (86).

# CONCLUSION

The year 1998 was something of a watershed year in the theatrical life of the Tennessee Williams repertoire, and also an eye-opening year for me. This was the year of the premiere production of *Not About Nightingales*, made possible through the collaboration of Vanessa and Corin Redgrave's independent theatre company Moving Theatre, the National Theatre of Great Britain, and Houston's Alley Theatre. I saw the production at the Circle in the Square when it came to New York. The production was a great success in London, in Houston, and in New York, demonstrating that, as we moved into the twenty-first century, Williams's reach in the theatre world was wide and deep, encompassing commercial and subsidized theatre; alternative, regional, and big-time London and New York theatre; serious "literary" theatre and public entertainment.

This was a long way from the situation at the time of his death in 1983, when a new play by Williams could barely get an Off-Broadway premiere. If the 1939 play was not exactly hailed as a newly discovered masterpiece, it was rightly seen, as Matt Wolf put it, as a play "that extends critical understanding of Williams" (Wolf 1998: E2). Director Trevor Nunn set the tone for a decade of new discoveries and insights when he told Wolf: "We're first of all correcting the notion that Tennessee sprang fully formed out of nowhere as a writer of masterpieces; of course he didn't, any more than Arthur Miller did or Shakespeare did. The apprenticeship is long and fascinating, and what the writer rejects is as interesting as what the writer chooses" (E2). The *New York Times*'s Vincent Canby sounded a similar note in recognizing that "'Not About Nightingales' is very much a Williams play. The splendid production not only finds the work's theatrically vivid life, it also deepens our appreciation of the playwright: how he saw himself and how he dueled with his demons" (Canby 1999: AR10). Mel Gussow noted that, as a "lost play," being produced for the first time, it "can now be approached in the context of Williams's other work. There are hints of themes that were to obsess him throughout his career, especially in the portraits of characters too sensitive to withstand the battering of malevolent forces in society" (Gussow 1999: E2).

At the same time as the "apprentice work" was being discovered in the theatre, scholarly attention to the later plays was bringing more and more of Williams's work to light. Annette Saddik's and Linda Dorff's dissertations on the later plays, in 1996 and 1997, and their subsequent critical presentations and publications, inspired a new engagement with his later work from the academic side, which led directly to productions and staged readings of many works that had not yet seen the light of day outside the archives. A particularly fruitful collaboration among Dorff, director Michael Wilson, and dramaturg Christopher Baker began the Tennessee Williams Marathon at Connecticut's Hartford Stage, a series of main stage productions, studio productions, play readings, talk-backs, lectures, and symposia that was to last for 10 years, from 1998 until 2008. As a Connecticut local, I was fortunate enough to see a good many of these events and to participate in a couple of them.

Besides the major works, the main stage productions included *8 by Tenn*, a revolving repertory of eight one-acts that included several premieres and plays that had been seen very little, such as *The One Exception, The Palooka, Now the Cats with Jewelled Claws, Something Unspoken*, and *The Chalky White Substance*. It was the brilliant performances of Amanda Plummer and Elizabeth Ashley in *The Gnädiges Fräulein* that forever convinced me of the importance of this play to fully understanding Tennessee Williams. In staged readings, even more rarely witnessed short works, like *Lord Byron's Love Letter, Auto-Da-Fe, I Rise In Flame, Cried the Phoenix, Steps Must Be Gentle, The Purification, Masks Outrageous, Lifeboat Drill*, and *The Demolition Downtown*, were presented, along with some longer plays that did not make it to the main stage, but which Baker and Wilson were committed to showing: *In the Bar of a Tokyo Hotel, You Touched Me!, Vieux Carré, The Two-Character Play*.

The value of such a program to a Williams scholar and teacher like me was of course immense, but it wasn't done just for the likes of me, and I was particularly attentive to the audience's response to the project during symposia and talk-backs. The Hartford Stage audience became confident, outspoken, and a bit possessive of Williams, empowered by an informed sense of his repertoire and an understanding of his work that deepened with each production and interpretive event. The actor Alyssa Bresnahan, who became part of a *de facto* Williams repertory company over the 10-year Marathon, said of the audience: "So many people talked about the relationship among the theater and the audience and the community. No matter what they thought of each production, they seemed to own it. Simply by virtue of the audience having seen more than one Tennessee Williams play, they naturally made connections and had a relationship on their own to the playwright, and to the actors. They'd say, 'Oh, this character is like that character from the other play.' Seeing them together gives them a sense of confidence in their participation in the theater" (Rizzo 2008). It also gave them a sense of confidence in their understanding of Tennessee Williams. In teaching seminars on Williams, I have found the same confidence and sense of ownership in my students, who typically have seen or read one isolated play by Williams—*Streetcar* or *Menagerie*—in secondary school, and achieve an understanding of his work that grows exponentially as they experience it as a whole, from the 30s to the 80s.

I see this book as another element in the project of seeing Tennessee Williams whole. Its core is the playwright at work on the plays, both the writing and the staging of them. Its analysis of the plays is always in the context of his whole career. His perennial obsessions and concerns are seen developing throughout his work, from 1936 to 1983. Seen in this context, his recognizable tropes and themes take on a resonance and depth that it is impossible to see if one only looks at the great plays he wrote between 1944 and 1961. Entrapment and escape—"the Wild of Heart Kept in Cages"; the plight of the artist, the bohemian, the romantic, and the misfit in contemporary America; the search for God, the gnawing of guilt, and the drive toward atonement; the struggle with sexuality and gender identity, or, as he put it, "loneliness, eroticism, repression, undefined spiritual longings" (N: 489); the indelible imprint of the family, in all its dysfunctional dynamics, on the artist; the need to express truth and the fight against mendacity, both external and internal; the constant battle against panic, anxiety, and the fear of death; the driving desire for success and the paralyzing fear of failure; these are concerns that inform Williams's work from beginning to end. In the twenty-first century, watching the ever-expanding Williams repertoire on stage and studying the texts, newly available works along with established classics, it is possible to gain a deeper understanding of this in many ways quintessential twentieth-century American artist than was ever possible during his lifetime. I have no doubt that future work on both fronts will continue to deepen our understanding and whet our interest.

# NOTES

## Critical Perspectives

1. See Phelan 1993, for one of the strongest statements on the ontological incommensurability of live stage performances and film.
2. For an introduction to dynamic systems theory, see Van Gelder and Port: 1–43 and Ward. One of the best recent books on the enaction paradigm is Stewart, Gapenne, and DiPaolo. On the link between emotional response and character appraisal, see Oatley: 118–22.
3. Kolin: 6–12, and Kazan: 344–7.
4. Grodal: 106–11, 154–6, 206–11.
5. All theatre reviews of the premiere of *Streetcar* in 1947 by Atkinson, Barnes, Chapman, Coleman, Garland, Hawkins, Morehouse, Kronenberger, and Watts may be found in the *New York Theatre Critics' Reviews.*
6. I consulted the following reviews on the 1951 film of *Streetcar: Commonweal* 54 (28 September 1951): 596–97; *Holiday* 10 (October 1951): 25–8; *Life* 31 (25 September 1951): 91+; *Nation* 173 (20 October 1951); *New Yorker* 27 (29 September 1951): 111; *Newsweek* 38 (1 October 1951): 87; *Saturday Review* 34 (1 September 1951): 28–31; *Time* 58 (17 September 1951): 105–6. The 4 images of Brando's Stanley are on p. 91 in *Life*. See Michaels: 52–5, 134–5, for information on the film.
7. Stewart, John, "Foundational Issues in Enaction as a Paradigm for Cognitive Science," 1–5, 12–18; Gapenne: 184–209; Engel: 219–43; and Hutchins: 423–50. As these essays make it clear, the enaction paradigm directly challenges earlier understandings about perception and cognition as representation and the reading of codes.
8. McConachie, *American Theater in the Culture of the Cold War:* 126–33. My research for the cold war book led me to emphasize the importance of social beliefs when I looked again at Tandy's Blanche and Brando's Stanley for a section in my *Engaging Audiences:* 102–5.
9. See, for example, Batson: 3–16.
10. Thompson: 382–402. Thompson actually discusses four stages of empathy in all, but the first two are the most relevant to *Streetcar*.
11. I am aware that several of the New York reviewers who disliked Tandy as Blanche found Uta Hagen's characterization more sympathetic in the summer of 1948. See Kolin's summary, 33–9. Although the intermission arrangements were the same as when the play opened with Tandy, Hagen avoided Tandy's hysteria and neurosis in the early scenes and her Blanche stood up, when she could, to Anthony Quinn's more sinister Stanley, instead of wilting before the power and charm of a Brando opposite her. Different acting and directing choices can lead audiences away from cultural

stereotypes. In the case of Hagen's performances, the intermission after Scene Four probably locked in mostly positive attributes about Blanche for the audience.

12. Kaier Curtin notes that "eighty-four plays with either gay characters or gay themes were seen on New York stages" in the 70s alone (1985: 328). No equivalent was ever possible in Hollywood. See also Russo, 1985.

13. As Palmer and Bray note,

> Williams . . . was a figure suited admirably to that period of transition in which Hollywood found itself situated almost immediately after the war. Within American culture, his was beyond question a new, unique voice, but though he challenged and, in the process, modified long-established protocols of the Broadway theatre (especially regarding the dramatization of erotic life), he also addressed time-honored subjects upon whose appeal the film industry had long depended. These included the ravaging effects of time on human destiny, the irregular passages of romantic life, the moral and psychological contradictions of sexual desire, the unavoidable discontents of family relations, and—in a more specifically national vein—the exotic, attractively perverse nature of southern culture. Williams, we show, provided ideal source materials for a cinematic age eager for the new, yet reluctant to let go of the tried and true. (ix)

14. Although bothered by the bad notices he received in the press, Williams was as livid when no notices appeared at all. See his letter to the editors of the *New York Herald Tribune Book Review* about their lack of reviewing his novel *The Roman Spring of Mrs. Stone*:

> I feel that I have worked very hard and very seriously over a considerable period, that I have not done anything cheap or meretricious, that regardless of my known limitations as a writer, I have shown taste and courage and do have honesty: and, consequently, have a right to receive from journals that have literary criticism, such as The Herald-Tribune, The New Yorker, Etc., the minimal courtesy of some space within two or three weeks of the publication date, a courtesy which I am sure they have extended time and again to writers who make far less effort than I to explore the world and experience our time with some truth and significance. (L2: 354)

15. All references to the over 30 pages that Williams wrote to Brustein correspond to two folders labeled "Reply to Professor Brustein," MS Thr 397 (756 and 757), at the Houghton Library, Harvard University. The square brackets indicate the order in which the manuscript appears in the folder, as none of the pages is numbered.

16. Mannes's title refers to the success of Alan J. Lerner and Frederick Lowes's 1956 Broadway musical, *My Fair Lady*, which ran for a then-record 2,717 performances.

17. Although "Too Personal?" was written at the time of *Small Craft Warnings*, it seemingly serves as a response to Clive Barnes's review of *In the Bar of a Tokyo Hotel*. Barnes commented: "The play seems almost too personal, and as a result too painful, to be seen in the cold light of public scrutiny. Mr Williams has, perhaps, never been overreluctant to show the world his wounds—but in this new play he seems to be doing nothing else" (12 May 1969: 54).

18. This is indicated in the play's stage directions, but Redgrave is hardly plump in the film.

19. Nance seems to be a composite of Williams, whose father called him "Miss Nancy," and his sister Rose, who was chastised by her mother for "inappropriate" expressions of sexual desire.

20. We see a more subtle, romanticized version of this contrast in *The Night of the Iguana*, when Hannah tells the story of the salesman who asked her to remove her underwear and began to masturbate with it. While Shannon sees the story as a "sad, dirty little episode" that should inspire "*disgust*," Hannah insists that "[n]othing human disgusts [her] unless it's unkind, violent" (T4: 363–4).

21. The play's connections to Williams's biography are overt. For more on the biographical connections, see Thomas Keith, "A House Not Meant to Stand: Tennessee's Haunted Last Laugh" and the "Introduction" to *A House Not Meant to Stand*.

22. In my essay "'Drowned in Rabelaisian Laughter': Germans as Grotesque Comic Figures in the Plays of Tennessee Williams," I use a similar term, "extra-realistic in the sense of being beyond realism" (358), to refer to the German tourists in *The Night of the Iguana*. See the corrected online version of this essay for the most accurate version, as the printed version contains several copy editing errors that were inadvertently created by the journal in the final print stages.

# CHRONOLOGY

**1911**  On 26 March, Thomas Lanier Williams III is born in Columbus, Mississippi to Edwina Dakin Williams and Cornelius Coffin (C. C.) Williams, a traveling salesman. His sister Rose Isabel was born in 1909.

**1911–1918**  The family lives with Edwina's parents, the Rev Walter Dakin, an Episcopal priest, and Rose Otte Dakin, in parish rectories in Nashville, Tennessee as well as Columbus, Canton and Clarksdale, Mississippi. At the ages of 5 and 6, Williams is confined to the house with diphtheria and then Bright's disease. He becomes very close to his sister Rose and attends school in Clarksdale.

**1918–1927**  C. C. Williams moves his family to an apartment in a lower-middle-class neighborhood in St Louis, where he has a job at the corporate headquarters of the International Shoe Company. Tom and Rose have difficulty adjusting to their new circumstances. The family will move to a series of new apartments and houses in increasingly better neighborhoods. Williams's brother Walter Dakin Williams is born in 1919. Williams attends local public schools. The family is troubled by C. C.'s alcoholism and the parents' constant fighting.

**1928**  Williams publishes "The Vengeance of Nitocris" in *Weird Tales* and tours Europe with his grandfather and a church group.

**1929–1932**  Williams enrolls at the University of Missouri in Columbia, where he wins an award for a one-act play, *Beauty Is the Word*. He is withdrawn at the end of his third year by his father for failing ROTC (Reserve Officer Training Corps).

**1932–1934**  Williams works as a clerk at the International Shoe Company during the day, writing at night, continuing to publish poems and winning a prize for the short story "Stella for Star."

**1935**  Williams is hospitalized after collapsing from exhaustion and spends the summer of 1935 in Memphis with his grandparents. On 12 July, *Cairo! Shanghai! Bombay!* is produced by the Rose Arbor Playhouse in Memphis.

**1936**  Williams enters Washington University in St Louis, meets the poet Clark Mills McBurney, with whom he sets up a "literary factory," and continues publishing poetry and writing plays. On 3 October, *The Magic Tower* is staged by the Webster Groves Theatre Guild.

**1937**  On 8 March, *Candles to the Sun* is produced by The Mummers in St Louis, directed by Willard Holland. Rose Williams is diagnosed with dementia praecox (schizophrenia) and confined to the state mental hospital in Farmington. Williams enters the playwriting program at the University of Iowa, supported by his mother and grandparents. There he writes *Spring Storm* and has his only heterosexual love affair with Bette Reitz. In December, *Fugitive Kind* is produced by the Mummers in St Louis.

**1938–1939**  Williams earns his B. A. degree from Iowa and makes first visit to New Orleans' French Quarter, where he lives a gay lifestyle for the first time and spends the majority of his time writing *Not About Nightingales*. He travels to California with his friend Jim Parrott, wins a $100 prize from the Group Theatre for his one-act plays, and engages Audrey Wood as his agent. She helps him to win a $1,000 grant from the Rockefeller Foundation.

**1940**  Williams falls in love with Kip Kiernan while on vacation in Provincetown, Massachusetts. On 30 December, The Theatre

Guild produces *Battle of Angels*, which closes in Boston before it reaches New York.

**1941–1943** Williams wanders among New York, New Orleans, St Louis, Macon, Georgia, and Jacksonville, Florida, writing and subsisting on small sums from occasional jobs and option money from producers. Rose Williams undergoes a prefrontal lobotomy in January, 1943, while Williams is in New York. In May, he goes to Hollywood, where Audrey Wood has gotten him a screenwriting job. He saves a good deal of his salary and works on his own script of "The Gentleman Caller" instead of studio projects he is assigned. He is fired after 6 months.

**1944** Williams is in St Louis for the death of his beloved grandmother, Rose Dakin, in January. On 26 November, *The Glass Menagerie*, the play developed from "The Gentleman Caller," is produced, running for 6 weeks in Chicago.

**1945** On 31 March, *The Glass Menagerie*, directed by Eddie Dowling and Margo Jones, premieres on Broadway with great success. On 25 March, *Stairs to the Roof* is produced by the Pasadena Playhouse. Williams goes to Mexico and works on the play that would become *A Streetcar Named Desire*. On 25 September, *You Touched Me!*, cowritten with Donald Windham, premieres in New York.

**1946** Williams lives with Amado (Pancho) Rodriguez y Gonzales in New Orleans and travels with him to Taos and Nantucket, where he and Carson McCullers write together, as he works on *Streetcar* and *Summer and Smoke*.

**1947** Williams meets Frank Merlo in Provincetown and breaks off with Pancho Rodriguez. On 8 July, the Dallas production of *Summer and Smoke*, directed by Margo Jones, opens. On 3 December, *A Streetcar Named Desire*, directed by Elia Kazan, opens in New York, Williams's greatest Broadway success, running for 855 performances and winning the Pulitzer Prize and Drama Critics Circle Award.

**1948** On 28 July, *The Glass Menagerie* opens in London, directed by John Gielgud. On 6 October, *Summer and Smoke* opens in New York, directed by Margo Jones. Frank Merlo moves in with Williams in October, beginning their 14-year relationship. Edwina and C. C. Williams separate.

**1949** On 12 October, *A Streetcar Named Desire* opens in London, with Vivien Leigh directed by Laurence Olivier. After traveling for a good deal of the year, Williams moves with Merlo and grandfather Dakin to Key West, Florida, where he buys the house that would become his home.

**1951** On 3 February, *The Rose Tattoo* premieres on Broadway. Williams transfers his sister Rose to Stony Lodge in Ossining, New York, which will be her permanent home, and visits her often. The film of *A Streetcar Named Desire*, for which Williams wrote the screenplay, is released, winning four Oscars.

**1953** On 19 March, *Camino Real* opens in New York, closing after 60 performances. Williams directs Donald Windham's *The Starless Air* at the Playhouse Theatre in Houston.

**1955** On 24 March, *Cat on a Hot Tin Roof*, directed by Elia Kazan, premieres on Broadway, a critical and commercial success which runs for 694 performances and wins the Pulitzer Prize and the Drama Critics Circle Award. On 14 February, Williams's grandfather Walter Dakin dies in St Louis at age 97.

**1956** The film *Baby Doll*, adapted by Williams from the one-act plays *27 Wagons Full of Cotton* and *The Unsatisfactory Supper* and directed by Elia Kazan, is released. It is nominated for four Oscars, including best screenplay, but is the subject of controversy when it is denounced by the Catholic Legion of Decency and Francis Cardinal Spellman of New York.

**1957** On 21 March, *Orpheus Descending* opens on Broadway, closing after 68 performances. C. C. Williams dies on 27 March, and Williams attends his funeral in Knoxville. On 8 April, the first London production of *Camino Real* opens, directed by Peter Hall. In June, Williams begins psychoanalysis with Dr Lawrence Kubie, who urges him to take a hiatus from writing.

**1958** On 7 January, *Garden District* (*Suddenly Last Summer* and *Something Unspoken*), directed by Herbert Machiz, is produced Off-Broadway in New York, a critical success. Williams ends his psychoanalysis in March. He works on the script for *The Fugitive Kind*, the film version of *Orpheus Descending*. On 30 January, the London production of *Cat on a Hot Tin Roof* premieres, and the film is released later in the year. On 16 September, the London production of *Garden District*, directed by Herbert Machiz, opens.

**1959** On 10 March, *Sweet Bird of Youth*, directed by Elia Kazan, opens on Broadway and runs for 375 performances, but is not a critical success. Williams meets Fidel Castro in Havana. The film of *Suddenly Last Summer*, directed by Joseph Mankiewicz, is released. On 14 May, *Orpheus Descending*, directed by Tony Richardson, opens at the Royal Court Theatre in London. Williams takes a 3-month trip around the world.

**1960** On 10 November, *Period of Adjustment*, directed by George Roy Hill, opens on Broadway. It runs for 132 performances.

**1961** On 28 December, *The Night of the Iguana*, directed by Frank Corsaro, opens. It is to be Williams's last success on Broadway, running for 316 performances and winning the Drama Critics Circle award for best play as well as three Tony nominations.

**1962** On 13 June, *Period of Adjustment*, directed by Tony Richardson, opens at the Royal Court Theatre in London. The successful production is transferred to Wyndham's Theatre in July.

**1963**   On 16 January, *The Milk Train Doesn't Stop Here Anymore* premieres on Broadway, closing after 69 performances. Frank Merlo, from whom Williams had been estranged, is diagnosed with cancer, and comes to live in Williams's New York apartment until he is hospitalized prior to his death in September. His death initiates Williams's long period of depression and ever-increasing abuse of drugs and alcohol.

**1964**   In February, the first British production of *Sweet Bird of Youth* opens at the Experimental Club in Manchester. The film of *The Night of the Iguana*, directed by John Huston, is released. Williams becomes a patient of "Dr. Feel Good," Max Jacobson, who supplies him with drugs.

**1965**   On 24 March, the first London production of *The Night of the Iguana*, directed by Philip Wiseman, is transferred to the West End from Croydon.

**1966**   On 22 February, *Slapstick Tragedy* (*The Gnädiges Fräulein* and *The Mutilated*) opens on Broadway, running for only seven performances.

**1967**   On 12 December, Williams attends the world premiere of *The Two-Character Play*, directed by James Roose-Evans, at the Hampstead Theatre Club in London.

**1968**   On 27 March, *The Seven Descents of Myrtle* (*Kingdom of Earth*) opens in New York, running for just 29 performances.

**1969**   On 10 January, Williams is received into the Roman Catholic Church at the urging of his brother Dakin. On 11 May, *In the Bar of a Tokyo Hotel* opens in New York and is cruelly panned by the critics. Williams travels compulsively until, in September, Dakin takes him from Key West to St Louis and persuades him to enter the psychiatric ward of Barnes Hospital, where he is confined for 3 months. Three seizures and two cardiac episodes follow his "cold turkey" withdrawal from alcohol and drugs.

**1970**    Williams famously comes out as gay by answering, "I've covered the waterfront" in response to a question about homosexuality on the David Frost television show.

**1971**    Williams fires Audrey Wood, his agent since 1939, in a fit of anger; she is replaced by Bill Barnes. On 8 July, *Out Cry*, a revised version of *The Two-Character Play*, is produced in Chicago. Williams speaks out against the Viet Nam War at a rally at the Cathedral of St John the Divine in New York.

**1972**    On 2 April, *Small Craft Warnings* opens at the Off-Broadway Truck and Warehouse Theatre; Williams makes several appearances as Doc.

**1973**    In January, *Small Craft Warnings* is produced at the Hampstead Theatre Club in London. On 1 March, *Out Cry* opens on Broadway, closing after 12 performances.

**1975**    On 18 June, *The Red Devil Battery Sign* opens in Boston and closes in 10 days. The novel *Moise and the World of Reason* and *Memoirs* are published. There are successful New York revivals of *Sweet Bird of Youth*, *Summer and Smoke*, and *The Glass Menagerie*.

**1976**    On 20 January, *This is (an Entertainment)* opens in San Francisco.

**1977**    On 11 May, *Vieux Carré* opens on Broadway, closing after 6 performances. On 8 June, *The Red Devil Battery Sign*, directed by Keith Baxter, opens at the Roundhouse in London; the production is transferred to the West End on 7 July.

**1978**    On 14 February, *Kingdom of Earth* opens in London. On 5 June, *Creve Coeur* is staged at the Spoleto Festival in Charleston, South Carolina. On 9 August, *Vieux Carrè* opens in London. In the winter, *Tiger Tale*, a play adapted from the film *Baby Doll*, is produced in Atlanta. Mitch Douglas becomes Williams's agent. The essay collection *Where I Live* is published.

**1979** On 10 January, *A Lovely Sunday for Creve Coeur* opens at the Hudson Guild Theatre in New York. *Kirche, Kutchen, und Kinder: An Outrage for the Stage* plays in repertory at the Jean Cocteau Repertory Theatre in New York.

**1980** On 25 January, *Will Mr. Merriwether Return from Memphis?* is the opening production for the Tennessee Williams Performing Arts Center in Key West. On 26 March, *Clothes for a Summer Hotel* opens in New York, the last of Williams's plays to be performed on Broadway during his lifetime. It closes after 15 performances. *Tennessee Laughs*, three short plays, is produced at the Goodman Theatre in Chicago. On 2 June, Edwina Dakin Williams dies.

**1981** On 24 August, *Something Cloudy, Something Clear* opens at the Jean Cocteau Repertory Theatre in New York. *A House Not Meant to Stand* is produced at the Goodman Theatre in Chicago. Luis Sanjurjo becomes Williams's agent.

**1982** Williams attends productions of several of his plays at the Williamstown Theatre Festival in Massachusetts. In November, he makes his last public appearance, at the 92nd Street Y in New York. He is hospitalized in December for drug toxicity in Key West.

**1983** On 24 February, Williams dies of asphyxiation at the Hotel Elysee in New York. Funeral Services, directed by his brother Dakin, take place at the St Louis Cathedral, and, despite his wish to be cremated and buried at sea near the site of the poet Hart Crane's death, Williams is buried next to his mother in the Calvary Cemetery in St Louis.

# FURTHER READING

## Works by Tennessee Williams

*American Blues* (New York: Dramatists Play Service, 1948).

*Candles to the Sun,* ed. Dan Isaac (New York: New Directions, 2004).

*The Collected Poems of Tennessee Williams*, eds. David Ernest Roessel and Nicholas Rand Moschovakis (New York: New Directions, 2002). (Cited as CP)

*Five O'Clock Angel: Letters of Tennessee Williams to Maria St. Just 1948–1982* (New York: Knopf, 1990).

*Fugitive Kind*, ed. Allean Hale (New York: New Directions, 2001).

*A House Not Meant to Stand*, ed. Thomas Keith (New York: New Directions, 2008).

"'I Have Rewritten a Play for Artistic Purity,'" *New York Times*, 21 November 1976, 77.

*The Magic Tower and Other Plays*, ed. Thomas Keith (New York: New Directions, 2011).

*Memoirs* (Garden City, NY: Doubleday, 1975). (Cited as M)

*Moise and the World of Reason: A Novel* (New York: Simon and Schuster, 1975).

*New Selected Essays: Where I Live*, ed. John S. Bak (New York: New Directions, 2009). (Cited as NSE)

*Not About Nightingales*, ed. Allean Hale (New York: New Directions, 1998).

*The Selected Letters of Tennessee Williams: Volume I 1920–1945*, eds. Albert J. Devlin and Nancy M. Tischler (New York: New Directions, 2000). (Cited as L1)

*The Selected Letters of Tennessee Williams: Volume II 1945–1957*, eds. Albert J. Devlin and Nancy M. Tischler (New York: New Directions, 2004). (Cited as L2)

*Something Cloudy, Something Clear* (New York: New Directions, 1995).

*Spring Storm*, ed. Dan Isaac (New York: New Directions, 1999).

*Stairs to the Roof*, ed. Allean Hale (New York: New Directions, 2000).

*A Streetcar Named Desire*: Acting Edition (New York: Dramatists Play Service, 1947).

*Tennessee Williams Collected Stories* (New York: New Directions, 1985). (Cited as CS)

*Tennessee Williams' Letters to Donald Windham 1940–1965*, ed. Donald Windham (New York: Penguin, 1980).

*Tennessee Williams: Notebooks*, ed. Margaret Bradham Thornton (New Haven: Yale University Press, 2006). (Cited as N)

*Tennessee Williams Plays: 1937–1955* (New York: Library of America, 2000). (Cited as P1) *Spring Storm, Not About Nightingales, Battle of Angels, I Rise in Flame, Cried the Phoenix, 27 Wagons Full of Cotton, The Lady of Larkspur Lotion, The Last of My Solid Gold Watches, Portrait of a Madonna, Auto-da-Fe, Lord Byron's Love Letter, This Property Is Condemned, The Glass Menagerie, A Streetcar Named Desire, Summer and Smoke, The Rose Tattoo, Camino Real, "Something Wild," Talk to Me Like the Rain and Let Me Listen, Something Unspoken, Cat on a Hot Tin Roof.*

*Tennessee Williams: Plays 1957–1980* (New York: Library of America, 2000). (Cited as P2)

*Orpheus Descending, Suddenly Last Summer, Sweet Bird of Youth, Period of Adjustment, The Night of the Iguana, The Eccentricities of a Nightingale, The Milk Train Doesn't Stop Here Anymore, The Mutilated, Kingdom of Earth (The Seven Descents of Myrtle), Small Craft Warnings, Out Cry, Vieux Carré, A Lovely Sunday for Creve Coeur*

*The Theatre of Tennessee Williams*, 8 Vols. (New York: New Directions, 1971–1992). (Cited as T and volume number).

VOLUME 1: *Battle of Angels, A Streetcar Named Desire, The Glass Menagerie*

VOLUME 2: *The Eccentricities of a Nightingale, Summer and Smoke, The Rose Tattoo, Camino Real*

VOLUME 3: *Cat on a Hot Tin Roof, Orpheus Descending, Suddenly Last Summer*

VOLUME 4: *Sweet Bird of Youth, Period of Adjustment, The Night of the Iguana*

VOLUME 5: *The Milk Train Doesn't Stop Here Anymore, Kingdom of Earth (The Seven Descents of Myrtle), Small Craft Warnings, The Two-Character Play*

VOLUME 6: *27 Wagons Full of Cotton, The Purification, The Lady of Larkspur Lotion, The Last of My Solid Gold Watches, Portrait of a Madonna, Auto-Da-Fé, Lord Byron's Love Letter, The Strangest Kind of Romance, The Long Good-bye, Hello from Bertha, This Property Is Condemned, Talk to Me Like the Rain . . ., Something Unspoken, The Unsatisfactory Supper, Steps Must be Gentle, The Demolition Downtown*

VOLUME 7: *In the Bar of a Tokyo Hotel, I Rise in Flame, Cried the Phoenix, The Mutilated, I Can't Imagine Tomorrow, Confessional, The Frosted Glass Coffin, The Gnädiges Fräulein, A Perfect Analysis Given by a Parrot, Lifeboat Drill, Now the Cats with Jewelled Claws, This is the Peaceable Kingdom*

VOLUME 8: *Vieux Carré, A Lovely Sunday for Creve Coeur, Clothes for a Summer Hotel, The Red Devil Battery Sign*

*The Traveling Companion and Other Plays*, ed. Annette J. Saddik (New York: New Directions, 2008).

*Vieux Carré* (New York: New Directions, 1979).

# Unpublished Manuscripts

["and in this way we fight the bang-bang"]. Fragment of the essay "Prelude to a Comedy" [c. 1960]. TWPC, Rare Book and Manuscript Library, Columbia University, n.d.

"The Good Men & the Bad Men." Fragment of an essay [c. 1960]. MS Thr 397 (725 & 726). TWPHL, Houghton Library, Harvard University, n.d.

["The last time I wrote . . ."]. Fragment of an essay [c. 1960].TWPC, Rare Book and Manuscript Library, Columbia University, n.d.

"A Playwright's Prayer in Rehearsal". Fragment of an essay [c. 1959]. MS Thr 397 (753). TWPHL, Houghton Library, Harvard University, n.d.

["Reply to Professor Brustein"]. Fragments of an essay [c. July 1959]. MS Thr 397 (756 & 757). TWPHL, Houghton Library, Harvard University, n.d.

"Some Philosophical Shop Talk, or An Inventory of a Remarkable Market". Fragments of an essay [c. 1960]. TWPC, Rare Book and Manuscript Library, Columbia University, n.d.

## Biographies, Interviews, Documentaries, and Memoirs

Brockway, Merrill et al. *Tennessee Williams: Orpheus of the American Stage*, American Masters Series, WNET Television (Princeton, NJ: Films for the Humanities and Sciences, 2003).

Cave, Mark, "Something Wild in the Country: The Fugitive Life of Tennessee Williams." *Southern Quarterly*, 48, 4 (Summer 2011): 11–31.

Devlin, Albert J. (ed.), *Conversations with Tennessee Williams* (Jackson: University Press of Mississippi, 1986). (Cited as C)

Kazan, Elia, *Elia Kazan: A Life* (New York: Knopf, 1988).

Leverich, Lyle, *Tom: The Unknown Tennessee Williams* (New York: Crown, 1995).

McHaney, Pearl Amelia, "Tennessee Williams," *American Dramatists: Contemporary Authors Bibliographic Series,* III, ed. Matthew Roudané (Detroit: Gale, 1989): 385–429.

Mielziner, Jo, *Designing for the Theatre: A Memoir and a Portfolio* (New York: Bramhall House, 1965).

Mitchell, Tom, "Tennessee Williams and the Mummers of St. Louis: The Birth of a Playwright." *Tennessee Williams Annual Review* 10 (2009): 91–104.

Rader, Dotson, *Tennessee: Cry of the Heart* (Garden City: Doubleday, 1985).

Smith, William Jay, *My Friend Tom: The Poet-Playwright Tennessee Williams* (Jackson: University Press of Mississippi, 2012).

Spoto, Donald, *The Kindness of Strangers: The Life of Tennessee Williams* (New York: Ballantine, 1986).

Steen, Mike, *A Look at Tennessee Williams* (New York: Hawthorn, 1969).

*Tennessee Williams: The Wounded Genius.* A&E Television, 1998.

Van Antwerp, Margaret A. and Sally Johns (eds), *Dictionary of Literary Biography*, Documentary Series, IV: *Tennessee Williams* (Detroit: Gale, 1984).

Williams, Dakin and Shepherd Mead, *Tennessee Williams: An Intimate Biography by His Brother* (New York: Arbor House, 1983).

Williams, Edwina Dakin, as told to Lucy Freeman, *Remember Me to Tom* (New York: Putnam, 1963).

Windham, Donald, *Lost Friendships: A Personal Memoir of Truman Capote, Tennessee Williams, and Others* (New York: Morrow, 1987).

## Bibliographies and Reference Works

Arnott, Catherine M., *Tennessee Williams on File* (London: Methuen, 1985).

Crandell, George W., *Tennessee Williams: A Descriptive Bibliography* (Pittsburgh: U of Pittsburgh P, 1995).

— (ed.), *The Critical Response to Tennessee Williams* (Westport: Greenwood, 1996).

Dony, Nadine, "Tennessee Williams: A Selected Bibliography." *Modern Drama* 1 (1958): 181–91.

Gunn, Dewey Wayne, *Tennessee Williams: A Bibliography* (Metuchen, NJ: Scarecrow, 1980).

Kolin, Philip C., *The Tennessee Williams Encyclopedia* (Westport, CT: Greenwood, 2004).

— (ed.), *Tennessee Williams: A Guide to Research and Performance* (Westport, CT: Greenwood Press, 1998).

McCann, John S., *The Critical Reputation of Tennessee Williams: A Reference Guide* (Boston: G. K. Hall, 1983).

Presley, Delma E., "Tennessee Williams: Twenty-Five Years of Criticism." *Bulletin Of Bibliography* 30 (1973): 21–9.

Smith-Howard, Alycia and Greta Heintzelman, *Critical Companion to Tennessee Williams: A Literary Reference to His Life and Work* (New York: Facts on File, 2005).

## Reviews and Criticism of Individual Plays

### *Battle of Angels* and *Orpheus Descending*

"Battle of Angels to Have Lines Cut." *Boston Post* (7 January 1941): 8.

Case, Claudia Wilsch, "Inventing Tennessee Williams: The Theatre Guild and His First Professional Production." *The Tennessee Williams Annual Review* 8 (2006): 51–71.

E. F. M., "Battle of Angels," *Christian Science Monitor* (31 December 1940).

Hastings, Morris, "Miriam Hopkins Returns," *Boston Transcript* (31 December 1940).

Libbey, "Battle of Angels," *Variety* (31 December 1940).

"Miriam Hopkins at Wilbur." *Boston Post* (31 December 1940): 8.

"Plays Here," *Boston Globe* (31 December 1940).

Watts, A. E., "Hopkins at Wilbur," *Boston Traveler* (31 December 1940).

Wheildon, Leonard, "Battle of Angels" Battle Called "Misunderstanding," *Boston Transcript* (7 January 1941).

Williams, Alexander, "The Theater," *Boston Herald* (31 December 1940).

### *Camino Real*

Atkinson, Brooks, "'Camino Real.'" *New York Times* (29 March 1953): section 2, 1.

Brown, John Mason, "Seeing Things: The Living Dead." *Saturday Review* 15 (April 1953): 28–30.

Kerr, Walter, "'Camino Real,'" *New York Herald Tribune* (20 March 1953).

—, Walter F. Kerr to Tennessee Williams, 13 April 1953, *Dictionary of Literary Biography: Documentary Series*, vol. 4, *Tennessee Williams*, eds. Margaret A. Van Antwerp and Sally Johns (Detroit: Gale, 1984): 139.

Murphy, Brenda, "Toward a Map for the Camino Real: Tennessee Williams's Cultural Imaginary." *The Southern Quarterly* 48, 4 (Summer 2011): 73–90.

—, "Williams and the Broadway Audience: The Revision of *Camino Real*," *Critical Essays on Tennessee Williams*, ed. Robert A. Martin (Boston: G. K. Hall, 1997): 107–19.

*New York Theatre Critics' Reviews*, 14 (1953): 330–2.

Parker, Brian, "A Developmental Stemma for Drafts and Revisions of Tennessee Williams's Camino Real." *Modern Drama*, 39, 2 (Summer 1996): 331–41.

—"Documentary Sources for *Camino Real.*" *Tennessee Williams Annual Review*, 1 (1998): 41–52.

Renaux, Sigrid, "The Real and the Royal in Tennessee Williams' Camino Real." *Ilha Do Desterro: A Journal Of Language And Literature*, 3, 7 (July 1982): 43–66.

## Cat on a Hot Tin Roof

Arrell, Douglas, "Homosexual Panic in *Cat on a Hot Tin Roof.*" *Modern Drama* 51, 1 (Spring 2008): 60–72.

Bak, John S., "'Sneakin' and Spyin' from Broadway to the Beltway: Cold War Masculinity, Brick and Homosexual Existentialism." *Theatre Journal* 56, 2 (May 2004): 225–49.

Bentley, Eric, "Theatre." *New Republic* 132 (4 April 1955): 22.

—, "Theatre." *New Republic* 132 (11 April 1955): 28–9.

Bibler, Michael P., "'A Tenderness Which Was Uncommon': Homosexuality, Narrative, and the Southern Plantation in Tennessee Williams's *Cat on a Hot Tin Roof.*" *Mississippi Quarterly,* 55, 3 (Summer 2002): 381–400.

"'Cat' Censored, But by Whom?" *Variety* (13 April 1955): 73.

Hawkins, William, "'Cat' Yowls on Hot Tin Roof," *New York World, Telegram, and Sun* (25 March 1955).

McConachie, Bruce, "*Cat* and the Grotesque in the Cold War." *Tennessee Williams Literary Journal* 5, 1 (Spring 2003): 47–64.

Murphy, Brenda, "Brick Pollitt Agonistes: The Game in 'Three Players of a Summer Game' and *Cat on a Hot Tin Roof.*" *Southern Quarterly* 38, 1 (Fall 1999): 36–44.

Nathan, George Jean, Review of *Cat on a Hot Tin Roof, New York Journal American* (5 April 1953).

*New York Theatre Critics' Reviews*, 16 (1955): 342–4.

Parker, Brian, "A Preliminary Stemma for Drafts and Revisions of Tennessee Williams's *Cat on a Hot Tin Roof* (1955)." *Papers Of The Bibliographical Society of America* 90, 4 (December 1996): 475–96.

Shackelford, Dean, "The Truth That Must Be Told: Gay Subjectivity, Homophobia, and Social History in *Cat on a Hot Tin Roof.*" *Tennessee Williams Annual Review* (1998): 103–18.

## Clothes for a Summer Hotel

Adler, Thomas, "When Ghosts Supplant Memories: Tennessee Williams' *Clothes for a Summer Hotel.*" *Critical Essays on Tennessee Williams*, ed. Robert A. Martin (New York: G. K. Hall, 1997): 175–87.

Anderson, Hilton, "Tennessee Williams' *Clothes for a Summer Hotel*: Feminine Sensibilities and the Artist." *Publications Of the Mississippi Philological Association*, 7 (1988): 1–8.

Clurman, Harold, "Clothes for a Summer Hotel." *The Nation* 209 (19 April 1980): 477.

Dorff, Linda, "Collapsing Resurrection Mythologies: Theatricalist Discourses of Fire and Ash in *Clothes for a Summer Hotel.*" *Tennessee Williams: A Casebook*, ed. Robert F. Gross (New York, London: Routledge, 2002): 153–72.

Herridge, Frances, "Quintero Finds 'Clothes' Suitable." *New York Post* (21 March 1980): 42.

Kakutani, Michiko, "Williams and Quintero Build a 'Summer Hotel.'" *New York Times* (23 March 1980): section 2: 1.

— "Williams, Quintero, and the Aftermath of a Failure." *New York Times* (22 June 1980): section 2: 1, 7.

Paul, "Shows Out of Town," *Variety* (6 February 1980): 132.

Saddik, Annette J., "Recovering 'Moral and Sexual Chaos' in Tennessee Williams's *Clothes for a Summer Hotel.*" *North Carolina Literary Review* 18 (2009): 53–65.

## The Glass Menagerie

Cassidy, Claudia, "Fragile Drama Holds Theatre in Tight Spell." *Chicago Daily Tribune* (27 December 1944): 11.

Kronenberger, Louis, "A Triumph for Miss Taylor." *PM* (2 April 1945): 16.

Krutch, Joseph Wood, "Drama." *The Nation* (14 April 1945): 424–5.

Murphy, Brenda, "Tennessee Williams's Silent Movie: *The Glass Menagerie* in Production,' *One Hundred Years of Desire: Tennessee Williams, 1911–2011*, ed. Alessandro Clericuzio (Perugia: Guerra Edizione, 2012): 13–22.

*New York Theatre Critics' Reviews*, 6 (1945): 234–7.

Nathan, George Jean, "The Glass Menagerie," *Theatre Book of the Year, 1944–1945* (New York: Knopf, 1946): 324–7.

Nolan, Paul T., "Two Memory Plays: *The Glass Menagerie* and *After the Fall.*" *Mcneese Review* 17 (1966): 27–38.

Scheye, Thomas E., "*The Glass Menagerie*: It's No Tragedy, Freckles," *Tennessee Williams: A Tribute,* ed. Jac Tharpe (Jackson: University Press of Mississippi, 1977): 207–13.

## In the Bar of a Tokyo Hotel

Barnes, Clive, "Williams Play Explores Decay of an Artist," *New York Times* (12 May 1969): 54.

Display Ad, *New York Times* (10 June 1969): 96.

Kanfer, Stefan, "White Dwarf's Tragic Fade-Out," *Life* (13 June 1969): 10.

Kelly, Kevin, "Is Tennessee Williams Through?" *Boston Globe* (1 June 1969): A22, A24.

Kerr, Walter, "The Facts Don't Add Up to Faces," *New York Times* (25 May 1969): D5.

Ruckel, Terri Smith, "*Ut Pictura Poesis, Ut Poesis Pictura*: The Painterly Texture of Tennessee Williams's *In the Bar of a Tokyo Hotel,*" *The Undiscovered Country: The Later Plays of Tennessee Williams,*" ed. Philip C. Kolin (New York: Peter Lang, 2002): 80–92.

"Torpid Tennessee," *Time* (23 May 1969): 75.

## The Night of the Iguana

Brustein, Robert, "A Little Night Music," *The New Republic* (22 January 1962): 20, 22–3.

Haake, C. Allen, "Exorcizing Blue Devils: *The Night of the Iguana* as Tennessee Williams's Ultimate Confession." *Mississippi Quarterly* 58, 1–2 (2004 Winter–2005 Spring): 105–18.

Isaac, Dan, "Love in Its Purest Terms: Williams, Hepburn, and *Night of the Iguana*," *The Village Voice* (14 May 1996): 82.

Kelly, Kevin, "'Tennessee Williams' 'The Night of the Iguana': Familiar Themes and Symbols Echo in His New Drama," *Boston Globe* (18 February 1962): 61.

Parker, Brian, "A Provisional Stemma for Drafts and Revisions of Tennessee Williams's *The Night of the Iguana* (1961)." *The Papers of the Bibliographical Society of America*, 98, 1 (2004): 54–89.

Peck, Seymour, "Williams and 'The Iguana,'" *New York Times* (24 December 1961): X5.

Saddik, Annette, "'Drowned in Rabelaisian Laughter': Germans as Grotesque Comic Figures in the Plays of Tennessee Williams," *Modern Drama* 55, 3 (Fall 2012): 356–72.

## Not About Nightingales

Brantley, Ben, "Williams, a Youth Confined," *New York Times* (17 June 1998): E1.

Canby, Vincent, "'Nightingales' Sings of Williams's Promise," *New York Times* (7 March 1999: AR 10.

Gianakaris, C. J., "Tennessee Williams and *Not about Nightingales*: The Path Not Taken." *American Drama* 9, 1 (Fall 1999): 69–91.

Gussow, Mel, "In the Plays of Fledglings, Intimations of Immortality," *New York Times* (8 March 1999): E2.

Hale, Allean, "*Not about Nightingales*: Tennessee Williams as Social Activist." *Modern Drama* 42, 3 (Fall 1999): 346–62.

Nightingale, Benedict, "'The Redgraves' 'Nightingales' Sings Grandly," *New York Times* (5 April 1998): AR3.

Nunn, Trevor, "Discovering the Tennessee in Young Tom Williams," *New York Times* (21 February 1999): AR13.

Wolf, Matt, "Finding Out How Tennessee Williams Got That Way," *New York Times* (21 April 1998): E2.

## Slapstick Tragedy (The Gnädiges Fräulein and The Mutilated)

Cassidy, Claudia, "On the Aisle," *Chicago Tribune* (14 March 1966): C7.

Kauffmann, Stanley, "About Williams: Gloom and Hope," *New York Times* (6 March 1966): X1.

Kelly, Kevin, "One-Act Plays Fold: Tennessee Williams at His Worst," *Boston Globe* (6 March 1966): A15, A19.

Kolin, Philip C., "*The Mutilated*: Tennessee Williams's Apocalyptic Christmas Carol." *American Drama* 13, 2 (Summer 2004): 82–97.

Quinlan, Stefanie, "The Gnädiges Fräulein: Tennessee Williams's Southernmost Belle." *Tennessee Williams Annual Review* 11 (2010): 53–64.

Watt, Douglas, "Williams Play Breaks with Reality," *Chicago Tribune* (24 February 1966): B13.

## Small Craft Warnings

Barnes, Clive, "Stage: Williams Accepting Life as Is," *New York Times* (3 April 1972): 50.

De Jongh, Nicholas, *Not in Front of the Audience* (London: Routledge, 1992).

Gaver, Jack, "'Tennessee Williams' 'Small Craft' Opens," *Los Angeles Times* (5 April 1972): F16.

Kelly, Kevin, "'Wiliams' 'Warnings' Lacks Earlier Skill," *Boston Globe* (14 May 1972): B19.

Kerr, Walter, "Talkers, Drinkers and Losers," *New York Times* (16 April 1972): D8.

Parker, Jerry, "Tennessee Williams Debut," *Los Angeles Times* (8 June 1972): H19.

## Something Cloudy, Something Clear

Feingold, Michael, "The Playwright as Stinker," *Village Voice* (6–22 September 1981): 89.

Kerr, Walter, "A Comic at a Loss, a Playwright at Sea," *New York Times* (27 September 1981): D3.

Kolin, Philip C., "*Something Cloudy, Something Clear*: Tennessee Williams's Postmodern Memory Play." *Journal Of Dramatic Theory and Criticism* 12, 2 (Spring 1998): 35–55.

## A Streetcar Named Desire

Atkinson, Brooks, "First Night at the Theatre," *New York Times* (4 December 1947): 42.

Bak, John S., "Criticism on *A Streetcar Named Desire*: A Bibliographic Survey, 1947–2003." *Cercles* 10 (2004): 3–32.

Bak, John S., "A Streetcar Named Dies Irae?: Tennessee Williams and the Semiotics of Rape." *Tennessee Williams Annual Review* 10 (2009): 41–72.

Guilbert, Georges–Claude, "Queering and Dequeering the Text: Tennessee Williams's *A Streetcar Named Desire*." *Cercles* 10 (2004): 85–116.

Kolin, Philip C., *Williams: A Streetcar Named Desire*, Plays in Production (Cambridge: Cambridge University Press, 2000).

*New York Theatre Critics' Reviews*, 8, (1947): 249–52.

O'Connor, Jacqueline, "From 'Home–Place' to the Asylum: Confining Spaces in *A Streetcar Named Desire*." *Cercles* 10 (2004): 159–68.

"A *Streetcar* Runs on Electricity," *New York World-Telegram* (16 October 1947) clippings file, New York Public Library for the Performing Arts.

"'Streetcar Named Desire' Powerful Stage Drama," *Los Angeles Times* (5 December 1947): A9.

*A Streetcar Named Desire: The Original Director's Version*, DVD, Warner Brothers, 1993.

Trewin, J. C., "Plays in Performance." *Drama* 3, 15 (Winter 1949): 7.

## Suddenly Last Summer

Atkinson, Brooks, "Garden District," *New York Times* (19 January 1958): II: 1.

Crisp, Clement, "Garden District," *The Financial Times* (18 September 1958): 2.

Dettmer, Roger, "'Garden' Sends Civic Stock Up," *Chicago American* (8 April 1959): 28.

Gelb, Arthur, "Williams Explains His Move Off-Broadway," *New York Times* (15 December 1957): 129.

Gross, Robert F., "Consuming Hart: Sublimity and Gay Poetics in *Suddenly Last Summer*." *Theatre Journal* 47, 2 (May 1995): 229–51.

Harris, Sydney J., "Garden District," *Chicago Daily News* (8 April 1959): 38.

Kerr, Walter, "Williams' 'Garden District' Presented at York Theater," *New York Herald-Tribune* (8 January 1958): 16.

Oppenheimer, George, "On Stage," *Newsday* (17 January 1958): 7C.

Hope-Wallace, Philip, "Modern Clytemnestra in a Wheelchair," *Manchester Guardian* (18 September 1958).

Parker, Brian, "A Tentative Stemma for Drafts and Revisions of Tennessee Williams's *Suddenly Last Summer* (1958)." *Modern Drama* 41, 2 (Summer 1998): 303–26.

Saddik, Annette J., "The (Un)Represented Fragmentation of the Body in Tennessee Williams's 'Desire and the Black Masseur' and *Suddenly Last Summer*." *Modern Drama* 41, 3 (Fall 1998): 347–54.

Sofer, Andrew, "Self–Consuming Artifacts: Power, Performance and the Body in Tennessee Williams' *Suddenly Last Summer*." *Modern Drama* 38, 3 (Fall 1995): 336–47.

Tynan, Kenneth, "In Darkest Tennessee," *The Observer* (21 September 1958): clippings file, Billy Rose Theatre Collection, New York Public Library for the Performing Arts.

## *Summer and Smoke* and *Eccentricities of a Nightingale*

Atkinson, Brooks, "Work of Art," *New York Times* (17 October 1948): X1.

Carey, Ralph W., "Among New York Theaters," *The Hartford Courant* (17 October 1948).

Chapman, John, "Chapman Calls 'Summer and Smoke' Boring," *Chicago Daily Tribune*, 17 October 1948, clippings file, New York Public Library for the Performing Arts.

Clum, John M., "From *Summer and Smoke* to *Eccentricities of a Nightingale:* The Evolution of the Queer Alma." *Modern Drama* 39, 1(1996): 31–50.

Durgin, Cyrus, "'Mr. Roberts' and 'Summer and Smoke' Two More Broadway Hits," *Boston Globe* (28 November 1948).

Hammerman, Dan, "Theater-ing," *West Side News* (25 April? 1952): 8 clippings file, Billy Rose Theatre Collection, New York Public Library for the Performing Arts.

Khor, Neil Jin Keong, "The 'Gay' Spinster of Glorious Hill: A Queer Reading of Tennessee Williams' Summer and Smoke." *Southeast Asian Review Of English* 37 (December 1998): 57–73.

Marsh, W. Ward, Review of *Summer and Smoke*, *The Cleveland Plain Dealer* (28 September 1948), clippings file, Billy Rose Theatre Collection, New York Public Library for the Performing Arts.

Nadel, Norman, "Indifferent New Williams Play Gets Botched-Up Showing," *New York World-Telegraph and Sun* (27 June 1964): 19.

Simon, John, "Two from Williams' Menagerie," *The New Leader* (3 January 1977): 25–6.

Tallmer, Jerry, "Williams vs. Williams," *New York Post* (16 May 1968): 58.

Taylor, Harvey, "'Summer and Smoke' Is Far from Williams' Best," The *Detroit Times* (14 September 1948): C12.

## Sweet Bird of Youth

Brustein, Robert, "Sweet Bird of Success." *Encounter* 12 (June 1959): 59–60.

Clurman, Harold, "Sweet Bird of Youth." *The Nation* 188 (28 March 1959): 281–3.

Gunn, Dewey Wayne, "The Troubled Flight of Tennessee Williams's *Sweet Bird*: From Manuscript through Published Texts." *Modern Drama* 24, 1 (March 1981): 26–35.

*New York Theatre Critics' Reviews,* 20 (1959): 347–50.

"Old But New," Philadelphia *Inquirer* (22 March 1959).

Parker, Brian, "Problems with Boss Finley." *Tennessee Williams Annual Review* 9 (2007): 53–65.

Parker, Brian, "A Provisional Stemma of Drafts and Revisions for Tennessee Williams's Sweet Bird of Youth (1959)." *Papers Of The Bibliographical Society Of America* 103, 3 (September 2009): 357–90.

Tynan, Kenneth, "Sweet Bird of Youth." *The New Yorker* 35 (21 March 1959): 98–100.

## The Two-Character Play/Out Cry

Barnes, Clive, "Stage: A Static 'Out Cry,'" *New York Times* (2 March 1973): 18.

Campbell, Mary, "Tennessee Williams Is Writing Again," *Hartford Courant* (6 June 1971): 5A.

Londré, Felicia Hardison, "The Two-Character Out Cry and Break Out," *The Undiscovered Country: The Later Plays of Tennessee Williams,* ed. Philip C. Kolin (New York: Peter Lang, 2002): 93–106.

Marks, J., "Tennessee Williams Talks About His New Play." *Chicago Tribune* (9 May 1971): E1, E3.

Parker, R. B., "The Circle Closed: A Psychological Reading of *The Glass Menagerie* and *The Two Character Play.*" *Modern Drama* 28, 4 (December 1985): 517–34.

Philp, Richard, "Reviews: Theater On Broadway and Off," *After Dark* (August 1974), clippings file, Billy Rose Theatre Collection, New York Public Library for the Performing Arts.

Terry, Clifford, "The Playwright's Not for Roasting," *Chicago Tribune* (22 August 1971): G56–60.

"Williams Drama Baffles Critics," *New York Times* (13 December 1967): 54.

"Williams' Play Foggy to London," *Chicago Tribune* (13 December 1967): C5.

Wilson, Edwin, "A Writer's Cry of Desolation," *Wall Street Journal* (6 March 1973): 24.

## Vieux Carré

Barnes, Clive, "Stage: 'Vieux Carre' by Williams is Haunting," *New York Times* (12 May 1977): 70.

Bray, Robert, "*Vieux Carré:* Transferring 'A Story of Mood,'" *The Undiscovered Country: The Later Plays of Tennessee Williams,* ed. Philip C. Kolin (New York: Peter Lang, 2002): 142–54.

Clinton, Craig, "Finding the Way: The Evolution of Tennessee Williams's *Vieux Carré.*" *Resources For American Literary Study* 26, 1 (2000): 49–63.

Kerr, Walter, "A Touch of the Poet Isn't Enough to Sustain Williams's New Play," *New York Times* (22 May 1977): 65.

## Other Williams Criticism

Bak, John S., *Homo Americanus: Ernest Hemingway, Tennessee Williams, and Queer Masculinities* (Madison, NJ: Fairleigh Dickinson University Press, 2010).

Bray, Robert (ed.), *Tennessee Williams and His Contemporaries* (Newcastle: Cambridge Scholars Press, 2009).

Clericuzio, Alessandro (ed.), *One Hundred Years of Desire: Tennessee Williams, 1911–2011* (Perugia: Guerra, 2012).

Bredeson, Kate, "Sometimes Cloudy, Sometimes Clear: God, Religion, and the Williams Passion Play." *Tennessee Williams Literary Journal* 5, 1 (Spring 2003): 71–9.

Cluck, Nancy Anne, "Showing or Telling: Narrators in the Drama of Tennessee Williams." *American Literature* 51, 1 (March 1979): 84–93.

Clum, John M., "The Sacrificial Stud and the Fugitive Female in *Suddenly Last Summer, Orpheus Descending*, and *Sweet Bird of Youth*," *The Cambridge Companion to Tennessee Williams*, ed. Matthew C. Roudané (Cambridge: Cambridge University Press, 1997): 128–46.

Clum, John, *Still Acting Gay: Male Homosexuality in Modern Drama* (New York: Palgrave Macmillan, 2000).

Debusscher, Gilbert, "'Minting Their Separate Wills': Tennessee Williams and Hart Crane." *Modern Drama* 26, 4 (December 1983): 455–76.

Dorff, Linda, "Theatricalist Cartoons: Tennessee Williams's Late, 'Outrageous' Plays." *The Tennessee Williams Annual Review* 2 (1999): 13–33.

Fleche, Anne, "When a Door Is a Jar: Or, Out in the Theatre: Tennessee Williams and Queer Space." *Theatre Journal* 47, 2 (May 1995): 253–67.

Gale, Steven H., "Tennessee Williams' Tiger Tail." *Theatre Journal* 32, 2 (October 1980): 397–98.

Gilman, Richard, "Mistuh Williams, He Dead." *Commonweal* 77 (1963): 515–17.

Holditch, Kenneth, and Richard Freeman Leavitt, *Tennessee Williams and the South* (Jackson, MS: University Press of Mississippi, 2002).

Hooper, Michael S. D., *Sexual Politics in the Work of Tennessee Williams: Desire over Protest* (Cambridge, England: Cambridge University Press, 2012).

Hynds, Reed, Review of *Fugitive Kind*, *St. Louis Star-Times* (1 December 1937): 17.

Keith, Thomas, "A House Not Meant to Stand: Tennessee's Last Laugh," *The Undiscovered Country: The Later Plays of Tennessee Williams*, ed. Philip C. Kolin (New York: Peter Lang, 2002): 201–20.

Kolin, Philip C., *The Influence of Tennessee Williams: Essays on Fifteen American Playwrights* (Jefferson, NC: McFarland, 2008).

—"Sleeping with Caliban: The Politics of Race in Tennessee Williams's *Kingdom of Earth*." *Studies In American Drama, 1945-Present* 8, 2 (1993): 140–62.

—"*The Remarkable Rooming-House of Mme. Le Monde*: Tennessee Williams's Little Shop of Comic Horrors." *The Tennessee Williams Annual Review* 4 (2001): 39–48.

—(ed.), *The Undiscovered Country: The Later Plays of Tennessee Williams* (New York: Peter Lang, 2002).

Kolin, Philip C. and Douglas B. Chambers., "Special Issue: The Legacy of Tennessee Williams." *Southern Quarterly* 48, 4 (Summer 2011): 5–138.

Londré, Felicia Hardison, *Tennessee Williams* (New York: Ungar, 1979).

Londré, Felicia, *Tennessee Williams: Life, Work, Criticism* (Fredericton, N.B.: York, 1989).

Martin, Robert A., *Critical Essays on Tennessee Williams* (New York: G. K. Hall, 1997).

McPherson, Colvin, Review of *Fugitive Kind*, *St Louis Post-Dispatch* (1 December 1937).

Monteiro, George, "Tennessee Williams Misremembers Hemingway." *The Hemingway Review* 10, 1 (Fall 1990): 71.

Moschovakis, Nick, Bray, Robert, Allean Hale, Philip Kolin, George Crandell, and Nick Moschovakis, "The Early Plays of Tennessee Williams." *Tennessee Williams Annual Review*, 7 (2005).

Murphy, Brenda, *Tennessee Williams and Elia Kazan: A Collaboration in the Theatre* (Cambridge: Cambridge University Press, 1992).

Murphy, Brenda (ed.), *Tennessee Williams*, Critical Insights Series (Pasadena, CA: Salem, 2011).

Paller, Michael, *Gentleman Callers: Tennessee Williams, Homosexuality, and Mid-Twentieth-Century Broadway Drama* (New York: Palgrave Macmillan, 2005).

—"'I've Come Back to Something That I Went Away From': Spring Storm and Its Children." *Valley Voices: A Literary Review* 10, 1 (Spring 2010): 39–57.

—"A Playwright with a Social Conscience." *Tennessee Williams Annual Review* 10 (2009): 105–10.

Palmer, R. Barton and William Robert Bray, *Hollywood's Tennessee: The Williams Films and Postwar America* (Austin: U of Texas P, 2009).

Parker, Brian, "Tennessee Williams and the Legends of St. Sebastian." *University Of Toronto Quarterly* 69, 3 (Summer 2000): 634–59.

Parker, Brian, Saddik, Annette, Philip Kolin, Jacqueline O'Connor, and Brian Parker, "Williams and the Grotesque." *Tennessee Williams Annual Review* 8 (2006): 175–92.

Prosser, William, *The Late Plays of Tennessee Williams* (Lanham, MD: Scarecrow, 2009).

Radavich, David, "You Can Go Home Again: Tennessee Williams's *A Lovely Sunday for Creve Coeur.*" *Midwestern Miscellany* 33 (Fall 2005): 7–21.

Rizzo, Frank, "The Tennessee Williams Marathon Train Stops Here," McClatchy-Tribune Business News [Washington] (18 May 2008).

Roudané, Matthew C., *The Cambridge Companion to Tennessee Williams* (Cambridge: Cambridge University Press, 1997).

Saddik, Annette J., *The Politics of Reputation: The Critical Reception of Tennessee Williams' Later Plays* (Cranbury, NJ: Associated University Press, 1999).

—"'Blueprints for the Reconstruction': Postmodern Possibility in *Stairs to the Roof.*" *Tennessee Williams Annual Review* 9 (2007): 67–75.

Saddik, Annette, "'The Inexpressible Regret of All Her Regrets': Tennessee Williams's Later Plays as Artaudian Theater of Cruelty," *The Undiscovered Country: The Later Plays of Tennessee Williams*, ed. Philip C. Kolin (New York: Peter Lang, 2002): 5–24.

Savran, David, *Communists, Cowboys, and Queers: The Politics of Masculinity in the Work of Arthur Miller and Tennessee Williams* (Minneapolis: University of Minnesota Press, 1992).

Schiavi, Michael R., "Effeminancy in the *Kingdom*: Tennessee Williams and Stunted Spectatorship." *Tennessee Williams Annual Review*, 2 (1999): 99–113.

Schlatter, James, "*Red Devil Battery Sign*: An Approach to a Mytho–Political Theatre." *Tennessee Williams Annual Review*, 1 (1998): 93–101.

Siegel, Robert, "The Metaphysics of Tennessee Williams." *American Drama* 10, 1 (Winter 2001): 11–37.

Smith, Harry W., "Tennessee Williams and Jo Mielziner: The Memory Plays." *Theatre Survey* 23, 2 (November 1982): 223–35.

Spector, Susan, "Alternative Visions of Blanche DuBois: Uta Hagen and Jessica Tandy in *A Streetcar Named Desire*." *Modern Drama* 32 (1989): 545–60.

Tharpe, Jac (ed.), *Tennessee Williams: A Tribute* (Jackson, MS: University Press of Mississippi, 1977).

Tischler, Nancy M., *Student Companion to Tennessee Williams* (Westport, CT: Greenwood, 2000).

—, *Tennessee Williams: Rebellious Puritan* (New York, NY: Citadel, 1961).

## Other Works Cited

Ames, Daniel R., "Everyday Solutions to the Problem of Other Minds: Which Tools are Used When," *Other Minds: How Humans Bridge the Divide Between Self and Others,* eds. Bertram R. Malle and Sara D. Hodges (New York: Guilford Press, 2005): 158–73.

Bakhtin, Mikhail, *Rabelais and His World*, trans. Hélène Iswolsky (Bloomington: Indiana University Press, 1984).

Batson, C. Daniel, "These Things Called Empathy: Eight Related But Distinct Phenomena," *The Social Neuroscience of Empathy*, eds. Jean Decety and William Ickes (Cambridge, MA: MIT Press, 2009): 3–16.

Curtin, Kaier, *"We Can Always Call Them Bulgarians": The Emergence of Lesbians and Gay Men on the American Stage* (Boston: Alyson, 1987).

Freud, Sigmund, "The 'Uncanny,'" *The Standard Edition of the Psychological Works of Sigmund Freud,* ed. and trans. James Strachey, vol. 16 (London: Hogarth, 1953): 219–52.

Engel, Andreas K., "Directive Minds: How Dynamics Shapes Cognition," *Enaction: Toward a New Paradigm for Cognitive Science*, eds. John Stewart, Olivier Gapenne, and Ezequiel A. DiPaolo (Cambridge, MA: MIT Press, 2010): 219–43.

Frye Northrop, *Anatomy of Criticism: Four Essays* (Princeton: Princeton University Press, 1957).

Gapenne, Olivier, "Kinesthesia and the Construction of Perceptual Objects," *Enaction: Toward a New Paradigm for Cognitive Science*, eds. John Stewart, Olivier Gapenne, and Ezequiel A. DiPaolo (Cambridge, MA: MIT Press, 2010): 183–218.

Jentsch, Ernst, "On the Psychology of the Uncanny," trans. Roy Sellars, *Angelaki*, 2, 1 (1996): 7–23.

Grodal, Torben, *Embodied Visions: Evolution, Emotion, Culture, and Film* (New York: Oxford University Press, 2009).

Hutchins, Edwin, "Enaction, Imagination, and Insight," *Enaction: Toward a New Paradigm for Cognitive Science*, eds. John Stewart, Olivier Gapenne, and Ezequiel A. DiPaolo (Cambridge, MA: MIT Press, 2010): 423–50.

Jackson, Esther M., *The Broken World of Tennessee Williams* (Madison: U of Wisconsin P, 1965).

Kristeva, Julia, *Powers of Horror: An Essay on Abjection*, trans. Leon S. Roudiez (New York: Columbia University Press, 1982).

Malle, Bertram F., "Three Puzzles of Mindreading," *Other Minds: How Humans Bridge the Divide Between Self and Others*, eds. Bertram R. Malle and Sara D. Hodges (New York: Guilford Press, 2005): 26–43.

Mannes, Marya, "Plea for Fairer Ladies," *New York Times Magazine* (29 May 1960): 16, 26.

May, Elaine Tyler, *Homeward Bound: American Families in the Cold War Era* (New York: Basic Books, 1988).

McConachie, Bruce, *American Theater in the Culture of the Cold War: Producing and Contesting Containment* (Iowa City: University of Iowa Press, 2003).

McConachie, Bruce, *Engaging Audiences: A Cognitive Approach to Spectating in the Theatre* (New York: Palgrave Macmillan, 2008).

Michaels, Lloyd, *Elia Kazan: A Guide to References and Resources*, A Reference Publication in Film (Boston: GK Hall, 1985).

Miller, Arthur, *After the Fall: A Play in Two Acts* (New York: Viking, 1964).

Oatley, Keith, *Such Stuff as Dreams: The Psychology of Fiction* (Chichester: Wiley-Blackwell, 2011).

O'Connor, Flannery, "Some Aspects of the Grotesque in Southern Fiction," *Mystery and Manners: Occasional Prose*, eds. Sally Fitzgerald and Robert Fitzgerald (New York: Farrar, Straus & Giroux, 1961).

Odets, Clifford, *Awake and Sing!*, Famous American Plays of the 1930s, ed. Harold Clurman (New York: Dell, 1968): 19–93.

Phelan, Peggy, *Unmarked* (London: Routledge, 1993).

Read, Stephen J. and Lynne C. Miller, "Explanatory Coherence and Goal-Based Knowledge Structures in Making Dispositional Inferences," *Other Minds: How Humans Bridge the Divide Between Self and Others*, eds. Bertram R. Malle and Sara D. Hodges (New York: Guilford Press, 2005): 124–39.

Reed, John Shelton, *Minding the South* (Columbia, MO: University of Missouri Press, 2003).

Russo, Mary, *The Female Grotesque: Risk, Excess, and Modernity* (London: Routledge, 1994).

Russo, Vito, *The Celluloid Closet: Homosexuality in the Movies*, rev. ed. (New York: Harper & Row, 1985).

Stewart, John, "Foundational Issues in Enaction as a Paradigm for Cognitive Science," *Enaction: Toward a New Paradigm for Cognitive Science*, eds. John Stewart, Olivier Gapenne, and Ezequiel A. DiPaolo (Cambridge, MA: MIT Press, 2010): 1–31.

Stewart, John, Olivier Gapenne, and Ezequiel A. DiPaolo (eds), *Enaction: Toward a New Paradigm for Cognitive Science* (Cambridge, MA: MIT Press, 2010).

## Further Reading

Thompson, Evan, *Mind in Life: Biology, Phenomenology, and the Sciences of Mind* (Cambridge, MA: Harvard University Press, 2007).

Van Gelder, Timothy and Robert F. Port, "It's About Time: An Overview of the Dynamical Approach to Cognition," *Mind as Motion: Explorations in the Dynamics of Cognition*, eds. Robert F. Port and Timothy van Gelder (Cambridge, MA: MIT Press, 1995): 1–43.

Ward, Lawrence M., *Dynamical Cognitive Science* (Cambridge, MA: MIT Press, 2002).

# NOTES ON CONTRIBUTORS

**John S. Bak** is *Professeur* at the Université de Lorraine in France, where he teaches courses in literary journalism and American drama and theatre. His articles on Williams have appeared in such journals as *Theatre Journal, Mississippi Quarterly, Journal of American Drama and Theatre, The Tennessee Williams Literary Journal, American Drama, South Atlantic Review* and *Studies in Musical Theatre.* His edited books include *Post/modern Dracula: From Victorian Themes to Postmodern Praxis* (2006), *New Selected Essays: Where I Live* (2009), and (with Bill Reynolds) *Literary Journalism across the Globe: Journalistic Traditions and Transnational Influences* (2011). He is the author of the monographs *Ernest Hemingway, Tennessee Williams, and Queer Masculinities* (2009) and *Tennessee Williams: A Literary Life* (2013).

**Felicia Hardison Londré**, Curators' Professor of Theatre at the University of Missouri-Kansas City, currently serves as Dean of the College of Fellows of the American Theatre. She received ATHE's Outstanding Teacher of Theatre in Higher Education Award (2001) and The Betty Jean Jones Award for an Outstanding Teacher of American Theatre and Drama (2011). Her first book was *Tennessee Williams* (Ungar 1979). Her 12th book, *The Enchanted Years of the Stage: Kansas City at the Crossroads of American Theatre, 1870–1930*, won the Theatre Library Association's 2007 George Freedley Memorial Award.

**Bruce McConachie** is the director of Graduate Studies for Theatre and Performance Studies at the University of Pittsburgh. His scholarship ranges from US theatre and drama to cognitive approaches to performance. Recent books include *American Theater in the Culture of the Cold War: Producing and Contesting Containment* (2003), *Engaging Audiences: A Cognitive Approach to Spectating in the Theatre* (2008), and *Theatre and Mind* (2012). He coedits the Cognitive Studies in Literature and Performance series for Palgrave Macmillan.

**Annette J. Saddik** is professor of Theatre and English at the City University of New York. She is the author of two books and one edited collection: *Contemporary American Drama* (2007), *The Politics of Reputation: The Critical Reception of Tennessee Williams' Later Plays* (1999), and *Tennessee Williams: The Traveling Companion and Other Plays* (2008). She has also published several essays on twentieth-century drama in various anthologies and journals such as *Modern Drama* and *TDR*, and serves on the editorial boards of *Theatre Topics* and the *Tennessee Williams Annual Review*. She is currently completing her latest book manuscript, *"The Strange, The Crazed, The Queer": Tennessee Williams' Late Plays and the Theatre of Excess*.

# INDEX

Major discussions of plays are indicated in **bold type**. Williams's works are entered under their titles. Plays by other authors are listed under authors' names.